AFTER JENA

Topics in Historical Philosophy

General Editors David Kolb
John McCumber

Associate Editor Anthony J. Steinbock

AFTER JENA

New Essays on Fichte's Later Philosophy

Edited by Daniel Breazeale and
Tom Rockmore

Northwestern University Press
Evanston, Illinois

Northwestern University Press
www.nupress.northwestern.edu

Printed in the United States of America

10 9 8 7 6 5 4 3 2 1

Library of Congress Cataloging-in-Publication Data

After Jena : new essays on Fichte's later philosophy / edited by Daniel Breazeale and Tom Rockmore.
p. cm. — (Topics in historical philosophy)
Includes bibliographical references.
ISBN-13: 978-0-8101-2407-3 (cloth : alk. paper)
ISBN-10: 0-8101-2407-6 (cloth : alk. paper)
ISBN-13: 978-0-8101-2408-0 (pbk. : alk. paper)
ISBN-10: 0-8101-2408-4 (pbk. : alk. paper)
1. Fichte, Johann Gottlieb, 1762–1814. I. Breazeale, Daniel. II. Rockmore, Tom, 1942– III. Series: Northwestern University topics in historical philosophy.
B2848.A38 2008
193—dc22

2007035883

∞ The paper used in this publication meets the minimum requirements of the American National Standard for Information Sciences—Permanence of Paper for Printed Library Materials, ANSI Z39.48-1992.

Contents

Introduction

Tom Rockmore

In recent years, attention has increasingly been paid to the writings of the German idealist philosopher J. G. Fichte, a central figure in German idealism and one of the small number of truly significant philosophical thinkers. Fichte's career divides easily into two parts: the Jena period (1794–99), where he assumed the recently vacated chair of critical philosophy at the University of Jena, which at the time was rapidly emerging as the capital of the new German philosophy; and the post-Jena period, after he left Jena for Berlin.

The focus of Fichte studies in French and German and in the English-speaking world is very different. In Europe, Fichte's complex German and dense writing style present comparatively less of an obstacle than in the English-speaking world. Over the last decade, European Fichte studies have increasingly shifted toward Fichte's post-Jena writings. Yet in part because of their relative inaccessibility for someone whose grasp of German texts is either nonexistent or at least not strong—much of Fichte's philosophical output has still not been translated—students of Fichte working in English tend to focus on his Jena writings, especially the *Foundation of the Entire Wissenschaftslehre* (1794–95), which was originally not intended for publication but was written as an aid for Fichte's students, while neglecting his later texts.

In the English-language community, Fichte's post-Jena work has received comparatively little attention. This is unfortunate since Fichte is a major thinker, whose position continued to develop in a number of important texts after he left Jena. These include (but are not limited to) "popular" writings such as the well-known *The Vocation of Man* (1800); an interesting text on political economy (*The Closed Commercial State,* 1800); a number of further versions of the *Wissenschaftslehre* (*The Science of Knowledge;* 1804, 1805, 1807, 1810, 1811, 1812, 1813, and 1814) that, with the exception of the *Presentation of the General Outlines of the Wissenschaftslehre* (1810), were unpublished during his lifetime and are only now appearing in German in the definitive complete edition of his writings edited by the Bavarian Academy of Sciences;[1] a text intended to show the implications of his view of freedom for the philosophy of history (*The Characteristics of the Present Age,* 1806); a treatise on religion (*Guide to the Blessed Life, or the Doctrine of Religion,* 1806), and his celebrated but controversial *Addresses to the German Nation* (1808). Hence, there is much material to attract the attention of a scholar of German idealism, or of someone merely interested in the work of a first-rate philosophical mind.

The papers collected in this volume, which are drawn from a biennial meeting of the North American Fichte Society held in Montreal in 1999, all focus in different ways on Fichte's post-Jena philosophy. Most of the authors are established Fichte scholars, some are on the way to making a name for themselves in this domain, and others are considered among the ranking students of Fichte in the world today.

These essays fall into three related categories: Fichte's development, his view of religion, and other aspects of his "popular" (or not so popular) philosophy. Fichte's complex development reflects the overall philosophical concerns at the time he was active, the specific debates to which he contributed and which he influenced, and the complex events of his own philosophical career.

The first part of the volume, which is devoted to Fichte's development, contains contributions by Daniel Breazeale, Violetta Waibel, Günter Zöller, Steven Hoeltzel, Michael Vater, and George Seidel. Breazeale's "Toward a *Wissenschaftslehre more geometrico* (1800–1801)" provides a close reading of Fichte's precise trajectory during the crucial period of 1800–1801, focusing especially on his *New Version of the Wissenschaftslehre* (*Neue Bearbeitung der Wissenschaftslehre*). Breazeale usefully turns to letters and unpublished manuscripts, as well as this particular version of the *Wissenschaftslehre,* in walking us painstakingly through the various objections to Fichte's earlier expressions of his philosophical project and in charting ways in which his responses to these objections impacted his thinking. In "Structures of Imagination in Fichte's *Wissenschaftslehre* 1794–1795 and 1804," Waibel offers a more schematic, but philosophically very interesting argument for the continuity of Fichte's Jena and Prussian periods. The chapter is organized into three parts: problems with Kant's philosophy, the theory of imagination in the early *Wissenschaftslehre,* and the changes in the structure and intent of the basic position in the 1804 *Wissenschaftslehre.* The first half of Zöller's "Thinking and Willing in the Later Fichte" gives a broad review of Fichte's treatment of the relation of thinking and willing, first in lectures of the late 1790s and then in the second Jena version of the *Wissenschaftslehre.* Zöller demonstrates the fundamental duality of the I throughout the attempt to think the absolute ground of subjectivity in the *Wissenschaftslehre nova methodo,* as well as the shift that occurs via the reclassification of the I, formerly the ground, as a form or mode and the identification of the ground as something independent of the I. The central contribution of this chapter is its sketch of the exciting contents of the *Transcendental Logic* and the later *System of Ethics* (1812).

Both Hoeltzel and Vater discuss the relation of Schelling and Fichte. In "Toward or Away from Schelling? On the Thematic Shift in Fichte's Later Philosophy," Hoeltzel makes a persuasive case for the fascinating claim that Fichte's 1801 *Wissenschaftslehre* has strong affinities with the position Schelling had initially adopted around 1795. Further light on the relation between Schelling and Fichte is thrown by Vater's "Fichte's Reaction to Schelling's Identity Philosophy in 1806." This controversial claim is tempered by Vater, who argues that after he left Jena, Fichte explicitly targeted Schelling among those who misunderstood his position. Vater, who analyzes a text Fichte wrote in 1806, but which was unpublished in his lifetime, focuses on Fichte's reaction to early critics of his position as well as on his partly vitriolic denunciation of Schelling's philosophy of identity. He concludes by suggesting that despite the interest of Schelling's philosophy of being, it can only illuminate the objective pole of cognition. In Kant's wake, Fichte must be preferred to Schelling for his potential contribution in bringing together the disunity left by Kant's three *Critiques.*

Seidel's "The Light That Lights the Seeing of the Light: The Second *Wissenschaftslehre* of 1804" examines the relation between the view in this text and its earlier formulations. According to Seidel, despite the many changes, two aspects remain constant in the *Wissenschaftslehre* of 1804. First, being is still posited being, and second, there is still the *Sollen* (or "ought") of Fichte's moral idealism. In Seidel's account, Fichte answers the question about what we seek in seeking the truth by suggesting that religion, above all Christianity, is the content of which philosophy is the form.

The second part of this volume contains chapters by Yolanda Estes, Ernst-Otto Onnasch, Kevin Zanelotti, Johannes Brachtendorf, and Holger Zaborowski that discuss Fichte's philosophy of religion. Fichte initially made a name for himself when his early *Attempt at a Critique of All Revelation* (1792), for reasons that have never been satisfactorily explained, was published without the author's name and preface. This book, which was mistaken as Kant's long-awaited work on religion, immediately called attention to Fichte and led quickly to a prestigious chair at the University of Jena for him. Fichte, who then turned aside from the philosophy of religion in working out his theoretical philosophy, came back to this theme near the end of his stay in Jena, when he was suddenly accused of atheism. It is then ironic that in the wake of the so-called Atheism Controversy (*Atheismusstreit*) of 1798–99, the very thinker who had initially called attention to himself because of his interest in religion was forced to resign his post on suspicion of impiety.

After he left Jena, Fichte returned to and further worked out his philosophy of religion. Indeed, some observers believe he strengthened his personal link to religion in the wake of this controversy. In their respective chapters, Estes, Onnasch, and Zanelotti address the complicated theme of how best to interpret Fichte's *Guide to the Blessed Life, or the Doctrine of Religion* (*Die Anweisung zum seligen Leben oder auch Religionslehre*). In "After Jena: Fichte's *Religionslehre*," Estes identifies points of continuity between Fichte's later philosophy of religion and his overall Jena philosophical perspective. She argues that Fichte's position, despite some alterations in his views of morality and religion, remains consistent with his earlier, Jena views of God and philosophy. She begins by reviewing the account of blessedness in the *Religionslehre* before comparing it with earlier discussions of moral consciousness. She then reviews the transcendental philosophy of religion presented in the *Religionslehre* with the *Wissenschaftslehre nova methodo.* The chapter concludes with a differentiation of the *Religionslehre* from absolute idealism, mysticism, and dogmatic theology. Onnasch offers, in "Fichte's Conception of the System of Philosophy in *Die Anweisung zum seligen Leben*," a careful study of Fichte's 1805 lectures on philosophy of religion with particular attention to Fichte's metaphysical commitment in those lectures. He carefully navigates the way in which Fichte consistently presents two potentially conflicting conceptions of being: as determined by consciousness and as an externalized appearance of absolute being as manifested in and through consciousness. Zanelotti's "How Not to Read Fichte's *Die Anweisung zum seligen Leben* (1806): Against the Mystical Reading" provides a powerful attack *against* Anthony Perovich's well-known reading of the *Anweisung* and *for* the significance of Fichte's later work as a departure from the *Wissenschaftslehre.* After stipulating a canonically accepted conception of mysticism and elaborating Perovich's claim that Fichte espouses a weak, introverted mysticism, Zanelotti recounts Fichte's own statements that contrast mysticism with transcendental philosophy. In the second part of the chapter he makes a trenchant case for the incompatibility of the *Anweisung* with mysticism and that at the same time explains why it has been so interpreted. The explanation, on Zanelotti's reading, lies in the way in which the *Anweisung* departs from the *Wissenschaftslehre* by posing the problem of the one and the many in a way that transgresses transcendental idealism in countenancing "an ontology that grounds finite existence in the necessary manifestation of the Absolute from itself."

The second half of the section on religion contains more general essays by Johannes Brachtendorf and Holger Zaborowski. It is often claimed that in his later work Fichte reverts to a pre-critical metaphysical stance and thereby undermines the central contribution of his Jena writings. Brachtendorf's comparative study of Fichte's theory of being, "The Notion of Being in Fichte's Late Philosophy," brings much-needed clarity to this question, in the process clarifying some difficult sections in Fichte's texts. He offers a very clear account of the transition in Fichte's account of subjectivity. In "Fall and Freedom," Zaborowski provides a very well-written and extremely thorough survey of Fichte's mature philosophy of religion with a critical eye toward demonstrating the ways in which Fichte's philosophy of religion is developed in conversation with the doctrine of original sin. Zaborowski's theological analysis of Saint Paul's account of original sin shows how the issue of original sin informs Fichte's philosophy of history and his secularized account of human redemption.

The third and final section considers Fichte's later "popular" and not so popular philosophy in contributions by Andrew Fiala, Angelica Nuzzo, and Tom Rockmore that are devoted respectively to Fichte's views of language, history, and knowledge. In "Fichte and the *Ursprache*," Fiala points to the connection between Fichte's philosophy of language and human freedom and compares his early philosophy of language with the theory of language underlying his *Addresses to the German Nation* given during the French occupation. Fiala does a good job of showing the way in which language shapes human subjectivity. At the beginning of the last century, Emil Lask, who influenced Heidegger, Lukács, and Kroner in his short career, made an important contribution to our grasp of Fichte's view of history. Nuzzo examines " 'The Logic of Historical Truth': History and Individual in Fichte's Late Philosophy of History" in the course of concentrating on Fichte's *Characteristics of the Present Age* (1804). The result is a strong case for a certain reading of Fichte's philosophy of history, another important aspect of his work "after Jena." Nuzzo's reading supports Lask's and extends to include an inquiry into the general systematic conditions for a theory of history. Rockmore's "Fichte on Knowledge, Practice, and History" traces Fichte's treatment of knowledge and history against the background of the critical philosophy. He suggests that Fichte contributes to this movement in reformulating the ahistorical Kantian position on the basis of the primacy of practical reason, which is finally understood historically. He further suggests that though Fichte differs from Kant, Fichte's conceptions of knowledge and history are a priori, and hence ahistorical.

Note

1. See J. G. Fichte, *Johann Gottlieb Fichte: Gesamtausgabe der Bayerischen Akademie der Wissenschaften,* ed. Reinhard Lauth, Hans Jacobs, Hans Gliwitzky, and Erich Fuchs (Stuttgart-Bad Cannstatt: Frommann, 1964–), 32 volumes to date. This complete edition of Fichte's writings is cited as *GA* in the notes.

Abbreviations

Works by Johann Gottlieb Fichte are cited in the notes (and occasionally in text) by the following abbreviations:

AGN *Addresses to the German Nation,* trans. R. F. Jones and G. H. Turnbull (Chicago: Open Court, 1922).

ASL *Die Anweisung zum seligen Leben, oder auch Religionslehre,* ed. Hansjürgen Verweyen (Hamburg: Felix Meiner, 1994).

CPA *Characteristics of the Present Age,* in *Significant Contributions to the History of Psychology, 1750–1920,* ed. Daniel N. Robinson, vii–290 (Washington, D.C.: University Press of America, 1977).

EPW *Fichte: Early Philosophical Writings,* ed. and trans. Daniel Breazeale (Ithaca: Cornell University Press, 1988).

FTP *Fichte: Foundations of Transcendental Philosophy (Wissenschaftslehre) nova methodo (1796/99),* ed. and trans. Daniel Breazeale (Ithaca: Cornell University Press, 1992).

FW *Fichtes Werke,* ed. Immanuel Hermann Fichte, 11 vols. (Berlin: De Gruyter, 1971). This is an integrated reprint of *NW* and *SW* (see below).

FZR *J. G. Fichte in zeitgenössischen Rezensionen,* ed. Erich Fuchs, Wilhelm G. Jacobs, and Walter Schieche (Stuttgart-Bad Cannstatt: Frommann-Holzboog, 1995).

GA *Johann Gottlieb Fichte: Gesamtausgabe der Bayerischen Akademie der Wissenschaften,* ed. Reinhard Lauth, Hans Jacobs, Hans Gliwitzky, and Erich Fuchs (Stuttgart-Bad Cannstatt: Frommann, 1964–), 32 volumes to date. Successive numbers (separated by periods) designate the series and the volume of this edition, respectively, and the number (or numbers) after the colon refer to the page numbers; for example, *GA* 1.4:183.

GGZ *Die Grundzüge des gegenwärtigen Zeitalters* (Hamburg: Felix Meiner, 1978).

IWL *Introductions to the Wissenschaftslehre and Other Writings (1797–1800),* ed. and trans. Daniel Breazeale (Indianapolis: Hackett, 1994).

NW — *Johann Gottlieb Fichtes nachgelassene Werke,* ed. Immanuel Hermann Fichte, 3 vols. (Bonn: Adolph-Marcus, 1834–35).

RL — *Die Anweisung zum seligen Leben, oder auch der Religionslehre* (1806), ed. Fritz Medicus (Hamburg: Meiner, 1910).

SW — *Johann Gottlieb Fichtes sämmtliche Werke,* ed. Immanuel Hermann Fichte, 8 vols. (Berlin: Veit, 1845–46).

TL — *Über das Verhältniß der Logik zur Philosophie oder transscendentale Logik,* ed. Reinhard Lauth and Peter K. Schneider, with the collaboration of Kurt Hiller (Hamburg: Meiner, 1982).

VM — *The Vocation of Man,* ed. and trans. Peter Preuss (Indianapolis: Hackett, 1987).

VOM — *The Vocation of Man,* trans. William Smith, rev. and ed. Roderick M. Chisholm (Indianapolis: Bobbs-Merrill, 1956).

WBL — *The Way Towards the Blessed Life, or the Doctrine of Religion,* trans. William Smith, in *Significant Contributions to the History of Psychology, 1750–1920,* ed. Daniel N. Robinson, 291–496 (Washington, D.C.: University Press of America, 1977).

WLNM — *Wissenschaftslehre nova methodo: Kollegnachschrift K. Chr. Fr. Krause 1798/99,* ed. Erich Fuchs (Hamburg: Felix Meiner, 1982; 2nd ed., 1994).

WZV — *Die Wissenschaftslehre: Zweiter Vortrag im Jahre 1804 vom 16. April bis 8. Juni,* ed. R. Lauth et al., 2nd ed. (Hamburg: Meiner, 1986).

AFTER JENA

Toward a *Wissenschaftslehre more geometrico* (1800–1801)

Daniel Breazeale

On the "Development" of Fichte's Philosophy and the Problematic "Unity of the *Wissenschaftslehren*"

The issue of the development of Fichte's philosophy—sometimes referred to as the problem of the "unity of the *Wissenschaftslehren*"—has long been central to Fichte studies. Even during his own lifetime, Fichte had to respond to charges—notably Schelling's—that he had abandoned the standpoint of his early, Jena system for a radically different one.[1] Though some excellent scholars—for example, Loewe, Fischer, Léon, and Wundt[2]—have agreed with Fichte on this point, and have argued that the differences between the various presentations of the *Wissenschaftslehre* concern only the external "form" of a philosophical system the underlying principles and content of which remained unchanged from beginning to end, many others have been convinced that the striking differences of vocabulary and of presentation between, for example, the *Grundlage der gesamten Wissenschaftslehre* of 1794–95, the *Darstellung der Wissenschaftslehre* of 1801–2, and the *Wissenschaftslehre* of 1810, are indications of profound differences in the underlying contents of the same. These same interpreters, however, disagree among themselves concerning the precise number of significantly different "stages" or "periods" to assign to the development of the *Wissenschaftslehre.* Should one, for example, in the manner of Erdmann, Windelband, Medicus, Weischedel, Schmid, Heimsoeth, Janke, Rohs, and many others, simply distinguish between "earlier" and "later" *Wissenschaftslehren,* separated by an alleged "turn toward the absolute"?[3] Or should one, in the manner of Rickert, Lask, and Drechsler, also distinguish a "middle period"?[4] Or should one make even finer-grained distinctions within each of these two (or three) main periods,[5] emphasizing the distinctive character of *each* of Fichte's fifteen or so individual presentations of his philosophy?[6]

Even among those who concede that there are substantial differences among at least some of Fichte's presentations of his philosophy there is disagreement concerning the precise *significance* of these differences, with some concluding that they represent sharp breaks in the continuity of Fichte's thinking and others arguing for the slow and continual "evolution" of the *Wissenschaftslehre* from one presentation to the next. Interpreters of the former sort, of whom Gueroult is a good example, sometimes associate Fichte's apparent shift from one standpoint to another with certain external events, such as the "Atheism Controversy," or with the criticisms or initiatives of other philosophers, such as Jacobi or Schelling.[7] In contrast, those who emphasize the continuity between the various *Wissenschaftslehren* usually interpret the differences between them as expressions of a certain *immanent*—"logical" or "dialectical"—development of Fichte's own thinking, and thus they try to show how each successive version represents an effort on Fichte's part to clarify issues left obscure in earlier versions and to solve new problems raised by his previous solutions to older ones. This is the course taken by, among others, Gurwitsch, Hartmann, Radrizzani, and Lauth.[8]

What most "evolutionary" approaches to the *Wissenschaftslehre* have in common is a tendency to view the later versions as the more "definitive" ones and thus to interpret the earlier ones in their light[9]—which is, no doubt, how Fichte himself eventually came to view them. This, however, does not mean that *we* have to read these texts in this way. Indeed, one might well argue that the "spirit" of the various versions is so different that one does irreparable violence to the same when one uses, say, the second *Wissenschaftslehre* of 1804 for clues for interpreting the 1794–95 *Grundlage*—a point to which I shall return at the conclusion of my remarks.

The scholarly debate over the relationship between the earlier and later *Wissenschaftslehren* has been complicated by several factors, including the incomplete and unsatisfactory state of the documentary evidence. Not only were many of the later manuscript versions of the *Wissenschaftslehre* unavailable to earlier scholars, but those that were available were often published in incomplete and defectively edited form. Another complicating factor is a tendency to confuse questions concerning the internal, systematic development of the *Wissenschaftslehre* with biographical issues concerning external, often highly dramatic, changes in Fichte's external circumstances and career. Dazzled by the visibility and drama of many of these biographical events, some scholars have felt an almost irresistible temptation to employ Fichte's biography as the key to his philosophy.

Though it would be absurd to suggest that the dramatic changes in Fichte's external circumstances had *no* consequences whatsoever for the development of his philosophy, the dangers of such an approach should also be readily apparent. Whereas it is impossible to overlook the direct connections between, on the one hand, the dramatic changes in Fichte's political views between his 1793 *Beitrag zur Berichtigung der Urtheile des Publicums über die französische Revolution* and his 1808 *Reden an die deutsche Nation* and, on the other, certain even more dramatic events in European history that occurred during this same period, there is no such clearly evident linkage between, for example, Fichte's loss of his position at Jena in 1799 and his decision, more than two years later, to begin the 1801–2 *Darstellung der Wissenschaftslehre* with the concept of *Wissen* rather than with an injunction to "think the I." At the very least, it is the responsibility of those who would appeal to the influence of such external factors upon the internal development of Fichte's philosophy to demonstrate—in detail—the linkage in question.

The remarks that follow are intended as a modest contribution to the ongoing discussion of the evolution and unity of Fichte's thought. They are concerned with what is surely one of the least-known and most neglected versions of the *Wissenschaftslehre:* namely, the fragmentary and unfinished *Neue Bearbeitung der Wissenschaftslehre,* or, as I shall more often refer to it, "the *Wissenschaftslehre* of 1800–1801"—a designation that includes both the unpublished *Neue Bearbeitung* and the published *Sonnenklarer Bericht,* a text that was originally intended by Fichte to bear precisely the same "introductory" relationship to the *Neue Bearbeitung* that the two "Einleitungen" of 1797 have to the unfinished *Versuch einer neuen Darstellung der Wissenschaftslehre.* Reasons for the relative neglect of the *Neue Bearbeitung* are, of course, not difficult to identify, beginning with the fact that this text remained wholly unknown to scholars for almost two centuries and was first published in 1979.[10] Furthermore, the manuscript itself, which occupies only seventy-one pages in the *Gesamtausgabe,* was evidently abandoned by its author after only a few months' work and is thus no more than a fragment of the full-scale "New Presentation" confidently described by Fichte in a public announcement dated "4 November 1800" and published in January 1801.[11]

For all of its shortcomings, the *Wissenschaftslehre* of 1800–1801 is of special interest not only in its own right, but also to anyone concerned with Fichte's philosophical development, since it was written precisely during the period which, for many scholars, represents the dividing line between the "early *Wissenschaftslehre,*" with its focus upon the structure of self-consciousness and its elaborate account of the I and the "later *Wissenschaftslehre,*" with its focus upon the structure of *Wissen* or *Wahrheit* and its new emphasis on the relationship of these to "the absolute." As Günter Meckenstock, in one of the rare scholarly publications devoted explicitly to the *Neue Bearbeitung,* puts it: "Between the fragmentary *Neue*

Bearbeitung der Wissenschaftslehre and the *Wissenschaftslehre* of 1801/2 that followed it, there lies a gap."[12] The purpose of the following remarks is to explore this "gap" in some detail.

"Streiferein im Gebiete der Philosophie"

Despite certain misgivings about appealing to external or extra-philosophical circumstances to explain or to illuminate the doctrinal development of the *Wissenschaftslehre,* I now propose to call attention to a series of public criticisms that are, I believe, of special importance for understanding the internal evolution of Fichte's conception of his own project during the period that concerns us—namely, the period between his conclusion of his final series of lectures on the *Wissenschaftslehre nova methodo,* in Jena in the spring of 1799, and his commencement of a new series of private lectures on the *Wissenschaftslehre* in Berlin at the end of 1801.[13]

Fichte's philosophy was, of course, controversial from the start, and it seems he was always being criticized from one side or another and always making plans to reply to such criticisms. But the years 1799–1801 were surely something of a high point in this respect. The public criticism advanced against the *Wissenschaftslehre* during these years is distinguished not only by its enormous *volume* and often intemperate *tone,* but also by the *philosophical stature* of many of Fichte's critics, who included Kant, Jacobi, Reinhold, Hamann, Herder, Nicolai, Schleiermacher, and Jean Paul, in addition to a host of lesser-known professional philosophers. In the following survey I shall ignore the purely personal attacks on Fichte by critics such as Nicolai, as well as the public ridicule to which his philosophy was subjected by authors such as Jean Paul and Schleiermacher.[14] I shall also ignore the specific charge of "atheism" and the baroque details of the Atheism Controversy. Instead, I shall focus on a few of the more significant *theoretical* objections to the *Wissenschaftslehre.* I will then try to indicate how Fichte, in his writings of this period, responded to these criticisms. The point of this exercise will be to determine whether such information helps to illuminate the peculiarities of the unfinished *Neue Bearbeitung* of 1800–1801.

The temptation to interpret transcendental claims as factual, empirical claims about the human mind, and hence to view philosophy as a branch of psychology or as a kind of introspective anthropology, is as old as transcendental philosophy itself. Indeed, some of Fichte's earliest polemical works were directed against efforts to base philosophy on "the facts of consciousness."[15] In the wake of the *Atheismusstreit,* the *Wissenschaftslehre* was once again criticized on precisely this score by several authors, beginning with Johann Heusinger, whose 1799 tract, *Über das idealistisch-atheistische System des Herrn Profeßor Fichte,* was judged by Fichte himself to be one of the more philosophically substantial contributions to the *Atheismusstreit.*[16] As is clear from his later comments, Fichte was particularly provoked by Heusinger's charge that the *Wissenschaftslehre's* account of the self-construction of the I, *qua* intellectual intuition, as presented in chapter 1 of the *Versuch einer neuen Darstellung,* was based on nothing more than a series of "psychological delusions."[17]

Nor was Heusinger the only critic to interpret the *Wissenschaftslehre* in a straightforwardly "psychological" manner; this was also how it was often characterized by empiricists and *Popularphilosophen.* Thus Nicolai, in his book of 1799, *Ueber meine gelehrte Bildung,*[18] describes transcendental idealism as teaching that each person creates his own, private world by the mere association of ideas. A similar charge was eventually repeated by Reinhold, an erstwhile exponent of the *Wissenschaftslehre.*[19]

More worrying to Fichte than Reinhold's endorsement of the charge of psychologism, however, was the latter's startling conversion, in the spring of 1799, to C. G. Bardili's conception of philosophy as a system of "rational realism," based purely upon "thinking *qua* thinking." According to this conception, philosophy should be understood as a type of pure logic, which stands in no need of any appeal whatsoever to the evidence of "intuition" (*Anschauung*). In embracing this new conception of philosophy, Reinhold publicly announced that the *Wissenschaftslehre* had been superseded by Bardili's system, which he described as occupying a standpoint "between Fichte's philosophy and Jacobi's."[20]

Ironically, at the very moment that Reinhold was chastising Fichte for his failure to embrace Bardili's conception of philosophy as pure logic, others were interpreting the *Wissenschaftslehre* in precisely this manner: namely, as a purely "formal philosophy," or system of pure logic, and were criticizing it accordingly. This was the gravamen of Kant's charge against Fichte in his public "Declaration" of August 28, 1799.[21] A similar charge was also made by critics such as Jean Paul and Nicolai, who accused Fichte of illicitly smuggling all of the *Wissenschaftslehre*'s alleged "conclusions" into its first principle, from whence they were subsequently "derived" by nothing more than sheer logical analysis.[22]

The publication, in 1799 and 1800, of Herder's and Hamann's "Metacritiques" of transcendental philosophy[23] was viewed by Fichte as yet another attack upon the *Wissenschaftslehre.* Herder and Hamann criticized transcendental philosophy for failing to recognize the extent to which all thought is conditioned by natural language and thus for its failure to preface its critique of reason with a critique of language. Another linguistically based criticism was applied explicitly to the *Wissenschaftslehre* by Jean

Paul, who characterized Fichte's philosophy as "mere language, free of concepts and intuitions."[24]

But of all the philosophical criticisms to which Fichte was subjected during the period 1799–1801, none seems to have affected him more deeply and more personally than the famous charge of "nihilism" leveled against the *Wissenschaftslehre* by Jacobi in his "open letter" of 1799.[25] No sooner, according to Jacobi, does transcendental reflection set to work on reality than it transforms the latter into a mere "construction," lacking any reality of its own. Adding insult to injury, Jacobi rebuked Fichte for his "logical enthusiasm" and characterized him derisively as motivated by "the solitary spirit of the philosopher for whom there is only one possible philosophy."[26]

Hostile reviews of *Die Bestimmung des Menschen* began to appear in the spring and summer of 1800, and some of these were very fresh in Fichte's mind as he set to work on the *Neue Bearbeitung* later that year. Of these critical reviews, he seems to have taken most seriously one that appeared anonymously in the Erlangen *Literatur-Zeitung*, the author of which was probably Johann Heinrich Abicht.[27] This reviewer rejected the account of "knowing" (*Wissen*) found in book 2 of *Die Bestimmung des Menschen* on the grounds that it presupposes something that is in fact impossible: namely, that we can be consciously aware of our own activity of intuiting. Instead, this critic claimed that we are only passively conscious of external "perceptions" and never directly aware of our own inner acts and therefore issues to Fichte the following challenge: "Just explain your own explanation!"[28]

Another critical review of *Die Bestimmung des Menschen,* this one by Friedrich Ludwig Bouterwek,[29] deserves mention for its conclusion, which calls attention to what Bouterwek characterizes as the radical differences between each of Fichte's three different presentations of his philosophy: first, in the *Grundlage der gesamten Wissenschaftslehre,* where it is presented as a new metaphysics grounded on the principle of identity; second, in the *Versuch einer neuen Darstellung,* where the *Wissenschaftslehre* is grounded on intellectual intuition; and finally, in *Die Bestimmung des Menschen,* where it is presented as a form of *Glaubensphilosophie.* In suggesting that the system propounded by Fichte in 1800 was no longer the same one he had presented to the public in 1794, Bouterwek appears to have been the first to raise publicly the question concerning "the unity of the *Wissenschaftslehre.*" Indeed, his remarks on the subject may well have assisted Fichte in posing this problem more clearly for himself.

Last, but by no means least, one must mention Fichte's growing appreciation during this period of the ever-increasing divergence between his own philosophical standpoint and that of the person to whom he was still referring in public as "my talented co-worker, Prof. Schelling."[30] Though Fichte had long been concerned by Schelling's more extravagant forays into *Naturphilosophie,* it was his careful reading, sometime in the latter half of 1800, of the latter's *System des transscendentalen Idealismus,* and especially of the "Introduction" to the same, with its patronizing remarks concerning the "one-sided idealism" of the *Wissenschaftslehre,*[31] that seems to have made him fully aware of the growing gulf between his standpoint and Schelling's. Fichte's alarm on this score was only increased by his correspondence with Schelling during the period he was working on the *Neue Bearbeitung,* in the course of which their differences—concerning such matters as the relationship between consciousness and nature and the possibility of an "objective intellectual intuition"—became impossible to ignore.[32]

Fichte Responds to His Critics

When, in the fall of 1800, Fichte was finally able to set to work in earnest on the new presentation of the *Wissenschaftslehre* that he had described to his publisher nine months earlier,[33] he was, even more than usual, a thoroughly *embattled* thinker. As usual, his first inclination seems to have been to dismiss the foregoing criticisms either as evidence of simple misunderstanding, symptoms of an utter lack of philosophical ability, or expressions of pure malice. Yet some of these criticisms could not be so easily dismissed and demanded a genuinely philosophical response, and thus most of Fichte's publications during the period 1800–1801 include direct or indirect responses to specific, albeit usually unnamed, critics and opponents. Even *Die Bestimmung des Menschen* can be viewed in this light, for it represents Fichte's most sustained and direct philosophical response to the public charge of atheism and to Jacobi's charge of nihilism.

Consequently, the preparation of a new systematic presentation of the *Wissenschaftslehre* was closely associated with the project of defending the *Wissenschaftslehre* against the criticisms mentioned above. Indeed, these should not really be viewed as two separate tasks at all, inasmuch as Fichte seems to have concluded that the best way to *defend* his philosophy was to provide a new, clearer, and more convincing *presentation* of it (the *Neue Bearbeitung*), prefaced by a separate "critical" or metaphilosophical introduction, in which he would indeed "explain his explanation" (the *Sonnenklarer Bericht*).

An excellent illustration of how intimately Fichte associated the task of responding to his critics with that of providing a new presentation of his philosophy may be found in the lengthy public "Announcement" of the new presentation that he prepared in early November 1800.[34] In this neglected but important document he not only describes some of the distinctive features of his new presentation and relates it to previous presentations of the *Wissenschaftslehre,* but also responds indirectly to most of the specific criticisms mentioned above.

Has his theoretical position undergone radical alteration since 1794, as Bouterwek charged? No, responds Fichte, even as he apologizes for what he admits to be certain purely external deficiencies in the presentation contained in the *Grundlage der gesamten Wissenschaftslehre.*[35] Declining to argue the point, he instead offers to assume full blame for the obscurity of his earlier presentations, if his readers will promise to give the new presentation their full and unprejudiced attention, taking no account whatsoever of his earlier writings.[36]

Has Kant publicly disassociated himself from the *Wissenschaftslehre* and repudiated it as an abortive attempt to construct a new metaphysics on the basis of logic? Yes, he has, but this simply betrays his complete lack of acquaintance with Fichte's philosophy.[37] Though Fichte continues to insist on the underlying affinity between Kant's critical philosophy and the *Wissenschaftslehre*—and hence to imply that Kant could not really reject the latter without rejecting the former[38]—it is clear that he is no longer interested in insisting upon this point and is quite prepared to describe the *Wissenschaftslehre* as "a completely *newly discovered* science . . . the very idea of which did not exist before."[39]

Far more important than any argument over the adequacy of Kant's understanding of the *Wissenschaftslehre* or the true relationship between the latter and the critical philosophy, however, is the claim, voiced variously by Kant, Nicolai, and Jean Paul, that the *Wissenschaftslehre* is a purely "formal philosophy" or "logical" system, consisting of nothing but the logical analysis of its own (undemonstrated) first principle. To rebuff this charge was also to refute those philosophers—above all Bardili and Reinhold—who explicitly championed just such a conception of philosophy, understood as the logical analysis of pure concepts, based on nothing but "thinking as thinking."

Against such critics, Fichte explicitly denies that his philosophy is nothing more than "rational cognition *on the basis of concepts.*" Instead, he maintains, genuine philosophy, like mathematics, must be conceived as "rational cognition *on the basis of intuitions.*"[40] In fact, by far the largest and most interesting portion of the November 4 "Announcement" is devoted to a discussion of the parallels between the methods of mathematics (especially geometry) and philosophy and to an examination of the essential roles therein of construction and intuition. By describing the *Wissenschaftslehre* as "the *mathesis* of reason itself,"[41] Fichte clearly means to distance himself in the strongest possible terms from the conception of philosophy propounded by Bardili in his *Grundriss der Logik,* of which Fichte wrote a highly unflattering review immediately before setting to work on the *Neue Bearbeitung.*[42]

Though Fichte had defended the role of intuition within philosophy in some of his earlier writings, most notably, in the *Versuch einer neuen Darstellung der Wissenschaftslehre,* the claims put forward in the "Announcement" and the Third Lesson of the *Sonnenklarer Bericht* (which were written at about the same time) go well beyond anything he had previously published on this topic, and, as we shall see, point to one of the most characteristic and distinctive features of the 1800–1801 *Wissenschaftslehre.* This point is expressed as follows in the "Announcement":

> A "critique of reason" involves a cognition *of* reason, which is here the *object of cognition;* and thus reason has been assigned the task, prior to anything else, of examining itself. Only after it has done this can it then go on to examine how it may be able to cognize anything beyond itself. Consequently, from the moment that a "critique of reason" became a topic of conversation, it should have been obvious that reason does not grasp itself and cannot apprehend itself by means of anything else (such as a concept) that has to be derived from something else and that does not possess its foundation or ground within itself. Instead, reason can grasp and apprehend itself only immediately—and there is nothing immediate but *intuition.* Hence, if philosophy is from now on to be synonymous with *reason's own self-produced cognition of itself,* then philosophy can by no means be considered to be cognition based upon concepts, but must instead be cognition based upon intuition.[43]

The opposition between the *Wissenschaftslehre* and any "pure logic," or philosophy based merely upon concepts, could scarcely be plainer. Indeed, this is precisely what distinguishes a "*reele Philosophie,*" such as Fichte's, from all types of "*FormularPhilosophie.*" This distinction will be highlighted in the *Neue Bearbeitung.*

The parallels between philosophy and mathematics are developed still further in the November 1800 "Announcement," which also includes a sustained account of the intuitive foundation of all universally valid truth claims, as well as an explication of the role of "construction" in establishing and verifying such claims. The method of philosophy is explicitly identified as that of "intellectual intuition," and Fichte makes a sustained effort to explain what he means by "intuition" in general and by "intellectual intuition" in particular. The explanation in question, however, does not consist of new definitions, for definitions deal with concepts, which must, in turn, be grounded in intuitions. Thus, Fichte maintains, the only way in which one can "explain" the method of the *Wissenschaftslehre* is by assisting others in *producing* for themselves the requisite "intuitions."

From this it follows that the "metacritics'" proposal that philosophy be preceded by a critique of language should be rejected as betraying a faulty conception of the nature of philosophical evidence. According to Fichte's theory of language, linguistic signs serve only to designate concepts, and are thus even further removed from intuitions than are concepts. The very *fact* of mutual understanding and of our recognition of "universally valid" truths (for example, in mathematics) is, according to Fichte, sufficient to demonstrate that there must be a ground of evidence that is higher and more certain than anything that depends on words or concepts.[44] In an aside that seems to anticipate not only the *Neue Bearbeitung* of 1800, but the later presentations of 1801–2 and 1804, Fichte remarks that no one should approach the *Wissenschaftslehre* without first reflecting carefully on the nature of "immediate evidence" and "universal validity in general."[45]

In the context of 1800, however, it is probable that Fichte's comments on the distinctive role of intuitive evidence in philosophy and mathematics are largely intended to rectify the confusion on the part of some of his critics concerning the difference between transcendental philosophy and "psychology." As the parallel with mathematics is intended to make clear, the "intuitions" to which the *Wissenschaftslehre* appeals are not sensible "perceptions" and do not constitute passively received facts of empirical consciousness. Instead, like the intuitions of the geometer, those of the transcendental philosopher are inner intuitions of consciously intended mental *acts*. This explains why the concepts introduced within the *Wissenschaftslehre* can be understood only by one who *constructs them for himself* by actually *performing* the corresponding acts of intuition.[46] Fichte employs this same argument against the charge of psychologism in several other writings of this period, such as "Aus einem Privatschreiben," which includes a note responding directly to Heusinger's charge that the *Wissenschaftslehre*'s concept of the I is based on a "psychological illusion."[47] Another example may be found in the brief note, "An das philosophische Publikum,"[48] in which Fichte repeats Heusinger's charge, with the comment, "as if the *Wissenschaftslehre* were psychology and proceeded from the facts of consciousness, instead of from a freely produced product of speculation." This, he says, would be like claiming that geometry is based on a psychological illusion, inasmuch as mathematical points and lines cannot be presented in outer perception.[49]

With regard to Schelling, the "Announcement" continues to display a certain tact, and Fichte explicitly excuses himself from making any comment on Schelling's recent publications.[50] The well-informed reader will nevertheless recognize a thinly veiled criticism of Schelling's entire project only a few pages later, where Fichte explicitly endorses Kant's rejection of Schlosser's notion of an "objective" intellectual intuition of an independently existing "something" outside the mind. Indeed, Fichte spells out for his readers the implications of his agreement with Kant on this point: "For me, intellectual intuition is not the intuition of a persisting 'something' [*eines bestehenden Etwas*], and there can therefore be no 'objective intuition' of 'nature in itself.'"[51]

Considering that he had just published a book-length reply to Jacobi's charge of "nihilism," it is perhaps not surprising that the only allusion to Jacobi's "Open Letter" in the 1800 "Announcement" is a short comment on the dispute between *Viel-Philosophen* (such as Jacobi), who countenance the possibility of many different philosophies, and *Allein-Philosophen* (such as Fichte), for whom there can be only one genuine philosophy. Rather than a sign of modesty and tolerance, the laissez-faire attitude of the former is, according to Fichte, merely a sad indication of their ignorance concerning the true nature of all scientific claims. The dispute in question is therefore not really a *philosophical* dispute at all, but is one between philosophers and non-philosophers, inasmuch as "one is either an *Allein-Philosoph* or *no philosopher at all*."[52] A similar point is reiterated in the very first sentence of the *Sonnenklarer Bericht,* where Fichte maintains that "just as there is only one mathematics, so is there only one philosophy."[53]

This concludes our survey of Fichte's 1800 "Announcement," a document that shows just how determined he was to provide a new presentation of the *Wissenschaftslehre* that would silence, once and for all, his philosophical critics. The *Wissenschaftslehre* is neither psychology nor logic, but transcendental idealism. Its method is neither empirical generalization nor logical analysis, but "construction in intuition." As in the case of geometry, there can be but one universally valid system of philosophy, though of course there may be many different presentations of the same. Without renouncing his own earlier presentations, Fichte promised his readers a new and improved one, one that would possess the immediate evidence, the thoroughgoing determinacy, and the irrefutability of mathematics. A note from his publisher announced that the new presentation would appear "around the middle of this year."[54]

The New Version of the *Wissenschaftslehre*

We are at last prepared to consider the text of the *Neue Bearbeitung,* as well as some passages from the work originally conceived as a companion piece or popular introduction to it, the *Sonnenklarer Bericht.* In terms of its content and general structure, the *Neue Bearbeitung* is quite obviously based on Fichte's own manuscript (now lost) of his lectures on the *Wissenschaftslehre nova methodo*[55] and corresponds—albeit only roughly—to sections 1–6 of the latter, though some of the contents of sections 7–10 are discussed as well.[56] Like the *Wissenschaftslehre nova methodo,* the *Neue Bearbeitung* begins with a "summons" to "think the I," and it proceeds from there to a discursive derivation of all the other "acts of the mind" that must be accomplished as conditions for the possibility of the act of pure and immediate self-awareness (or intellectual intuition) with which the reader is supposed to begin. Accordingly, the *Neue Bearbeitung* contains discussions of such familiar topics as the relationship between activity and non-activity, intuitions and concepts, intuiting and thinking, determinability and determinacy, real and ideal activity, and feeling and striving, as well as "deductions" (or rather, "constructions") of the categories of relation, quality, and quantity. With the introduction of the problem of the origin of goal concepts and the relation of these to the construction of space and time, however, the manuscript suddenly breaks off.

From this bare inventory of topics one might conclude there is nothing all that novel or original about the new version and might therefore agree with those interpreters, such as Reinhard Koch, who read this text primarily as a continuation and clarification of the Jena presentation of the *Wissenschaftslehre nova methodo.*[57] Indeed, the same "spirit" seems to animate both. The starting point is the same; the account of the structure of selfhood is the same, at least in its general outlines; and the method of presentation is also the same: construction grounded in a series of "inner intuitions" guided by the "principle of determinacy" or "law of reflective opposition."

Yet it is also true that certain thematic and methodological features of the *Neue Bearbeitung* seem to point beyond any of the earlier versions of the *Wissenschaftslehre*—including the *Wissenschaftslehre nova methodo*—and to anticipate and even to prepare the way for some of the innovations characteristic of the *Wissenschaftslehren* of 1801–2 and 1804. Before considering these features, however, let us first attend to the many specific ways in which this new presentation addresses and responds to some of the preceding criticisms of and misconceptions concerning the *Wissenschaftslehre.*

Though the November 1800 "Announcement" was surprisingly silent on the subject of philosophy's relationship to reality and to the practical standpoint of ordinary life (which is, of course, the issue at the heart of Jacobi's nihilism charge), the same cannot be said of the new presentation of the *Wissenschaftslehre,* and particularly of the new, popular introduction to it. A detailed and extended discussion of the essential *differences* between the standpoints of philosophy and of life is, in fact, one of the most conspicuous features of the *Sonnenklarer Bericht,* nearly half of which is devoted to precisely this issue.[58]

Though the *Sonnenklarer Bericht* represents Fichte's clearest and most sustained reply to Jacobi's—and, as Fichte was complaining privately, Friedrich Schlegel's[59]—confusion of the standpoints of life and of speculation, remarks on this subject are also scattered throughout the *Neue Bearbeitung* itself,[60] which, like the *Sonnenklarer Bericht,* employs the language of "powers" or "levels" (*Potenzen*) in order to clarify the essential differences between philosophical reflection and the practical, everyday standpoint and to make it clear to the reader "that [here] we *never enter [the realm] of actual consciousness,* but always hover philosophically at a higher level."[61] The reader is thus explicitly warned against confusing philosophical constructions and reconstructions (*Nachkonstruktionen*) of reality with reality itself, of which philosophy can provide us with no more than an "image" (*Bild*) or "replica" (*Abbild*).[62] Fichte was obviously determined that his new presentation should remove every source of misunderstanding on this score and leave no room whatsoever for a future revival of the charge of nihilism.

He also seems to have been equally determined to produce a new presentation of the *Wissenschaftslehre* that would provide no further occasion for any confusion between transcendental philosophy and introspective psychology, a difference he explained as follows: whereas empirical psychology merely *observes* certain passively discovered facts (in this case, facts of "inner experience"), the *Wissenschaftslehre* always requires one to *act* in a certain manner, while simultaneously paying attention to how this act is accomplished. "We begin with postulates," Fichte writes: "Here, therefore, it is never a matter of psychology."[63] It is therefore utterly mistaken to interpret the I of the *Wissenschaftslehre* psychologically or to dismiss it as based on some sort of "psychological illusion."[64]

The *Wissenschaftslehre* of 1800–1801 also includes a direct response to the complaints of the linguistically oriented "metacritics" of transcendental philosophy, including Jean Paul. On the one hand, Fichte concedes that people may sometimes be misled by the terminology of the *Wissenschaftslehre,* since the words it employs will inevitably have a history that includes usages incompatible with the technical meanings they are assigned within philosophy. The solution, however, is not to pretend to engage in a linguistic metacritique prior to philosophizing, but rather to use ordinary language for an extraordinary purpose; namely, as an *aid* or *occasion* or even *provocation,* intended to help readers philosophize for themselves the means of "construction in intuition."

Here again, Fichte insists upon the importance of performing—for oneself, in the "first person," as it were—certain inner acts of reflection and then observing what happens. The purpose of the *Wissenschaftslehre* is not to convey ready-made truths, but to help others perform their own philosophical "experiments" and draw their own conclusions accordingly. The test of any particular philosophical vocabulary, as of any particular presentation of the *Wissenschaftslehre,* is simply whether it can successfully perform this heuristic function. Rather than setting up language—or commonsense understanding—as the proper judge of reason, one must always appeal to inner intuition as the final philosophical criterion. On this point too, the practice of the philosopher resembles that of the mathematician. Both employ technical terminology (or ordinary terms, used in a non-ordinary, technical manner) simply as "signs" or "pointers" (*Zeichen*) for specific—and uncommon—acts of imaginative construction and intuition. It is therefore just as inappropriate to raise "metacritical" objections against philosophy as it would be to criticize mathematics from the standpoint of ordinary language.[65]

Such considerations help explain the strong new emphasis in the *Wissenschaftslehre* of 1800–1801 on the essential roles of *intuition* and *construction* within philosophy. Not only does this reveal the misguided nature of the call for a linguistic metacritique of philosophy, but it also responds to Bardili's and Reinhold's project of reducing philosophy to logic and basing it on "thinking *qua* thinking."[66] The problem with such a project, as Fichte explained in his review of Bardili's *Grundriß* and then reiterated in his *Antwortschreiben an Herrn Prof. Reinhold,*[67] is this: a philosophy that limits itself to the realm of "pure thinking" can claim for itself only a purely analytic type of "universality" and "necessity," and it can claim this only because it sacrifices all real content. Such a "FormularPhilosophie" is therefore nothing but a "desiccated conceptual game."[68] If, on the other hand, Bardili's "rational realism" can lay any claim to possessing real content, this is only because it has surreptitiously imported this content from ordinary sense experience. This new, "purely logical" system thus turns out to be "the most crass form of dogmatic dualism," based entirely upon empirical evidence.[69] It can claim to be a system of "real thinking" only if it forfeits its claims to universality and necessity.

Only through its *object,* and not through its mere form, can philosophical speculation obtain any "reality" of its own, and only thereby can the *Wissenschaftslehre* distinguish itself from philosophy as a formal game (*spielende Formal-Philosophie*).[70] The only way human beings, philosophers included, can obtain access to objects is through intuition. Since knowledge claims based on sensible intuition must lack the necessity and universality demanded of philosophy, it follows that philosophy, like mathematics, must base its claim to "objective reference" on another, "purer" type of intuition: namely, "inner" or "intellectual intuition."[71] Intuition of this sort, however, is possible only of one's own deliberate *acts*—for example, one's act of drawing a line (in imagination) between two points in space or of constructing a concept, for example, the concept of the I.[72] Philosophy can never dispense with concepts, but it cannot limit itself to conceptual analysis. What makes both philosophy and its concepts "real" is that the latter are based on *construction in intuition*. This is a point emphasized over and over again in the *Neue Bearbeitung:* intuition is not only the source of all "real cognition," it is also the source of all real necessity—and *hence* of all universality as well.

Whereas Kant had generally derived necessity from universality, Fichte now proceeds in precisely the opposite direction: "Necessity and universality from intuition. The universality follows from the *necessity* (what is absolutely *original;* everything else is merely derived)."[73] What is necessarily true is necessarily true in every case. Thus, what I discover (via intuition) to be necessarily true must necessarily be found to be true by everyone else who possesses the same intuition. Hence, the kind of intuition that occurs within philosophy (and geometry) can also be described as "universal intuition," a term that, so far as I have been able to discover, occurs only in the *Neue Bearbeitung.*[74]

The *Wissenschaftslehre* can thus be described as "nothing more than a continuous, albeit systematic inner self-observation of the mind [*Hineinschauen des Geistes in sich selbst*], without argumentation or anything similar."[75] The evidence to which such a philosophy appeals is that of "immediate consciousness," which can therefore be confirmed by all of those who are able to "look within themselves" while reflecting in a certain, specific manner. The capacity to do this can therefore be described as "the genuine locus of transcendental and poetic talent."[76] In order to accomplish the kind of *Hineinschauen* posited by the *Wissenschaftslehre,* one has to make a free effort to think or to construct this philosophy for oneself. In other words, one can understand the *Wissenschaftslehre* only by *performing* or *enacting* it; and this is something no one can be forced to do, just as the "object" with which this philosophy is concerned and which is supposed to warrant its claim to "reality" is not one that can simply be passively discovered within consciousness. Philosophical reflection must be *freely undertaken;* its object must be *freely produced* (or constructed) and freely *observed.*[77]

As we have now seen, the great majority of the misunderstandings and criticisms to which the *Wissenschaftslehre* was subjected in the period 1799–1800 are based on the failure to recognize the distinctive *method* of this kind of philosophy and the distinctive character of the *evidence* to which it appeals. Since this method and evidence resemble, in certain important respects, the method and evidence of a science with which Fichte's readers could be assumed to be acquainted, namely geometry, it is not surprising that the *Wissenschaftslehre* of 1800–1801 should include a new and stronger stress upon the similarities between philosophy and geometry. The situation of the *Wissenschaftslehre,* Fichte explains in the *Sonnenklarer Bericht,* is "like that of geometry, in which each new proposition adds something new to the preceding one, the necessity of which can likewise only be exhibited in intuition. This must be the case in every real science that makes actual progress and does not simply revolve in a circle."[78] In philosophy, "the manner of proceeding is exactly the same as in *mathematics.* It is demonstrated in intuition. I can do nothing else. Mathematical demonstrations too are only devices for leading one to the point of intuition [*nur Hinleitungen auf den Punkt der Anschauung*]."[79]

This new emphasis on the parallels between philosophy and mathematics is reflected in the altered *form* of the *Neue Darstellung,* in which each of the eight sections begins with a new *theorem* or *Lehrsatz,* such as: "We are aware of self-determination only as a determination in accordance with a freely constructed concept of the specific determinacy in question."[80] The mere statement of such a theorem is then followed by a specific *postulate,* describing the particular internal *act* that has to be accomplished in order to demonstrate the theorem in question, such as: "To intuit correctly the act of self-determining as an absolute movement of transition from sheer determinability to determinacy, a movement of transition *grounded* in its own movement."[81] This intuitive "demonstration" is, in turn, usually followed by one or more "corollaries." All of these terms, Fichte explains, are to be understood in precisely the sense in which they are employed within Euclidean geometry (as interpreted by Kant): the theorem asserts a proposition that claims for itself necessary and universal truth; the postulate describes a specific intellectual act, the performance and observation of which is supposed to provide apodictic evidence for the theorem; and the corollaries are propositions derived from the theorem by means of logical or conceptual analysis, sometimes with the assistance of additional secondary postulates (or *Hilfs-Postulaten*).

Such a procedure is described as one of intellectual *construction.* Just as geometry freely constructs the various, necessary ways in which space can be delineated, so transcendental philosophy constructs the various necessary ways in which the I can and—if it is to conceive of itself as an I at all—*must* act. In both cases, the results are expressed in terms of concepts, but they are produced and confirmed in and by means of inner (or intellectual) intuition.[82]

The method of the 1800–1801 *Wissenschaftslehre* is therefore characterized by Fichte as "construction in intuition."[83] To be sure, a similar method was often employed in the 1796–99 *Wissenschaftslehre,* but with far less rigor and consistency than in the incomplete *Neue Bearbeitung*.[84] Instead of the single postulate with which the *Wissenschaftslehre nova methodo* begins, each section of the *Neue Bearbeitung*, as noted, includes its own distinct postulate (and sometimes several). This is why I have described the unfinished *Wissenschaftslehre* of 1800–1801—with apologies to Spinoza—as an attempt at a "*Wissenschaftslehre more geometrico*." By 1800 Fichte had become acutely aware of the fact that many of his readers were sincerely confused about the "reality" of the acts and objects described within the *Wissenschaftslehre*, about the type of knowledge this kind of philosophy was supposed to provide, and about how such knowledge was supposed to be obtained. It was, I suggest, precisely in response to such questions that he began, at about this same time, to characterize his philosophy as "the *mathesis* of the mind" (*Mathesis des Geistes*).[85] Just as anyone who truly wishes to *understand* geometry cannot simply memorize Euclid's theorems, but must, so to speak, "reinvent" (*nacherfinden*) the science for himself, so too, anyone wishing to engage in informed discussion about the *Wissenschaftslehre* "must himself invent the entire system."[86]

The most celebrated paradigm of a system of philosophy *more geometrico* is, of course, Spinoza's (which, however, is not to imply that Spinoza understood the "geometrical method" in precisely the same way as Fichte); and it is possible that Fichte's decision to employ such a method in his new presentation of the *Wissenschaftslehre* was in part a response to Jacobi's sardonic characterization of the *Wissenschaftslehre* as an "inverted Spinozism."[87] It may also have been inspired by Schelling's public endorsement of a broadly "Spinozistic" conception of philosophical systematicity.

Whatever the origins of this new way of describing the method of the *Wissenschaftslehre*, most of the elements of Fichte's new "geometrical method"—including the appeal to intuition and the characterization of philosophy as a kind of "construction"—were, of course, already present in earlier presentations of the *Wissenschaftslehre*. What is new is the attempt to purge the new presentation of other "methods" (such as the "dialectical" method of inquiry that occupies most of part 2 of the *Grundlage der gesamten Wissenschaftslehre*) and the new, concentrated effort on Fichte's part to make the external form of the new presentation resemble as closely as possible that of mathematical or geometrical proofs. Perhaps Fichte thought that by casting his system in such a form he would have the last laugh on Jacobi, while also demonstrating that the adoption of such a method of presentation did not commit one to anything like Schelling's—or Spinoza's—conclusions.

Indeed, one of the more striking features of the new presentation is the presence throughout of a strongly anti-Schellingean undertone, even though Schelling himself is seldom mentioned by name.[88] An exception can be found in chapter 1 of the *Neue Bearbeitung*. Here, immediately after identifying "immediate intuition" or "immediate self-consciousness" as "the absolutely *highest*, which comprises everything else," Fichte adds: "against Schelling's idea of a separate philosophy of nature."[89] This same point—that philosophy has to begin with immediate self-consciousness—is equally incompatible with the strategy of Schelling's still-emerging "system of identity."[90]

The irreparable philosophical rupture between Fichte and Schelling, which is only hinted at in the *Sonnenklarer Bericht*,[91] is painfully evident in the *Neue Bearbeitung*.[92] Both texts reveal Fichte's unequivocal rejection of any concept of "objective intellectual intuition" or of "reality in and for itself." Instead, he reiterates that "reality" is always reality *for consciousness*, and reaffirms that the only possible type of intellectual intuition is *self*-intuition. Indeed, it is only because intellectual intuition is always *self-intuition* that it can claim for itself the necessity and universality required by philosophy. It is difficult to avoid the conclusion that one of the chief goals of the new presentation of the *Wissenschaftslehre* was to reveal, more clearly than before, the untenability of rival conceptions of philosophy, particularly those of Jacobi, Bardili, and Schelling.[93]

Abandonment of Work on the *Neue Bearbeitung*

However much its more explicitly "geometrical" form of presentation may represent an advance on the *Wissenschaftslehre nova methodo*, the *Neue Bearbeitung* quite plainly began as a mere revision of the former, though major differences in content, argument, and order of presentation began to emerge almost at once and become more and more frequent as the manuscript proceeds. Beginning in section 4, the manuscript is interrupted with ever-increasing frequency by self-critical observations, expressions of self-doubt, and anxious speculations concerning alternate deductive strategies. At the end of section 5, for example, Fichte comments as follows on his own attempt to show how ideality and reality are united in the categories of causality, substantiality, and reciprocal interaction: "The absolute confusion first comes to light here. . . . In short, here I am very wrong, and nothing makes sense."[94] Here, as in most of the self-critical remarks that occur in this manuscript, Fichte's doubts and objections are directed not at his *conclusions* so much as at the adequacy of his *demonstrations* of the same. Thus he comments as follows upon his own complex effort to account for how the I constructs a concept of its goal: "The results seemed clear to me, but they [are] not yet demonstrated."[95]

This rising note of frustration becomes more and more evident as Fichte confesses to his growing uncertainty about how best to proceed in order to clarify the crucially important relationship between feeling and the infinitely divisible manifold of time and space: "A transition is lacking here, even though I know very well what I should say."[96] "I must go more deeply into this matter. If I only had some guiding thread!"[97] In section 8, the final section of the unfinished manuscript, he offers an unequivocally negative evaluation of his efforts to clarify the complex relationship between space, time, and productive imagination: "One still has no pure deduction of the same."[98] And this is precisely the point at which he finally abandons any further effort to continue his chain of derivations and constructions.

From this point on, the manuscript dissolves into a series of unsystematic questions and speculations on various subjects, including a possible connection between the intuition of space and a "pure intuition of God," which might, he speculates, serve as the necessary "band for connecting the entire intelligible world."[99] If this last suggestion seems to point in the direction of the later *Wissenschaftslehren,*[100] another hint in that direction may be detected in Fichte's increasing tendency, in the latter portions of the *Neue Bearbeitung,* to adopt a new, highly "imagistic" vocabulary, employing such terms as *das Bild, bilden, das Gebildete,* and *sich bilden,* and even to introduce the notion of "the eye [*Auge*] of intuition,"[101] until finally, near the end of manuscript, he expostulates that "I must therefore delve into the theory of the formation of images."[102] And, of course, one of the more distinctive features of Fichte's next effort to expound his philosophy, namely, the 1801–2 *Darstellung der Wissenschaftslehre,* is precisely the attention it gives to just this issue and its wholesale adoption of a new, more "visual" or "imagistic" technical vocabulary.

Though the final pages of the *Neue Bearbeitung* are filled with self-interrogatory remarks, such as, "Do I need to seek additional formulas?"[103] and poignant self-admonitions, such as "*clarify, elucidate, illuminate!*"[104] there is no trace of despair in such comments. Frustration, yes, but not despair. Instead, Fichte seems to have remained confident that the appropriate new formulas and clarifications would eventually be discovered—as indeed they were, though not for another year. In hindsight, it is not difficult to identify certain features of the *Neue Bearbeitung* that clearly presage the *Darstellung* of 1801–2, and interpreters such as Koch and Stolzenberg have called attention to some of these.[105] Yet the similarities in question are mostly a matter of terminology and stray comments, and rarely extend to the underlying structure of the two presentations. In the end, the links and the continuity between the *Neue Bearbeitung* and the *Wissenschaftslehre nova methodo* seem much stronger and more significant, which is hardly surprising, given the fact that the former evidently began as a thorough *revision* of the latter.

It is undeniable that there are many deep and striking differences between the 1801–2 *Wissenschaftslehre* and all the earlier versions—including the *Neue Bearbeitung*—just as it is also true that there are many points of continuity between the earlier presentations and that of 1801–2.[106] Moreover, as noted above, a few interesting and specific innovations and suggestions, which are usually associated with the 1801–2 presentation, are first introduced, albeit very tentatively, in 1800, yet none of these innovations are really developed in the unfinished *Neue Bearbeitung.*

For all of these reasons, I conclude that the *Neue Bearbeitung* of 1800–1801 can more accurately be described as the "last early" rather than as the "first late" *Wissenschaftslehre.* The *Sonnenklarer Bericht,* on the other hand, the first half of which was apparently written prior to the *Neue Bearbeitung* and the second half of which was written immediately after Fichte had abandoned work on the latter, offers a more complex case. This published text seems to straddle the divide (such as it is) between "early" and "late" *Wissenschaftslehren.* The Fourth Lesson, for example, contains an important passage that directly anticipates the deductive strategy of the 1801–2 *Darstellung,* inasmuch as it asserts that every genuine knowledge claim—and not merely those based on mathematical constructions or on "inner intuition" of the self-construction of the I—implies an "absolute assertion" of its own universal validity. Philosophical reflection upon such claims will, Fichte confidently predicts, reveal that all knowledge claims presuppose and are grounded upon a deeper, "fundamental" or "scientific" intuition.[107] This same claim, which clearly reflects the new strategy of the 1801–2 *Darstellung,* is reiterated in the postscript to the *Sonnenklarer Bericht,*[108] as well as in Fichte's *Antwortschreiben an Reinhold,*[109] which he wrote in early April 1801, immediately after completing the *Sonnenklarer Bericht.* According to this new claim, it is possible to *reverse* the order of the earlier presentations of the *Wissenschaftslehre:* rather than proceeding from intellectual intuition to an account of knowing (*Wissen*), one can instead, as in the *Wissenschaftslehre* of 1801–2, proceed from knowing to intellectual intuition—by way of the absolute. This, however, represents a significant alteration—or, if one prefers, advance—in Fichte's thinking since October 1800, when he was still publicly maintaining, in his Bardili review, that it is essential to begin philosophizing with the concept of I and was still denying the possibility of any alternative starting point.[110] There is, however, no hint of this new strategy in the *Neue Bearbeitung.*

Given its chronological place in Fichte's career, the *Neue Bearbeitung* surely merits Meckenstock's description of it as "the connecting link between the lecture transcripts of the *Wissenschaftslehre nova methodo* and the lectures on the *Wissenschaftslehre* from the winter of 1801/2."[111] But even a close study of the *Neue Bearbeitung* does not really solve the mystery of the "transition to the 1801/2 *Wissenschaftslehre,*" except insofar as this unfinished manuscript offers poignant testimony to Fichte's growing appreciation of some of the problems and difficulties implicit in his earlier conception of the appropriate "presentation" of his system. More interesting, perhaps, than the question of the relationship between the *Neue Bearbeitung* and later versions of the *Wissenschaftslehre* are the questions concerning Fichte's reasons, first of all, for *revising* his Jena manuscript on his lectures on *Wissenschaftslehre nova methodo* in the way that he did, and second, for *abandoning* this project before it was even half finished.

With respect to the first question, I have here tried to indicate that many of the specific revisions and innovations one finds in the *Wissenschaftslehre* of 1800–1801 appear to have been motivated by specific criticisms to which Fichte's philosophy had been subjected during the preceding eighteen months. The new, much stronger emphasis on the evidential role of intuition seems to be a response to the proposal, put forward by Bardili and championed by Reinhold, that philosophy should be conceived as "pure logic," based upon "thinking *qua* thinking." In contrast to such a purely "formal" philosophy, the *Wissenschaftslehre* claims *reality,* inasmuch as its objects or content are presented within *intuition.*[112]

The new insistence on the similarities between the method of proof within mathematics and that of philosophy seems, at least in part, to be a response to the objection, raised by various empiricists and "popular philosophers," that any philosophy based on intuition is really a form of introspective psychology, the claims of which are based upon an appeal to the passively perceived facts of inner sense and which are therefore lacking in universality and necessity. Following Kant, Fichte appealed to the peculiar character of mathematical proof, which employs a distinctive method of "construction" within the medium of pure (or, in the case of philosophy, "purified") intuition. This parallel with mathematical demonstration is clearly intended by Fichte to defend the universality and necessity of his own philosophical claims and conclusions.

The continued, explicit insistence on the *limits* of "philosophical" or "intellectual" intuition—namely, its limitation to the domain of the I itself and the originary acts of the same—seems to be an implicit rejection of the more extravagant claims that were being made on behalf of intellectual intuition by Schelling and Friedrich Schlegel. One of Fichte's new aims in the *Wissenschaftslehre* of 1800–1801 seems to have been to undermine, once and for all, any possibility of appealing to an "objective intellectual intuition."

Finally, in response both to Jacobi's characterization of transcendental philosophy as a life-denying "nihilism" and to the enthusiastic efforts by Friedrich Schlegel, Novalis, and other romantic philosophers to "apply" transcendental philosophy directly to everyday life and even to describe it as a kind of "magic," the new presentation of 1800–1801 distinguishes more carefully than any of the earlier versions of the *Wissenschaftslehre* between "the standpoint of life" and that of "philosophy." Indeed, this is the major theme of the *Sonnenklarer Bericht.*

Despite the fragmentary state of the 1800–1801 version of the *Wissenschaftslehre,* it is not without certain distinctive merits of its own. No one who reads the unfinished *Neue Bearbeitung* and the published *Sonnenklarer Bericht* can fail to be struck by a certain anxiety that pervades these writings: a new, heightened concern on Fichte's part to discover and to explain—in a manner that will "force the reader to understand"—the distinctive character and proper method or *Beweisart* of the *Wissenschaftslehre.* Again and again, he interrupts the flow of his manuscript to insert questions about the adequacy of his own "method of demonstration" and to engage in reflections about the possibility of a more adequate and convincing method of presenting and demonstrating his philosophy. To be sure, this was hardly a new concern on Fichte's part, but it is given a new prominence in the writings with which we are here concerned.

The solution adopted—or rather, attempted—by Fichte in the 1800–1801 *Wissenschaftslehre* was to model his new presentation as closely as possible upon that of the geometers. In my view, this is also the chief virtue of the *Neue Bearbeitung,* the specific "form" of which at least *promises* to be clearer and more accessible than any of the earlier—and perhaps any of the later—presentations of the *Wissenschaftslehre.* At each step of the way he makes a patient effort to distinguish: (1) precisely *what* he intends to demonstrate (theorem); (2) precisely *where*—that is, with which specific mental act—the demonstration of this conclusion must begin (postulate); (3) precisely *how* this conclusion is derived from this starting point (construction); and (4) exactly what *follows from* this conclusion (corollaries). By adhering closely to this pattern of exposition, the *Neue Bearbeitung* really does manage to dispel much of the confusion that still distracted readers of his earlier presentations.

This new, "geometrical" method also succeeds in clarifying the precise character of the *evidence* upon which the *Wissenschaftslehre* is ultimately grounded. Even if one is not persuaded by Fichte's account of philosophy as "construction in intuition" or as the "*mathesis* of reason," the *Neue Bearbeitung* nevertheless succeeds in explicating more clearly than ever before Fichte's own understanding of the role within philosophy of intuition and construction.

Despite the fact that it is an incomplete first draft, and despite the many false starts, repetitions, and second thoughts (which are not without a certain charm of their own), the *Neue Bearbeitung* is in some respects far easier to follow than any of the earlier presentations of the *Wissenschaftslehre.* Though the new presentation follows the general order of the *Wissenschaftslehre nova methodo,* it also sharpens some of the latter's key distinctions (above all, the distinction between "ideal" and "real" activities)[113] and introduces some helpful new ones, such as a proposed distinction between "reflection" (*Reflexion*) and "the pure reflex [*Reflex*] of consciousness"[114] and another between "the subjective object" and the "objective subject."[115]

Not all of the innovations contained in the *Neue Bearbeitung* are so ingenious or helpful, of course, and some, such as the awkward attempt in the final portion of the manuscript to "solve" the previously mentioned problem of the missing "highest synthesis" by appealing to a proposed intuition of totality or unity ("a pure intuition of *God*")[116] actually seem to be at odds with at least "the letter" of the rest of the *Neue Bearbeitung*—however well such suggestions may comport with the alleged "spirit" of the work and however clearly they may anticipate what is soon to come.

With regard to our second question—*why* did Fichte abandon work on the *Neue Bearbeitung* sometime at the end of 1800 or beginning of 1801, and why did he not return to this project later?—the evidence is, I believe, ultimately *inconclusive.* Here again, one might appeal to certain new criticisms that appeared about this time—above all, those contained in Reinhold's "Sendschreiben an den Herrn Professor Fichte," which appeared in January 1801 in the first issue of Reinhold's *Beyträge zur leichtern Übersicht des Zustandes der Philosophie beym Anfange de 19. Jahrhunderts,* along with certain other articles that may well have had an influence on Fichte—above all, Reinhold's discussion of Descartes' conception of *philosophia prima* in part 1 of his treatise on "Die erste Aufgabe der Philosophie."[117] Or one might seek to understand Fichte's change of heart concerning the proper starting point and formal structure of his new presentation by studying his ongoing correspondence with Schelling during the first half of 1801, which includes several letters of great philosophical significance. In any case, his publications during the spring of 1801—including, as indicated above, the *Antwortschreiben an Reinhold* and the final portions of the *Sonnenklarer Bericht*[118]—strongly suggest that by this point he had already turned his back on the rigorous "geometrical method" with which he had experimented in the *Neue Bearbeitung*[119] and was actively seeking a new starting point for the next presentation of the *Wissenschaftslehre.*

Though a close reading of the *Neue Bearbeitung* certainly reveals serious internal-systematic tensions within this new presentation, the same could easily be said of *all* of Fichte's earlier presentations of his philosophy. One must therefore exercise extreme caution in speculating about Fichte's precise reasons or motives for abandoning this project and making a radically new start. It may have been that he found the new, rigorously geometrical and discursive method of presentation to be ultimately unsuited for expounding the fivefold synthesis of productive imagination (which is, in fact, the point at which the *Neue Bearbeitung* breaks off). Or he may have abandoned the manuscript because he finally concluded that his favorite strategy of beginning with the I was in fact responsible for some of the most widespread and persistent misunderstandings of his project and that an altogether new starting point (by appealing, for example, to the fact of "knowledge," as in the 1801–2 presentation, or to what is implied by any "truth claim," as in the lectures on the *Wissenenschaftslehre* of 1804) might fare somewhat better. Or, as many of Fichte's marginal comments in the manuscript of the *Neue Bearbeitung* suggest, he may simply have encountered too many specific internal difficulties and technical problems in working out the all-important details of his new presentation, even as he remained confident concerning the overall soundness of his conclusions.

Perhaps, finally, the tradition that posits a major difference between the "spirit" of the earlier and the later *Wissenschaftslehren* is correct after all. Perhaps Fichte's conception of his own project did undergo a fundamental shift or "turn toward the absolute" sometime between 1799 and 1801, and perhaps he abandoned the *Neue Bearbeitung* because he was simply unable to do justice to his new conception of the *Wissenschaftslehre* within the framework of even a heavily revised version of his earlier presentation, *Wissenschaftslehre nova methodo.*

Notes

1. Schelling raised this charge publicly in his 1806 *Darlegung des wahren Verhältnisses der Naturphilosophie zu der verbesserten Fichteschen Lehre.* Adding insult to injury, he explained the alleged changes in the standpoint of the *Wissenschaftslehre* as signs of plagiarism on Fichte's part.

For Fichte's response, see his own comment in the 1806 "Preface" to his *Anweisung zum seligen Leben:* "These [changes] are wholly the result of my own continuing and more strenuous and mature efforts, over the past six or seven years, to develop within myself those same philosophical views that I acquired, in part, thirteen years ago. Though I hope that many things may have changed for me over this period, these views have not altered in any respect since that time" (*GA* 1.9:47).

See also Fichte's unpublished "Bericht über das Schicksale der *Wissenschaftslehre,*" also written in 1806, in which he maintains: "Since I have declared the previous presentation of the *Wissenschaftslehre* [i.e., the *Grundlage der gesamten Wis-*

senschaftslehre] to be good and correct, it goes without saying that a different theory is never to be expected from me than the one I presented to the public at that time" (*GA* 2.10:29). This is the same policy that Fichte had pursued from the start: explaining the obvious changes in each successive presentation of the *Wissenschaftslehre* as affecting merely the outer form of his philosophy, while staunchly maintaining the underlying identity of the same. See, for example, his comments on the relationship between the *Wissenschaftslehre nova methodo* and the *Grundlage der gesamten Wissenschaftslehre* (*Wissenschaftslehre nova methodo,* in *GA* 4.2:17 and 4.3:329; in English, *FTP,* 85–86).

Furthermore, he often defended and explained these differences as stemming from a conscious, pedagogic decision on his part to present the "same thought" in a dramatically different format, thereby freeing it from any attachment to "the letter." See, for example, his comment in his third series of lectures on the *Wissenschaftslehre* from 1804: "It is impossible for me to lecture in the same way. Advantage for the listener: fresh, lively thinking. Advantage for me (for I must also be concerned with my own self-development): I want to possess it in a manner that is absolutely independent of all expressions and forms [and to be] constantly able to create it out of its inner life [*aus dem inneren Leben*] and in any desired form. In my case, the *Wissenschaftslehre* is quite possible, for it is only one thought that has been lifted out of a countless, and in certain respects infinite number of possibilities, and one can link it to whatever one wishes within this infinity. For this reason [it can be expressed in] an infinite number of ways. Only then is one a master; and if I were to establish a seminary for future teachers of philosophy, this is how I would attempt to raise them to such mastery" (*GA* 2.7:316).

2. Johann Friedrich Loewe, *Die Philosophie Fichtes nach dem Gesammtergebnisse ihrer Entwicklung und in ihrem Verhälnisse zu Kant und Spinoza* (1862; Hildesheim: Olms, 1978); Kuno Fischer, *Geschichte der neueren Philosophie,* 4th ed., vol. 6 (Heidelberg: Winter, 1914), 657–70 and 704–7; Xavier Léon, *La philosophie de Fichte* (Paris: Alcan, 1902) and *Fichte et son temps,* vol. 1 (Paris: Colin, 1922), 6–13; and Max Wundt, *Fichte-Forschungen* (Stuttgart: Frommann, 1929), 3–9.

3. Johann Eduard Erdmann, *Versuch einer wissenschaftlichen Darstellung der Geschichte der neueren Philosophie,* vol. 3, pt. 2, *Geschichte der deutschen Spekulation seit Kant* (1853; Stuttgart: Frommann-Holzboog, 1973), 25–40; Wilhelm Windelband, *Die Geschichte der neueren Philosophie in ihrem Zusammenhange mit der allgemeinen Kultur und den besonderen Wissenschaften,* 3rd ed., vol. 2, *Geschichte der Philosophie der Neuzeit* (Leipzig: Breitkopf und Härtel, 1904), 197–227; Wilhelm Weischedel, *Der Zwiespalt im Denken Fichtes* (Berlin: De Gruyter, 1962); Fritz Medicus, *Fichtes Leben* (Leipzig: Meiner, 1914); F. A. Schmid, *Die Philosophie Fichtes mit Rücksicht auf die Frage nach der "veränderte Lehre"* (inaugural dissertation; Freiburg im Breisgau: Epstein, 1904), see esp. 109–12; Hans Heimsoeth, *Fichte* (Munich: Ernst Reinhardt, 1923), 219–21; Wolfgang Janke, *Fichte: Sein und Reflexion—Grundlagen der kritischen Vernunft* (Berlin: De Gruyter, 1970), 207–22; and Peter Rohs, *Johann Gottlieb Fichte* (Munich: Beck, 1991), 149–56. The phrase "Wendung zum Absoluten" is Janke's (see p. 221).

4. Heinrich Rickert, *Fichtes Atheismusstreit und die Kantische Philosophie: Eine Säkularbetrachtung* (Berlin: Reuter und Reichard, 1899); Emil Lask, *Fichtes Idealis-*

mus und der Geschichte (Tübingen and Leipzig: Mohr, 1902), 135–64 and 172–91; and Julius Drechsler, *Fichtes Lehre vom Bild* (Stuttgart: Kohlhammer, 1955).

For general discussions of the "periodization" of Fichte's philosophy, see Schmid, *Die Philosophie Fichtes;* Georges Gurwitsch, *Fichtes System der konkreten Ethik* (Tübingen: Mohr, 1924), 2–64; Dreschler, *Fichtes Lehre vom Bild,* 31–37; and Wundt, *Fichte-Forschungen,* 3–8.

5. See, for example, Christian Klotz's study of major, systematic differences between the *Grundlage der gesamten Wissenschaftslehre* and the *Wissenschaftslehre nova methodo,* "Reines Selbstbewußtsein und Reflexion in Fichtes Grundlegung der *Wissenschaftslehre* (1794–1800)," *Fichte-Studien* 7 (1995): 27–48.

6. This seems to be the course followed by, for example, Peter Baumanns, *J. G. Fichte: Kritische Gesamtdarstellung seiner Philosophie* (Freiburg and Munich: Alber, 1990).

The different presentations of the *Wissenschaftslehre* include:

1. *Über den Begriff der Wissenschaftslehre* (1794; *GA* 1.2:107–67) + *Grundlage der gesamten Wissenschaftslehre* (1794–95; *GA* 1.2:249–451) + *Grundriss des Eigenthümliche der Wissenschaftslehre in Rücksicht auf das theoretische Vermögen* (1795; *GA* 1.3:141–208). In English, *Concerning the Concept of the Wissenschaftslehre,* in *EPW,* 87–135 + *Foundations of the Entire Science of Knowledge,* in Fichte: *Science of Knowledge,* ed. and trans. Peter Heath and John Lachs (Cambridge: Cambridge University Press, 1982), 89–206 + *Concerning the Distinctive Character of the Wissenschaftslehre with Respect to the Theoretical Faculty,* in *EPW,* 233–306.
2. *Wissenschaftslehre nova methodo* [Kollegnachschriften] (1796–99; *GA* 4.2:17–267) + (1796–97; *GA* 4.3:151–96) + (1798–99; *GA* 4.3:321–535) + *Versuch einer neuen Darstellung der Wissenschaftslehre* (1797–98; *GA* 1.7:183–281). In English, *FTP.*
3. *Neue Bearbeitung der Wissenschaftslehre* (1800–1801; *GA* 2.5:331–402) + *Sonnenklarer Bericht* (1801; *GA* 1.7:183–268). In English, *A Crystal Clear Report to the General Public,* trans. John Botterman and William Rasch, in *Philosophy of German Idealism,* ed. Ernst Behler (New York: Continuum, 1987), 39–115.
4. *Darstellung der Wissenschaftslehre* (1801–2; *GA* 2.6:129–324). + [*Zur Ausarbeitung der Wissenschaftslehre*] (1801; *GA* 2.6:51–103).
5. *Vorlesungen der W.L. im Winter 1804* (January–March 1804; *GA* 2.7:66–235).
6. *Die Wissenschaftslehre* (April–June 1804; *GA* 2.8:2–421). In English, *The Science of Knowing: J. G. Fichte's 1804 Lectures on the Wissenschaftslehre,* trans. Walter E. Wright (Albany: State University of New York Press, 2005).
7. *3ter Cours de W.L. 1804* (November–December 1804; *GA* 2.7:289–368).
8. *4ter Vortrag der Wissenschaftslehre—Erlangen im Sommer 1805* (June–September 1805; *GA* 2.9:179–311).
9. *Wissenschaftslehre, Königsberg* (1807; *GA* 2.10:111–202).

10. *Die Wissenschaftslehre, in ihrem allgemeinen Umrisse dargestellt* (March 1810; *GA* 1.10:335–45). In English, *The Science of Knowledge in Its General Outline,* trans. Walter E. Wright, *Idealistic Studies* 6 (1976): 106–17.
11. *Wissenschaftslehre 1810* (1810; *GA* 2.11:293–392).
12. *Wissenschaftslehre 1811* (1811, *GA* 2.12:143–299).
13. *Die Wissenschaftslehre [aus dem Jahre 1812]* (1812; *GA* 2.13:43–179).
14. *Die Wissenschaftslehre 1813* (Spring 1813; *SW* 10:1–86).
15. *Wissenschaftslehre 1814 (Erste bis Fünfte Vorlesung)* (January 10–14, 1814; in *Ultima Inquirenda: J. G. Fichtes letzte Bearbeitungen der Wissenschaftsehre, Ende 1813/Anfang 1814,* ed. Reinhard Lauth (Stuttgart-Bad Cannstatt: Frommann-Holzboog, 2001).

7. See, for example, Martial Gueroult, *L'Évolution et la structure de la Doctrine de la Science de Fichte,* 2 vols. (Paris: Sociéte d'Édition, Les Belles Lettres, 1930). Though Gueroult tries to emphasize the "unity" of the *Wissenschaftslehre,* he nevertheless argues that the Atheism Controversy, combined with Jacobi's "Open Letter" and Fichte's growing differences with Schelling, signaled "un tournant décisif dans la vie et dans la pensée du philosophe" (Gueroult, "La destination de l'homme," in *Études sur Fichte* [Paris: Aubier Montaigne, 1974], 72.

For others, such as Xavier Léon and Ernst Cassirer, these same factors produced only a "change in accent" in what remained the same underlying system. See Ernst Cassirer, *Das Erkenntnisproblem in der Philosophie und Wissenschaft der neueren Zeit,* vol. 3, *Die nachkantischen Systeme* (Darmstadt: Wissenschaftliche Buchgesellschaft, 1974; repr. of second ed., 1923), 161–74 and 213–16.

8. Georges Gurwitsch, *Personal- und Gemeinschaftswert in der Ethik Fichtes: Eine Studie über Fichtes Lehre vom sittlichen Ideal—Die Einheit der Fichteschen Philosophie* (Berlin: Collingnon, 1922); and *Fichtes System der konkreten Ethik,* 2–64; Nicolai Hartmann, *Die Philosophie des deutschen Idealismus,* 3rd ed. (1923; Berlin: De Gruyter, 1974), 69–80; Ives Radrizzani, "Place de la *Destination de l'Homme* dans l'oeuvre Fichtéenne," *Revue Internationale de Philosophie,* no. 206 (December 1998): 665–96; Reinhard Lauth, "Einleitung" to Johann Gottlieb Fichte, *Darstellung der Wissenschaftslehre aus den Jahren 1801/2* (Hamburg: Meiner, 1977), xix–xxx.

9. A striking exception to this generalization is Gueroult, who concludes his two-volume study of the internal evolution of the *Wissenschaftslehre* by conjuring up the distinctive spirit of the 1794–95 presentation, with its ultimately untenable "promotion of subjective consciousness to the absolute," as Fichte's real, historical, and heroic achievement, containing within itself the germ of all the later developments. It is in this first presentation that Gueroult finds most clearly expressed what he considers to be the heart of Fichte's philosophy: "L'affirmation de la liberté et du Moi absolu étant considerée non comme le moyen, mais comme la *cause* et le *principe* de toute l'evolution" (Gueroult, *L'Évolution et la structure,* 2:242).

10. In *GA* 2.5:331–402. According to the editors of *GA,* Fichte began working on the *Neue Bearbeitung der Wissenschaftslehre* in early October 1800 and had abandoned the project by February 1801 at the latest, and probably before the end of December 1800.

11. "[Ankündigung:] Seit sechs Jahren" (*GA* 1.7:153–64); in English, "Public Announcement of a New Presentation of the *Wissenschaftslehre*," in *IWL*, 186–201.

12. Günter Meckenstock, "Fichtes Fragment 'Neue Bearbeitung der *Wissenschaftslehre*,'" in *Der transzendentale Gedanke: Die gegenwärtige Darstellung der Philosophie Fichtes*, ed. Klaus Hammacher (Hamburg: Felix Meiner, 1981), 89.

Other authors who have written on the 1800–1801 *Wissenschaftslehre* include Michael Rath, Jürgen Stolzenburg, and Reinhard Koch. See Michael Rath, *Selbstbewusstsein und Wille: Untersuchungen zu Fichtes Wissenschaftslehre nova methodo* (inaugural dissertation; Heidelberg, 1985); Jürgen Stolzenberg, *Fichtes Begriff der intellektuellen Anschauung: Die Entwicklung in den Wissenschaftslehren von 1793/94 bis 1801/02* (Stuttgart: Klett-Cotta, 1986), esp. 230–45; and Reinhard Koch, *Fichtes Theorie des Selbstbewußtseins: Ihre Entwicklung von den 'Eignen Meditationen über Elementar Philosophie' 1793 bis zur 'Neuen Bearbeitung der W.L.' 1800* (Würzburg: Königshausen und Neumann, 1989), esp. 289–481. Koch's book contains by far the most detailed and extended discussion of the *Neue Bearbeitung*.

13. This was, of course, a very eventful period in Fichte's life. Not only did he lose his position at Jena, relocate himself and his family to Berlin, and have to begin supporting himself as a private author and teacher, but he also became involved in personal disputes of various sorts—for example, with Feßler and Feldmann concerning Freemasonry, with Friedrich and August Schlegel over their failed plans for a jointly edited journal, and with his publisher regarding royalties and other financial claims.

14. See Schleiermacher's rather cruel parody of Fichte in his "review" of *Die Bestimmung des Menschen*, published in the summer of 1800 in the *Athenaeum*, vol. 3, no. 2 (repr. in *FZR* 3:66–75), and Jean Paul's *Clavis Fichteana seu Leibgeberiana* (Erfurt: Henningsschen Buchhandlung, 1800 [repr. in *Aus der Frühzeit des deutschen Idealismus: Texte zur Wissenschaftslehre Fichtes 1794–1804*, ed. Martin Oesch (Würzburg: Königshausen und Neumann, 1987), 199–216]). For a discussion of Nicolai's many personal attacks upon Fichte, see the editors' introduction to Fichte's *Friedrich Nicolai's Leben und sonderbare Meinungen* (*GA* 1.7:326–63).

15. See, for example, his 1796 "Vergleichung des vom Herrn Prof. Schmid aufgestellten Systems mit der *Wissenschaftslehre*" (*GA* 1.3:235–66).

16. Johann Henrich Gottlieb Heusinger, *Über das idealistisch-atheistische System des Herrn Profeßor Fichte* (Dresden: Perthes, 1799). See Fichte's comments on this work in his unpublished note from the spring of 1799, "[Gegen Heusinger]" (*GA* 2.5:193). His first public response to Heusinger's charge that the *Wissenschaftslehre* is based upon "psychologische Täuschungen" came almost a year later, in a note to "Aus einem Privatschreiben," published in January 1800 (*GA* 1.6:385–87; in English, "From a Private Letter," in *IWL*, 156–76). For Fichte's response to Schleiermacher's review, see his letter to Friedrich Schlegel, August 16, 1800.

17. Heusinger, *Über das idealistisch-atheistische System*, 14–19.

18. Christoph Friedrich Nicolai, *Über meine gelehrte Bildung, über meine Kenntniß der kritischen Philosophie und meine Schriften dieselbe betreffend, und über die Herren Kant, J. B. Erhard, und Fichte.* (Berlin and Stettin, 1799). Nicolai had been a thorn in Fichte's side for many years, and attacked him once again in late 1800 in the pages of the *Neuen allgemeinen deutschen Bibliothek*, in a collective review of recent

writings by Schelling and others (vol. 56, no. 1, installment 2, 142–76 and installment 3, 177–206). Fichte first became aware of Nicolai's attack in February 1801 and responded by dropping work on everything else and preparing for publication his polemical tract *Friedrich Nicolai's Leben und sonderbare Meinungen.*

19. Karl Leonhard Reinhold, "Ueber die Autonomie als Principle der praktischen Philosophie der Kantische—und der gesammten Philosophie der Fichtisch-schellingschen Schule," *Beyträge zur leichtern Übersicht des Zustandes der Philosophie beym Anfange des 19. Jahrhunderts,* installment 2. (Hamburg: Perthes, 1801).

20. See Karl Leonhard Reinhold, *Sendschreiben an J. C. Lavater und J. Fichte über den Glauben an Gott* (Hamburg, 1799).

21. Immanuel Kant, "Erklarung," *Allgemeine Literatur-Zeitung,* August 29, 1799.

22. See Jean Paul, *Clavis Fichteana;* and Nicolai, *Über meine gelehrte Bildung.*

23. Johann Georg Hamann, "Metacritik über den Purismum der Vernunft," in *Mancherley zur Geschichte der metacritischen Invasion,* ed. F. T. Rink (written 1784; Königsberg, 1800); and Johann Gottfried von Herder, *Verstand und Erfahrung: Eine Metakritik zur Kritik der reinen Vernunft* (Leipzig: Hartknoch, 1799).

24. See Jean Paul, *Clavis Fichteana,* section 10.

25. Friedrich Heinrich Jacobi, *Jacobi an Fichte* (Perthes, 1799); repr. in *GA* 3.3:224–81. This "open letter" was sent to Fichte in March 1799 and published in September of that year.

26. "die Alleingeist der Alleinphilosophen" (*GA* 3.3:228–30).

27. Erlangen *Literatur-Zeitung,* May 19–20, 1800; repr. in *FZR* 3:35–53. Other critical reviews of *Die Bestimmung des Menschen* include, in addition to the previously mentioned parody by Schleiermacher and Bouterwek's review (which is discussed below), anonymous reviews in the *Neue nürnbergischen gelehrten Zeitung,* no. 39 (May 16, 1800); repr. in *FZR* 3:32–35; and *Neue theologische Annalen* 1800, installment 2; repr. in *FZR* 3:12–20.

28. *FZR* 3:45.

29. Bouterwek's review of *Die Bestimmung des Menschen* appeared in the *Göttingische Anzeigen von gelehrten Sachen,* no. 92 (June 9, 1800) and is reprinted in *FZR* 3:53–56. That Fichte was aware of Bouterwek's work may be inferred from his November 22, 1800, letter to Gottfried Ernst Mehmel, in which he accuses Bouterwek, along with Abicht and several others, of "stealing" his ideas.

30. *[Ankündigung:] Seit sechs Jahren,* in *GA* 1.7:154; *IWL,* 187.

31. See Fichte, "Bei der Lectüre von Schellings tr. Idealismus" (*GA* 2.5:413–15). Some of the differences between Schelling and Fichte were, to be sure, already apparent to Fichte several years earlier, and some of these are tacitly referred to by Fichte in his 1797 introductions to the *Wissenschaftslehre.* See the "Editor's Introduction" to *IWL,* xxv–xxx. See also Reinhard Lauth, *Die Entstehung von Schellings Identitätsphilosophie in der Auseinandersetzung mit Fichtes Wissenschaftslehre* (Freiburg: Alber, 1975).

32. Fichte read and made notes on Schelling's *System des transscendentalen Idealismus* sometime between the spring and fall of 1800. But according to the editors of *GA* 2.5, it was only in November 1800 that he finally realized the true significance and scope of Schelling's project and the extent of his departure from the standpoint of the *Wissenschaftslehre.* Evidence for this may be found in the letters

exchanged between Fichte and Schelling during this period; for example, Fichte to Schelling, November 15, 1800; Schelling to Fichte, December 19, 1800; and Fichte to Schelling, December 27, 1800. The most important and philosophically significant exchange of letters, however, did not occur until later in 1801. See, above all, Fichte's letter to Schelling, May 31–August 7, 1801.

33. See Fichte's January 12, 1800, letter to Cotta (his publisher), in which he describes his impending literary projects, including both *Sonnenklarer Bericht* and *Neue Bearbeitung*. Other projects, including *Der geschloßne Handelsstaat,* intervened, however, and it was not until the end of the summer that he was finally able to work on the new presentation. Apparently he composed the first three "Lehrstunde" of *Sonnenklarer Bericht* in August, but he did not actually begin work on the *Neue Bearbeitung* until October 1800. This effort on his part coincided with a *privatissima* on the *Wissenschaftslehre* that he was simultaneously conducting for the Berlin banker, Salomon Levy. (See Fichte's letter to Reimer, October 21, 1800, which is the same letter in which he describes *Sonnenklarer Bericht* as the "introduction" to the *Neue Bearbeitung*.)

34. *GA* 1.7:153–64; *IWL,* 186–201.

35. *Seit sechs Jahren,* in *GA* 1.7:153; *IWL,* 186–87.

36. *Seit sechs Jahren,* in *GA* 1.7:155; *IWL,* 188. This should not be considered any concession on Fichte's part to those critics who had accused him of changing his philosophy. On the contrary, he continues to deny this; instead, he is simply announcing that it is less important to him to insist upon this point than to lead readers to an understanding of his new presentation—at which point, he confidently predicts, they will view his earlier writings in a new and clearer light and will grasp the underlying unity of his philosophy.

37. Though this point is implicit in the November 4 "Announcement," it is made explicit in a letter Fichte sent to Schelling in September 1799, which he directed Schelling to have published and which appeared in the September 28, 1799, issue of the "Intelligenzblatt" of the *Allgemeinen Literatur-Zeitung.*

38. See *Sonnenklarer Bericht,* in *GA* 1.7:193–94.

39. *Seit sechs Jahren,* in *GA* 1.7:153; *IWL,* 186.

40. *Seit sechs Jahren,* in *GA* 1.7:156; *IWL,* 189.

41. *Seit sechs Jahren,* in *GA* 1.7:160; *IWL,* 195. It is interesting to note that Jacobi had previously described the *Wissenschaftslehre* as "eine Mathesis pura" (*GA* 3.3:227).

42. Fichte first read Bardili's book (at Reinhold's insistence) in February 1800. He prepared his review in September and early October of that year. (See the notes published in *GA* 2.5:243–318.) The review was completed on October 11 and appeared in the October 30–31 1800 issue of the Erlangen *Literatur-Zeitung* (*GA* 1.6:433–50).

43. *Seit sechs Jahren,* in *GA* 1.7:157–58; *IWL,* 191.

44. *Seit sechs Jahren,* in *GA* 1.7:158–61; *IWL,* 191–97. Fichte expounded his theory of language in a lengthy two-part essay he published in the *Philosophisches Journal* in 1795, "Von der Sprachfähigkeit und dem Ursprung der Sprache" (*GA* 1.3:97–127). For a thorough examination of this theory, as well as for an English translation of Fichte's essay, see Jere Paul Surber, *Language and German Idealism* (New Jersey: Humanities, 1996).

45. *Seit sechs Jahren,* in *GA* 1.7:159–61; *IWL,* 196–97.

46. "The *Wissenschaftslehre* simply does not admit the validity of any concept whatsoever that it has not produced within its own boundaries from intuition; and none of its concepts count for it as anything more or other than what is contained within intuition" (*Seit sechs Jahren,* in *GA* 1.7:161; *IWL,* 197).

47. Published in the *Philosophisches Journal* in January 1800 (*GA* 1.6:385–87; English translation in *IWL,* 155–75).

48. Written in October 1800 and published November 1 1800, in the Erlangen *Literatur-Zeitung* (*GA* 1.6:457–60).

49. See *GA* 1.6:458.

50. *Seit sechs Jahren,* in *GA* 1.7:154; *IWL,* 187.

51. *Seit sechs Jahren,* in *GA* 1.7:159–60; *IWL,* 195.

52. *Seit sechs Jahren,* in *GA* 1.7:164; *IWL,* 200.

53. *Sonnenklarer Bericht,* in *GA* 1.7:185.

54. For over a year, Fichte kept postponing the projected publication date for the *Neue Bearbeitung der Wissenschaftslehre.* He originally intended to have it ready for publication by the end of 1800, and then announced that it would be published in the spring of 1801. When subscription fell short of expectations, however, Fichte and Cotta agreed to postpone publication until some unspecified later date. (See Fichte's letter to Cotta, December 26, 1800.) Finally, in a letter of February 14, 1801, to Cotta, Fichte announced that he had stopped working on the *Neue Bearbeitung* in order to devote his time to two other projects, the *Antwortschreiben an Reinhold* and the polemic against Nicolai.

55. Between 1796 and 1799 Fichte lectured three times on the *Wissenschaftslehre nova methodo.* For details concerning these lectures and the relationship between his own (lost) manuscript(s) and the various student transcriptions of his lectures, see the editor's introduction to *FTP.*

56. Section 1 of the *Neue Bearbeitung der Wissenschaftslehre* corresponds to section 1 of the *Wissenschaftslehre nova methodo;* section 2 corresponds to the first part of section 2 of *Wissenschaftslehre nova methodo;* section 3 corresponds in part to the rest of section 2 of *Wissenschaftslehre nova methodo;* section 4 corresponds to some of the material contained in sections 3 and 4 of *Wissenschaftslehre nova methodo;* section 5 corresponds to part of section 4 of *Wissenschaftslehre nova methodo;* section 6 corresponds to additional portions of section 4 and part of section 5 of *Wissenschaftslehre nova methodo;* section 7 corresponds to section 6 of *Wissenschaftslehre nova methodo;* section 8, which includes an ambitious "deduction of productive imagination," really has no precise parallel in *Wissenschaftslehre nova methodo,* but does discuss certain matters discussed in sections 7–10 of *Wissenschaftslehre nova methodo.*

57. "In der NBdWL . . . manifestiert sich die Kontinuität des systematisches Ansatzes der frühen Philosophie Fichtes, einschließlich der Darstellungs*form,* über den Atheismusstreit und die [*Bestimmung des Menschen*] hinaus. Darin liegt die historische Bedeutung dieser Darstellung. Systematisch, heißt dies, bietet sie nicht so sehr Neues, als sie vielmehr eine Klärung der bekannten Positionen, insbesondere Bereinigung von Anlässen zum Mißverständnis, schließlich Offenlegung inhärenter Probleme und Widersprüche erwarten läßt, die Anstoß zur

Weitererentwicklung des Ansatzes geben haben könnten" (Koch, *Fichtes Theorie des Selbstbewußtseins,* 289–90).

58. It is here, for example, that Fichte develops the famous analogy between an "explanation" or "deduction" of a clock and the clock itself, in order thereby to illustrate the difference between his own philosophical "construction"—or "reconstruction"—of reality and reality itself. (See the first, second, and fifth lessons of *Sonnenklarer Bericht,* esp. *GA* 1.7:212, 246–48.) Notice, however, that even here Fichte remains somewhat ambivalent on this question and, in the Sixth Lesson, cannot resist adding that the deepest "Tendenz" of his philosophy not only grows directly out of but also aims at improving life.

59. See his letter to Friedrich Schlegel, August 16, 1800, in which Fichte criticizes some of the aphorisms in Schlegel's *Ideen* collection (as well as his recently published *Gespräch über die Poesie*) as betraying a confusion between "the *philosophical manner of thinking* [*philosophischen Denkart*], which must of course be transferred to life, and philosophy itself, in the objective sense of the word, as a science," and adds, "The scientific-idealistic standpoint can never infuse life; that would be totally unnatural." This confusion is directly addressed in *Sonnenklarer Bericht,* which was completed after Fichte's break with Schlegel in the fall of 1800. See Fichte's letters to Schelling, September 13, 1800, and October 3, 1800, in the latter of which he complains about the Schlegel brothers' "loathing for everyone who does not completely share their views and does not make the move from *literature* to *life.*"

60. See, for example, *Neue Bearbeitung der Wissenschaftslehre,* in *GA* 2.5:334: "The reader is here invited to engage in a completely *free* act of thinking. Nothing that he produces here is actual thinking, sensing, perceiving, willing, etc., in life. For the reader was previously alive, and he continued to live without any effort or freedom on his part, and he was not engaged in philosophizing."

61. *Neue Bearbeitung der Wissenschaftslehre,* in *GA* 2.5:331. See also Fichte's *Atwortschreiben an Prof. Reinhold,* where he reiterates that the *Wissenschaftslehre* has nothing to do with ordinary experience and most certainly cannot improve life (*GA* 1.7:300–301).

62. See *Neue Bearbeitung der Wissenschaftslehre,* in *GA* 2.5:334–35.

63. *Neue Bearbeitung der Wissenschaftslehre,* in *GA* 2.5:333. See also *Sonnenklarer Bericht,* in *GA* 1.7:222: "Here we are not concerned with the discovery of something already finished, but rather with the discovery of something that first has to be produced by a free act of thinking. The *Wissenschaftslehre* is not psychology, which is nothing at all."

64. See *Sonnenklarer Bericht,* in *GA* 1.7:187–89, 221–22, 225, and 262.

65. *Sonnenklarer Bericht,* in *GA* 1.7:187–89 and 236–37.

66. "It is false to consider philosophy to be rational cognition on the basis of concepts. A concept is never an original image [*Urbild*], never the *matter* [*Sache*] itself, but only a copy [*Nachbild*]. The original image is an intuition. A concept (and therefore too *its* copy, a *word*), must justify itself before intuition, which must show that what is combined in the concept is present and inseparably connected within intuition. A *philosophy of concepts* can only *clarify* and make *consistent* a system that is

already *finished*. It cannot correct fundamental errors, however, since it never touches the foundation" (*Neue Bearbeitung der Wissenschaftslehre,* in *GA* 2.5:338).

67. "Rezension Bardili," Fichte's review of C. G. Bardili's *Grundriss der ersten Logik,* was written in October 1800 and published at the end of that month in the Erlangen *Literatur-Zeitung* (*GA* 1.6:433–50). His *Antwortschreiben an Herrn Prof. Reinhold* was written at the beginning of April 1801 and published later that month (*GA* 1.7:291–324).

68. "Rezension Bardili," in *GA* 1.6:435.

69. "Rezension Bardili," in *GA* 1.6:441 and 436. See also *Antwortschreiben,* in *GA* 1.7:298–99 and 308.

70. "Rezension Bardili," in *GA* 1.6:443.

71. The method of the new presentation, Fichte explains, "is *entirely* of the same sort as that of mathematical proofs. The *principium a quo* is intuition. It thus has no power to prove anything to someone who cannot *produce* or discover this within himself—though this is considered to be impossible [Wer diese nicht in sich *los machen* kann; oder nicht dasselbe darin fänd, welches für unmöglich gehalten wird—für den ist keine Beweiskraft]" (*Neue Bearbeitung der Wissenschaftslehre,* in *GA* 2.5:338).

72. In the course of explaining that the intuitions upon which the *Wissenschaftslehre* is grounded are intuitions of consciously executed inner *acts of construction,* rather than of "facts of consciousness," Fichte explicitly notes that his explanation is intended as a response to the anonymous reviewer (i.e., Abicht) of the *Bestimmung des Menschen* in the Erlangen *Literatur-Zeitung* (May 19 and 20, 1800), who had denied that he possessed any "Wahrnehmung" of the acts described in book 2 of *Die Bestimmung des Menschen.*

For a discussion of the various senses in which Fichte uses the term *intellectual intuition* and of the important differences between the present "methodological" usage and other Fichtean usages, see Daniel Breazeale, "Fichte's *nova methodo phenomenologica:* On the Methodological Role of 'Intellectual Intuition' in the later Jena *Wissenschaftslehre,*" *Revue Internationale de Philosophie* [Brussels] no. 206 (1998): 587–616.

73. *Neue Bearbeitung der Wissenschaftslehre,* in *GA* 2.5:349. See also *GA* 2.5:339: "*Universality* [*Allgemeinheit*] first follows from immediate necessity."

74. "It [the *Wissenschaftslehre*] is proven via the *necessity* of *thinking.* This necessity of thinking, however, is intuited, immediately intuited (precisely through universal intuition [*die universelle Anschauung*]). The latter is thus employed in order to seek out itself" (*GA* 2.5:349). See also the use of the term *wissenschaftliche Anschauung* in the Fourth Lesson of *Sonnenklarer Bericht,* in *GA* 1.7:243.

75. *Neue Bearbeitung der Wissenschaftslehre,* in *GA* 2.5:377.

76. *Neue Bearbeitung der Wissenschaftslehre,* in *GA* 2.5:359–60. See also *Sonnenklarer Bericht,* in *GA* 1.7:229: "Intuition would thus be the immediate grasping [*Aufassung*], all at once and in a single glance, of reason's overall modes of acting, through which it constructs itself as such. . . . One can comprehend how the immediate evidence, necessity, and universality of everything and for everyone—and hence, everything scientific—are based upon this intuition and upon it alone."

77. The arresting parallel between "transcendental and poetic talent" is perhaps an indication of how deeply Fichte's project was, as he himself admitted, influenced by his careful study of Kant's *Kritik der Urteilskraft.* The "universality" and "necessity" here attributed to philosophical judgments are closer to the kind of universality and necessity Kant attributes to "judgments of taste" than to the kind of universality and necessity he attributes (in the *Kritik der reinen Vernunft*) to properly "theoretical" judgments.

"The *Wissenschaftslehre* is concerned with what occurs in our consciousness as a result of a *free act of production*—not a *chance discovery*—of a determination [of consciousness]. Its entire demonstrative power is based on this inner intuition. (It is not based on the development of concepts, which are first brought into being from an intuition, that is, from the act of comprehending the latter. Before anything whatsoever can be demonstrated by the analysis of concepts, their correctness must be tested by reference to intuition.) The necessity and universal validity of what is found in this intuition by all rational consciousness is based, in part, on immediate consciousness and, in part, on insight into the subordination of everything that is subordinate to the condition discovered in intuition" (*Neue Bearbeitung der Wissenschaftslehre,* in *GA* 2.5:334).

See also *GA* 2.5:352–53: "That the sort of thinking just described provides something determinate is something that everyone must discover within his own intuition. It is by means of such intuition that the description just given first obtains its meaning and clarity."

78. *Sonnenklarer Bericht,* in *GA* 1.7:230.

79. *Neue Bearbeitung der Wissenschaftslehre,* in *GA* 2.5:335.

80. *Neue Bearbeitung der Wissenschaftslehre,* in *GA* 2.5:367.

81. *Neue Bearbeitung der Wissenschaftslehre,* in *GA* 2.5:368.

82. The *Wissenschaftslehre* "constructs the total, shared consciousness of all rational beings entirely a priori, according to its fundamental features, just as geometry constructs entirely a priori the universal ways in which space can be delimited by all rational beings" (*Sonnenklarer Bericht,* in *GA* 1.7:233).

83. See *Sonnenklarer Bericht,* in *GA* 1.7:233: "I posit 'I = A.' In the intuition of the act of constructing this 'A,' it is found [*so findet sich*] that a 'B' is inseparably connected with this 'A.' In the intuition of the act of constructing this B, it is, in turn, found that a 'C' is connected thereto, and so on, until one arrives at a finale extreme ('A'), to which full self-consciousness pertains and which appears to be self-enclosed and complete."

84. There are, of course, important differences between the method employed in the first ("ascending") half of the *Wissenschaftslehre nova methodo* and that employed in the second ("descending") half. Whether Fichte would have had to modify or to abandon his strict geometrical method in the second half of the *Neue Bearbeitung* is a question that cannot be answered, since the fragment stops well short of the completion of the first half of the presentation.

85. "The *Wissenschaftslehre* is *mathesis* of the mind. In actual mathematics one is concerned with the *products* of construction; here one is concerned with the act of construction itself" (*GA* 2.5:344).

86. *Sonnenklarer Bericht,* in *GA* 1.7:238.

87. Jacobi, *Jacobi an Fichte,* in *GA* 3.3:227.

88. Nevertheless, Fichte's point was certainly not lost on informed readers of the intended "introduction" to the new version of the *Wissenschaftslehre.* See, for example, Hegel's comment in his letter to Mehmel, August 1801, in which, after criticizing *Sonnenklarer Bericht,* he remarks that Fichte does do a good job of "distinguishing Fichte's and Schelling's enterprises [*Sache*]."

89. *Neue Bearbeitung der Wissenschaftslehre,* in *GA* 1.7:340.

90. On this point, see Fichte's unpublished "[Zu Schellings 'Darstellung meines Systems der Philosophie']" (*GA* 2.5:483–508; written in the spring or summer of 1801).

91. See, for example, the passing reference to "*another system of intellectual intuition, opposed to that of the Wissenschaftslehre*" (*GA* 1.7:239) See also Fichte's unequivocal rejection of anyone, "even though he might be a famous philosopher," who asserts that "the I *proceeds* from something that is real in and for itself, from *absolute being*" (*GA* 1.7:202), as well as *GA* 1.7:230.

92. *Sonnenklarer Bericht,* in *GA* 1.7:202.

93. See also the extended discussion, in the *Neue Bearbeitung,* of the distinction between "ideal" and "real" activity. In his November 15, 1800, letter to Schelling, Fichte mentions this distinction as one of the points most in need of clarification in the projected new presentation of the *Wissenschaftslehre,* and there appears to be a pointedly anti-Schellingean thrust to Fichte's clarification, inasmuch as he explicitly reminds his reader that the "identity of ideality and reality" affirmed in the *Wissenschaftslehre* is always an identity of the ideal and real dimensions *of the activities of the I* (see *GA* 2.5:361–62). From this it follows that the admission of the underlying identity of ideality and reality does not provide anyone (notably, Schelling) with a warrant for seeking a higher principle of the identity of the I and nature.

Another indication of Fichte's growing anti-Schellingeanism is his pointed criticism of recent efforts to interpret the "pragmatic history" provided by a transcendental-genetic account of consciousness (here described by Fichte as "a fiction") as an *actual* history of the genesis of the self, "the biography of a person prior to his birth" (*Sonnenklarer Bericht,* in *GA* 1.7:249). According to the editors of *GA* 1.7, this remark is explicitly directed against Schelling's account of the unconscious production of an objective subject-object. It is, however, just as likely that it is intended as a critique of Schelling's claim, in his *System of Transcendental Idealism,* that the latter provides a "narration" (*Erzählung*) of an actual "Odyssey of the Spirit."

94. "Ja wohl da kommt die absolute 'Verwirrung' erst zum Vorschein. . . . Kurz ich bin da sehr irre, u es gibt nichts geschietes" (*Neue Bearbeitung der Wissenschaftslehre,* in *GA* 2.5:374).

95. "Deutlich <wären> mir die Resultate so <ziemlich.> <nur> noch nicht bewiesen" (*Neue Bearbeitung der Wissenschaftslehre,* in *GA* 2.5:377). See also the following comment on the relationship between intuiting and thinking: "This is surely how it is; the question is simply how I want to direct the deduction" (*GA* 2.5:394).

96. *Neue Bearbeitung der Wissenschaftslehre,* in *GA* 2.5:391. A particular source of Fichte's dissatisfaction with his new presentation of the *Wissenschaftslehre* is its reliance on circular explanations, for example, of the relationship between free and

constrained activities (i.e., the relationship between striving and feeling), regarding which he writes: "This is a circular description, of which, unfortunately, I have many" (*GA* 2.5:386).

97. *Neue Bearbeitung der Wissenschaftslehre,* in *GA* 2.5:384.

98. *Neue Bearbeitung der Wissenschaftslehre,* in *GA* 2.6:394.

99. "Since the power of imagination is the capacity for the infinite, is there not a pure intuition of *God,* by means of which I could also help my philosophy?" (*GA* 2.5:401). "*God* is the band for connecting the entire intelligible world. Such an intuition simply must be demonstrated" (*GA* 2.5:385).

100. See Fichte's December 27, 1800, letter to Schelling, in which he confesses that transcendental philosophy still requires a certain "expansion," even with respect to its first principle, and adds: "I have not yet been able to elaborate these expanded principles scientifically. The clearest hint concerning them may be found in Book Three of my *Bestimmung des Menschen.* As soon as I have completed the new presentation of the *Wissenschaftslehre* [i.e., *Neue Bearbeitung der Wissenschaftslehre*], the elaboration of these principles will be my first task. In a word: what is still missing is a *transcendental system of the intelligible world.*"

This suggestion, however, needs to be balanced against Fichte's somewhat later assertion, in his May 31–August 7, 1801, letter to Schelling: "Though the *Wissenschaftslehre* is by no means lacking in its principles, it does indeed lack completion: namely, the highest synthesis, the synthesis of the spiritual world, is not yet accomplished. It was just as I was preparing to accomplish this that the charge of atheism was raised."

On the basis of these two assertions, one might conclude that Fichte abandoned work on *Neue Bearbeitung der Wissenschaftslehre* precisely because he discovered that it was essential to *incorporate* this new, "highest synthesis" within the new presentation and yet found himself unable to accommodate it within the framework of the older presentation (*Wissenschaftslehre nova methodo*) that he was still trying to revise. This might explain his decision to abandon work on the new version of 1800 and to make a fresh start from an altogether new starting point, which eventually led to the composition of the *Wissenschaftslehre* of 1801–2.

101. *GA* 2.5:394

102. "Ich müßte mich sonach auf die Bildungstheorie entlassen" (*GA* 2.5:397).

103. *GA* 2.5:395.

104. "*klärer machen, erhellen, leuchten*" (*GA* 2.5:395).

105. Koch (*Fichtes Theorie des Selbstbewußtseins,* 370) considers two different readings of the *Neue Bearbeitung.* Of the first, he writes: "Auf einen dieser Wege, der in die Richtung der späten WL führt, verweist NBdWL, ohne ihn schon zu betreten. Sie wägt eine Konzept der Einbildungskraft als Vermögen der Anschauung des Absoluten oder Gottes als des Inbegriff einer intelligiblen Welt ab, in welcher Interpersonalität und deren Darstellung in der sinnlichen Welt zu gründen waren." Nevertheless, Koch concludes that "das Konzept der WL 1801/02 ist noch fern. Fast könnte man Fichtes tastende Versuch am Ende der NBdWL auf die mit der WL 1804 beginnende Entwicklung der WL vorasubeziehen. Es sind Versuch einer Selbstverabschiedung der Reflexion vor dem Absoluten" (479). Koch himself locates "der Schritt über die Grenzen der *WLnm* hinaus" precisely in the new theory

of the productive imagination sketched by Fichte in very general terms in section 8 of the *Neue Bearbeitung,* in which, according to Koch, Fichte comes, for the first time, to identify intellectual intuition with productive imagination and thus goes beyond his previously limited concept of the latter (471–81). This is a very strong—and creative—reading of Fichte's extremely sketchy remarks on this topic, which are limited to a single page (*GA* 2.5:393).

See also Stolzenberg's conclusion that the analysis, in section 5 of the *Neue Bearbeitung,* of the relationship between intellectual intuition (*das Eine*) and ideal and real activity (*das Gegensatz*) is a clear anticipation of the way in which Fichte subsequently develops the first principle of his philosophy in the *Wissenschaftslehre* of 1801–2 (Stolzenberg, *Fichtes Begriff der intellektuellen Anschauung,* 245). See, however, Koch's (somewhat obscure) criticism of Stolzenberg on precisely this point (Koch, *Fichtes Theorie des Selbstbewußtseins,* 346–51).

106. For a brief but useful discussion of the relationship between the *Wissenschaftslehre* of 1801–2 and earlier versions of the same, see Wolfgang H. Schrader, "Der Übergang zur *Wissenschaftslehre* 1801," in *Transzendentalphilosophie als System: Die Auseinandersetzung zwischen 1794 und 1806,* ed. Albert Mues (Hamburg: Meiner, 1989), 199–211.

107. See *Sonnenklarer Bericht,* in *GA* 1.7:242.

108. "I am in search of science—not simply the outer, systematic form of the same, but the inner character of any *knowing* [eines *Wissens*]. I seek to grasp the original source of that on which alone it depends that any knowing, any conviction, anything unshakable occurs within consciousness" (*GA* 1.7:260).

109. Fichte's *Antwortschreiben an Herrn Prof. Reinhold* was written in three days in April 1801 as a direct response to Reinhold's "Sendschreiben an den Herrn Professor *Fichte* über die zweyte Recension von Bardilis Grundriß us.w. in der Erlang. Litt. Zeitung N. 214 und 215," which appeared in *Beyträge zur leichtern Übersicht des Zustandes der Philosophie beym Anfange de 19. Jahrhunderts,* installment 1 (January 1801), and which was itself a reply to Fichte's review of Bardili's book. See *GA* 1.7:292, 316–17, and 322–23.

110. See *GA* 1.6:448.

111. Meckenstock, "Fichtes Fragment," 80.

112. The editors of *GA* 2.5 argue that one of the reasons that Fichte abandoned work on the *Neue Bearbeitung* and began the new *Darstellung der Wissenschaftslehre* of 1801–2 was precisely because he felt the need for a "scientific refutation" of Bardili's and Reinhold's "dogmatism" (*GA* 2.5:327). It seems to me, however, that this is precisely what he was trying to accomplish in the *Neue Bearbeitung,* with its new emphasis on "intuition."

113. In fact, a large portion of the manuscript is devoted to explaining precisely this distinction. Fichte's dissatisfaction with the details of his own discussion of the distinction between ideal and real activities in the 1796–98 version of his system is evident from his November 15, 1800, letter to Schelling, in which he maintains that both he and Schelling have previously been guilty of some confusion on this score.

114. *Neue Bearbeitung der Wissenschaftslehre,* in *GA* 2.5:347

115. *Neue Bearbeitung der Wissenschaftslehre,* in *GA* 2.5:384–86. Another helpful innovation in the *Neue Bearbeitung* is a new distinction between the original

subject-object "duplicity" of the I and the "triplicity" that is the necessary product thereof: "Subject"—"Object"—"Object of this object"; or, the imaging subject, what is imaged, and what exists ("das Bildende"—"das Gebildete"—"das Seyende"). See *GA* 2.5:347 and 362–63.

116. *Neue Bearbeitung der Wissenschaftslehre,* in *GA* 2.5:401. See also *GA* 2.5:385.

117. Karl Leonhard Reinhold, "Die erste Aufgabe der Philosophie in ihren merkwürdigsten Auflösungen seit der Wiederherstellunge der Wissenschaften. Erste Abtheilung von Baco bis Kant," *Beyträge zur leichtern Übersicht des Zustandes der Philosophie beym Anfange de 19. Jahrhunderts,* installment 1 (1801): 1–65.

See Reinhard Lauth's thought-provoking suggestion that Fichte's reading of Reinhold's discussion of Descartes' *philosphia prima* in installment 1 of his *Beyträge* may have powerfully influenced Fichte's understanding of the relationship between the cogito and an intuition of God. See Lauth's introduction to "J. G. Fichte: Abriss. Aphorismen zur Geschichte der Philosophie (1801)," *Fichte-Studien* 1 (1990): 200.

118. Fichte's other major publication during this period, *Friedrich Nicolai's Leben und sonderbare Meinungen* (written February–April 1801 and published in May 1801), contains little of philosophical substance and is thus not significant for our present inquiry.

119. To be sure, certain features of the new method with which Fichte had experimented in 1800–1801 were incorporated in the 1801–2 *Darstellung* and became distinctive features of all the later versions of the *Wissenschaftslehre.* An example of this is the use of the terms "Konstruktion" and "Nachkonstruktion" to characterize the enterprise of the transcendental philosopher.

Structures of Imagination in Fichte's *Wissenschaftslehre* 1794–1795 and 1804

Violetta L. Waibel

At the beginning of the second series of lectures of the *Wissenschaftslehre* of 1804, Fichte announces that he aims to argue for the intrinsic unity of being and thinking, and moreover, for the unity of the three principles of knowledge given by the threefold *Critique* of Kant.[1] A first step in realizing this program is in my view the early *Wissenschaftslehre* of 1794–95, mainly in its theoretical part, whereas the *Wissenschaftslehre* of 1804 is to be regarded as a step of deeper engagement with this problem. What is in 1794 the construction of the fact of imagination is in 1804 the construction of the fact of reason or absolute knowledge, with both showing the intrinsic structure of unity and difference of being and consciousness on a certain level and both showing in some regard the common root of the Kantian principles of knowledge. My first step is to take a look at those elements in Kant's theory that Fichte intends to overcome. My second step is to look at the early *Wissenschaftslehre* and its theory of imagination. Finally I want to compare the theoretical *Wissenschaftslehre* of 1794 and 1804 in their structures and different intentions.

The concept of Kant's theory of cognition is to be described as justifying the objective validity of cognition by subjective principles, functions, and conditions of pure thinking. As is known, the unstructured manifold of experience, given to the subject by perception, is unified by several empirical and purely nomological synthetic functions of the mind. Most important in this context is the fact that only a few of these functions of synthesis are of interest with regard to founding an objective justification of cognition. These are, as is well known, the twelve categories. In Kant's opinion, there exists no kind of combination that could be given to the mind; instead they are always constituted by subjective conditions.[2] But whereas associations, for example, or customary successions of facts or other a posteriori synthetic unities are built by accidental conditions, the categories are absolutely necessary for each representation of a possible item of cognition. On the basis of this theory, there is a distinction of cognition in a narrow sense between the natural sciences (concerning the causal mechanisms of physics and so on) and mental acts in a broad sense, concerning each other meaningful way of saying. Two of these mental acts in a broader sense are of interest for the Kantian critical program: the lawgiving principle of practical reason, called the categorical imperative, and the principle of subjective and objective purposiveness in regard to the beautiful, the sublime, and the relations of part and whole or of species and genus in nature.

Although Kant was convinced that there is no unique principle or root of these three principles of knowledge, because the degree and source of obligation of each principle is quite different, Fichte in contrast laid stress on the thesis that there is one.[3]

The post-Kantian philosophy in the theories of Fichte, Schelling, and Hegel can be described as the project of explaining the unity and difference of the subjective and objective, being and thinking. First it was Fichte who tried to treat the problem of the subjective and the objective, to be sure, in the same vein as and in close connection to Kant, but also in a new way. His contribution to this philosophical issue is to be seen in the self-construction of the notion of imagination by means of the faculty of imagination, thus representing the unity in question.

Two things are important to be kept in mind. The faculty of imagination is said to be the faculty which is responsible for creating reality, and as Fichte stresses, it is the only one to do this. On the other hand, it is the nature of the absolute ego to be reality and to provide for or, literally translated, to "transport" (*übertragen*) reality to the contents of one's consciousness and knowledge.[4] So the interaction of the ego and the imagination has to guarantee every kind of claim of knowledge. But what does this mean?

With regard to the examples that Fichte gives in his essay *On the Concept of the Wissenschaftslehre,* the ego may correctly "transport" reality (= validity) on singular verifiable facts or coherent systems of history, nature, and so on, but not on fictional ideas, not even if they build a whole and absolutely consistent system of conditions and facts, as is the case for the possible and thinkable world of angels.[5] In intuition and in sound common sense we really agree. But what we want to know is the criterion, the principle which makes it possible to distinguish between the allowable and forbidden "transport" of reality.

If Fichte has given an answer to this question, then it is not quite obvious what it is. But my thesis is that it has to do with the paradigmatic structure in Fichte's *Wissenschaftslehre:* first in the ego in itself, which is described as the unity of being and positing; second, in the structure of the faculty of imagination, which unifies the objective with the subjective; and third, in the structure of pure reason or absolute knowledge in the *Wissenschaftslehre* of 1804, which unifies being and thinking. It is to this structure that we must look for the distinguishing element between really knowing and only fictionally thinking something.

Since I think that the structure of the early *Wissenschaftslehre* is paradigmatic for the Fichtean notion of knowledge, I'd like to sketch its construction in broad strokes, as given by Fichte.

Section 3 of the *Wissenschaftslehre* has shown that, on the basis of the categories of reality and negation, there is a relationship between the ego and the non-ego. This relation leads, as is well known, to a theoretical and a practical proposition, with only the former being of interest to my question. The theoretical proposition, "the ego posits itself, being determined by the non-ego,"[6] is analyzed in terms of the categories of relation. The ego, insofar as it posits itself, is interpreted as a relation of substantiality; the ego determined by the non-ego, however, is interpreted as a relation of causality. Relating these two relations, Fichte develops in arguments, which I will forgo, the notions of independent activities of the ego and the non-ego, the famous check and the spontaneity of the faculty of imagination.

Having reached this point, a series of contradictions and syntheses are meant to give the final synthesis of the imagination. These steps are often said to be dark, mechanical, and impenetrable, if not to say of unreasonable content. But an image given by Fichte himself helps to convey the point of this methodology, which is important for the attempt Fichte makes to understand the subject-object problem.

The distance of light and dark in continuous space and time can be assumed to have one point on its connection-line in which the light passes into dark.[7] At this point, light isn't light anymore and dark is not yet dark. In Fichte's language, there is a contradiction, solved by a synthesis that yields the notion of twilight. This game of language, as I interpret this methodology, can be expanded, searching for the passage point from light to twilight, twilight to dark, and so on. The intention of this game is in my view to give to the factual evidence, here of passing from light to dark, an advanced and developed conceptuality. The image of light and dark is an analogy of what Fichte develops in the artificial construction of the faculty of imagination, as he explicitly names his philosophical method. But what is the philosophical result of this construction? To give an answer, we have first to look at Kant's theory and then to examine further Fichte's construction of the faculty of the imagination.

Kant's fundamental claim in the transcendental aesthetic is that the only thing which could be given to mind is the sensible *material*, the given manifold, whereas the sensible *form* is the pure intuition of time and space and *in concreto* the inner and outer sense of the intellect, in which the given manifold is thought to stand together. The division of form and material is repeated on the level of concepts. The pure concepts of reason (the categories) are mere functions or forms of the intellect, whereas the empirical concepts, on which these forms are applied, give the content, or let's say, the material of the thinking.

In Fichte's construction we meet the division of form and material, which concerns the relation of substantiality and causality in a more abstract way, once again. With regard to the relation of causality, their division allows the difference of ideal and real to be inserted, or in other terms, of quantitative and qualitative elements within the relation of causality.[8] The check of the non-ego on the one hand is the material-giving realistic element, which serves to constitute the imagination, and, on the other, is a form-giving element which constitutes the idealistic aspects of the imagination.

The form-material division of the relation of substantiality refers to the form-giving and content-positing activities of mind. Thus the spontaneity of intellect opens the possibility of producing any kind of representational content, according to the subjective forms of mind. For my purposes at the moment it is only necessary to mention the different elements of form and material, of quality and quantity. I will forgo several steps of Fichte's account here.[9]

If we, for an instant, accept that Fichte's construction is absolutely controlled and anything but dark or impenetrable, we can identify its aim in putting together the extremes of empiricist and idealist models of explaining the fact of imagination, connecting being and consciousness, on the basis of the form-material division which Kant suggested earlier in the *Critique of Pure Reason*. Assuming that this interpretation is correct, we would have become acquainted with a theory of representation whose main intention is to show that the connection between the ego and the non-ego is thought to be continuous by a successive application of forms and functions (categories) of the intellect. As we have seen, this construction is led by the relational categories and by the opposition of empiricism and idealism, both of which give in some way plausible explanations, but each of which alone is unilateral as well. The result that Fichte offers is as follows.

Remembering the image of light and dark, we have filled the distance of the extremes with concepts, so that we can say they fill a space without any gap of understanding. As the *Wissenschaftslehre* is the expression of the original nature of mind, Fichte intends to show that we can get a concept of the essential elements of mind by mentally fulfilling the law that there is no unbridgeable hiatus between nature and consciousness.

The objective and the subjective are ordinarily of absolutely opposite nature, whatever their nature as such may be. For this reason, each of them has dominion over its own world. But there is also a frontier which not only divides these worlds but makes them touch. The frontier is the only thing they have in common, or let's say, the check is possible. It is the faculty of imagination that responds to this circumstance by picking up the different, completely opposite, and mutually exclusive elements but nevertheless grasping them together (*Zusammentreffen und Zusammenfassen*).[10] This is possible because of the nature of the ego, which is undetermined activity as well as substance, and as such is open to be determined by a check. Encountering a check, the ego gets to know its unlimited nature and thereby limits itself.

The result is the faculty of imagination oscillating between the unlimited and the self-limiting activity. The Fichtean construction of a conceptual continuity can be read as an answer to the Kantian question of how it could be possible that mere forms of the intellect such as categories can be said to determine factual matters of the world. If it is to be accepted that there are two worlds, foreign to each other but with a common frontier, then Fichte has intended to show that there is no unbridgeable hiatus. Fichte shows that the categories Kant identified as the same functions of the pure intellect which are analytically used in judgments and synthetically used in the synthesis of the given manifold to an intuition[11] are none other than those functions used to clarify and to understand identity and difference of the consciousness and its representations.

The nature of the intellect that was shown to have no unbridgeable hiatus is also thought to make possible the "transport" of reality. As the end of the early *Wissenschaftslehre* makes obvious, the possibility of transporting reality is accompanied by a feeling of pleasure (*Beifall*), its impossibility by a feeling of displeasure (*Mißfallen*).[12]

The construction of the concept of imagination by means of the faculty of imagination is the same structure involved in the constitution of any other concept of empirical objects. Fichte develops this in the "Deduction of Representation" at the end of the theoretical part of the *Grundlage*.

As stated previously, the ego was said to "transport" reality, and the faculty of imagination was said to constitute it in two ways: this faculty of imagination is responsible for the representation of the world, but also for the representation of its own. Therefore the faculty of imagination constitutes a material-guided realistic and a form-guided idealistic kind of reality, with both of them being contents of knowledge. We can say that the faculty of imagination is the concrete instantiation of the ego that finally has the same structure as the ego itself. On the one hand, we have the ego that is described as the identity and difference of pure spontaneity and being and on the other hand as the relation of substantiality and of causality. The ego is the condition of knowledge, whereas the faculty of imagination represents the conditions and possibility of pure intuition. What can be described as an identity of being and positing is the identity of a given (ideal or real) content and its being thought, and this structure is basic for any case of knowledge.

In some sense, we can read the *Wissenschaftslehre* of 1804 as a direct pursuit of the construction of the faculty of imagination which Fichte first undertook in 1794, though in another sense it is obvious that Fichte has attained a new perspective on the problem of founding knowledge.[13] A few points suffice to make the pursuit clear. First of all, there is the correlation of idealism and realism in both drafts of the *Wissenschaftslehre,* which are in the later version moreover distinguished as lower and higher idealism and realism. Furthermore, we twice meet the structure of self-reflection, first in terms of the faculty of imagination, and then in terms of the absolute knowledge. What is of most interest here is that the apparently new topic—namely the problem of the facticity of knowledge and Fichte's advanced suggestion of genetic insight into the factual matter of knowledge—can already be identified even in the *Wissenschaftslehre* of 1794. We have to remember that the developed concept of the faculty of imagination was indicated as the fact of consciousness (*Faktum des Bewußtseins*).[14] Ten years later Fichte reflects that the facticity of the concept of absolute knowledge must be genetically developed and understood. But this genetic development is in my view nothing more than a reformulation of the methodology of construction in 1794 and its application on the remained facticity.

So we have to examine the problem of facticity which Fichte attempts to overcome in 1804. Whereas the result of the earlier construction of the faculty of imagination was only given to the reader without any commentary concerning its philosophical implications, so that the reader was left alone without any explanation of the relationship between the evident but unexamined and the examined philosophical concept of imagination (the beginning and the end of the construction), later Fichte treats this problem as a new philosophical issue. It is precisely the undeveloped evidence of this relation which places the demand of overcoming facticity. The philosophical reflection produces for itself a content (*Gehalt*), for example, the facticity of imagination. This is why the theoretical part of 1804 is to be seen in the higher realism and its being which is deposited (*abge-*

setzt) by thought. This way the early theory of the ego and its condition of knowledge becomes a theory of absolute knowledge and its content of absolute being.

As Fichte now begins with the facticity of knowledge with the aim to show its vivid, non-factual "life," he replaces the Kantian question about the relation of the subjective and the objective with the question of a factual and vivid way of knowing. This is, I think, the proper question concerning the faculty of imagination. This step is legitimated by the assumption that every case of knowledge which is actually vivid has its reasonable content or object. This fact, which is only intuitively expressed in 1794, now receives conceptual clarification. A case of knowledge that is not reasonable never loses its facticity.

In 1804 Fichte not only renounces the reflection on the relation of the subject and the object, but also renounces the categorical-based theory of the faculty of imagination. Now it is the very relation of thinking and being which can be identified as a renewal of the absolute ego, and its unity of being and positing which finally represents the common structure of every case of knowledge.

Comparison of the two versions of the *Wissenschaftslehre* shows that the early language game of contradictions and syntheses, which results in new concepts, gives way to other methodological devices. Nevertheless the image of the connection-line, which is filled step-by-step with concepts, not, to be sure in a linear procession, but instead in a successive and reciprocal grasping of the one domain into the other (*Ineinandergreifen*), is in the background. Thus we can identify the two relations of substantiality and causality in a more abstract way by means of the concept of the "through" (*das Durch*). The "through" is, briefly, a description of the factual concept and its content vividly thought, which is the result of what the faculty of imagination together with the faculty of judgment have fixed in the concept.

Assuming that this classification of the different terminology but comparable structure of the philosophical issue is to be accepted, I finally will turn to the presentation of the conceptual movement which Fichte develops in 1804 once more in only broad strokes.

The metaphor of the "through" (*durch*) is the attempt to render vivid thinking, gathering the suitable forms and their contents. The "through" therefore is another image for the grasping together of the different moments of thinking into their unity. But since it is now the content of thinking itself which is at issue, the "through" provides not only an insight into its coherence. Instead, it is also aimed at making explicit the grasping together of the elements of knowing in any very act of thinking.

Lower idealism indicates the philosophical reflection on the content of thinking whereas realism, as is well known from 1794, represents the content of thinking in itself, giving insight into its "life." Fichte speaks therefore of the intelligible concept (idealism) and the intuitive light (realism).[15]

Philosophical thought is to be understood as a facticity which only produces an abstract concept of its content. But a concept of knowledge not only has to win insight into its construction, but also has to take account of that of which it is a theory. Solely reflecting on the content or the being of knowledge, which appears in thinking, is on the other side a factual realism.

The consequence for Fichte is to bring together the facticity of idealism and the facticity of realism, both being unilateral, independently regarded. Not only in 1794 but once again in 1804 it is the mutual dependency of the one-sided facticities which leads first to a higher idealism and then to a higher realism. Philosophical insight (idealism) has to become aware that the formal concept of knowledge (realism) has its aim in the knowing of something. The content-focused concept of knowledge has to be developed by taking account of the formal concept of knowledge. The idealism which reaches self-clarification of the concept of knowledge doesn't really accomplish the aim of the philosophical issue. It is reached only with the completely enlightened being of the concept of knowledge.

Thus what Fichte calls higher idealism is the philosophical reflection on the self-construction of reason that is aware of the aim of this construction, which is nothing but the knowledge itself. The vertical image of lower and higher philosophical standpoints would better be called the more embracing idealism and realism, thus joining to the horizontal connection-line of 1794 and moreover stressing the synthetic methodology of Fichte. Each step of the philosophical development brings the elements of knowledge into a stronger tie-up.

If we really can say that the theoretical result of the self-construction of the faculty of imagination remains in facticity because it didn't provide the synthetic unity of the evident imagination and the philosophical construction of its faculty Fichte now consequently produces the insight in the being of knowledge with his last step.

Idealism is always artificial with regard to the concept of knowledge it provides. Fichte calls the idealistic result of philosophy the sole image of knowledge, or, in Kantian terms, an ectype. The last step of higher realism intends to yield not only the concept of knowledge but the knowledge of knowledge in itself, or, let's say, the only case of archetypical knowledge. This is possible because the idealistic concept of knowledge is accompanied by an insight into itself. Therefore Fichte suggests finally to annihilate the artificial way of producing an insight in the concept of knowledge by means of pure reflection.

Thus the original evidence of knowing something is reflected by means of philosophical arguments and finally yields the evidence of the original evidence and its construction in their connection. The reconstitution of the evidence of the evidence is what is effected by the faculty of imagination producing reality and real and true images or contents of knowledge.

To sum up, the early *Wissenschaftslehre* can be read in the same vein as and in close connection to the Kantian problem of the subjective-objective duality. The faculty of imagination is responsible for bringing together the two worlds of consciousness and being.

Thereby the subject provides the synthetic forms of knowledge, and the object provides the material of any imagination. Fichte's claim to have shown the identity of the three Kantian principles of knowledge is not really obvious in 1794, or in Fichtean terms, it remains in facticity, because the hiatus-bridging self-construction of the faculty of imagination and its point of evidence remains undeveloped. When Fichte in 1804 intends to lay stress on the being of knowledge, he gives the reality-producing faculty of imagination its proper expression. The result of 1804 in terms of the being of knowledge, which has annihilated its own self-construction, is also the very proper expression for any kind of true knowledge and as such the unity of the threefold Kantian principles that, due to Fichte, can only be given by evident insight.

Notes

1. I owe special thanks to Theodore George, who patiently helped me find the correct and stylistically suitable expression for my ideas.

2. See Immanuel Kant, *Critique of Pure Reason,* ed. and trans. Paul Guyer and Allen W. Wood (Cambridge: Cambridge University Press, 1998), B 129/130.

3. In the *Grundlage* of 1794 Fichte doesn't make this explicit, but in a letter to Reinhold in April 1795 he clearly speaks about it. (See *GA* 3.2:304–17, 309 and 314–15; see also the *Wissenschaftslehre* of 1804, second lecture, *GA* 2.8:27ff.) I don't agree with the interpretation of the unification of the three Kantian principles suggested by Claudia Bickmann in "Zwischen Sein und Setzen: Fichtes Kritik am dreifachen Absoluten der kantischen Philosophie." In "Anfänge und Ursprünge: Zur Vorgeschichte der Jenaer Wissenschaftslehre," *Fichte-Studien* 9 (1997): 143–61. Bickmann interprets the unification in question by a concept that represents the totality of being, known by the absolute ego in the *Wissenschaftslehre* 1794–95 and expressed later by the genetic principle of light in the *Wissenschaftslehre* of 1804. She concludes by confirming that Kant's regulative idea of God as a principle of

totality of reality is more convincing than Fichte's notion of the absolute ego or the genetic principle of light. Against Bickmann, I think that the unique principle Fichte is looking for doesn't aim at a totality of being and knowing, but has to signify the claims of everything that deserves to be named an instance of knowledge. In my opinion, Fichte's theory of knowledge is close to the Kantian one, although Fichte equalizes the difference of objective knowledge by categories, ethical knowledge by the categorical imperative, and knowledge by the subjective and objective purposiveness. On this point, see also Wolfgang Janke, *J. G. Fichte: Wissenschaftslehre 1804: Text und Kommentar* (Frankfurt am Main, 1966), 100–103.

4. See *GA* 1.2:368 and 261–62.

5. See *GA* 1.2:112–13.

6. See *GA* 1.2:285.

7. See *GA* 1.2:301.

8. See *GA* 1.2:308–9.

9. For a more detailed reconstruction of the faculty of imagination in the *Grundlage,* see Violetta L. Waibel, *Hölderlin und Fichte: 1794–1800* (Paderborn: Schöningh, 2000), 200, 301–17; see also Wilhelm Metz, *Kategoriendeduktion und produktive Einbildungskraft in der theoretischen Philosophie Kants und Fichtes* (Stuttgart-Bad Cannstatt: Frommann, 1991).

10. See *GA* 1.2:356–57.

11. This point is well explained by Béatrice Longueness in her essay "The Divisions of the Transcendental Logic and the Leading Thread (A50/B74–A83/B109; B109–116)," in *Immanuel Kant: Kritik der reinen Vernunft,* ed. Georg Mohr and Marcus Willaschek (Berlin: Akademieverlag, 1998).

12. See *GA* 1.2:450–51.

13. The question of the unity or multiplicity of the different versions of the *Wissenschaftslehre* is treated by Daniel Breazeale in his paper "Toward a *Wissenschaftslehre more geometrico* (1800–1801)" in this volume. I generally agree with the critical view of Breazeale, although I think that the structure of the imagination is something that Fichte really developed further in this text.

14. See *GA* 1.2:362–64.

15. See the ninth lecture in the *Wissenschaftslehre* of 1804, in *GA* 2.8:131ff.

Thinking and Willing in the Later Fichte

Günter Zöller

Fichte understood his work on the ground and the forms of knowledge (*Wissen*) as such, which he undertook during some twenty years of thinking, teaching, and publishing under the project title *Wissenschaftslehre,* as a transformative continuation of Kant's transcendental philosophy.[1] A central feature of Fichte's systematic reliance on Kant is his thoroughgoing concern with the relation between theoretical and practical reason, which is continued in Fichte under the form of the relation between thinking and willing. Moreover, the original togetherness of thinking and willing constitutes one of Fichte's essential insights into the basic structure of knowledge in general.

As a basic theme of Fichte's transcendental philosophy, the relation between thinking and willing participates in the multiple changes and innovations in the presentation of the system of the *Wissenschaftslehre.* In fact, Fichte's understanding of thinking and willing offers a valuable indication of the direction as well as the extent of the development of the *Wissenschaftslehre* in its entirety and in its individual systematic components. The following chapter offers a modest contribution to the overall image of Fichte's doctrines of thinking and willing in his late cycle of systematic work, to be precise, in the *Transcendental Logic* of 1812 and the *System of Ethics* from the same year. For purposes of orientation, a summary presentation of Fichte's earlier extensive treatment of the relation between thinking and willing in the lectures on the *Wissenschaftslehre* from the years 1796 through 1799 precedes the later material in this chapter. Against the background of the pertinent positions of this second Jena *Wissenschaftslehre,* the orientation as well as the extent of Fichte's thought about thinking and willing in his later philosophy in general and especially in the *Transcendental Logic* and the late ethics will be discussed in successive sections of this chapter.

Thinking and Willing in the *Wissenschaftslehre nova methodo*

At the center of the *Attempt at a New Presentation of the Wissenschaftslehre* (*Versuch einer neuen Darstellung der Wissenschaftslehre*) of 1797–98, which is preserved only in student transcripts of the lectures on the *Wissenschaftslehre nova methodo*,[2] lies the "original duplicity" (*ursprüngliche Duplicität*)[3] of the I as the principle of Fichte's transcendental philosophy. Fichte uses this term to characterize the radical twofold division that constitutes the essence of the finite rational being—a division that at once refers backward to an elusive, lost unity and refers forward to the equally elusive complete restitution of that unity. The duality in origin manifests itself as the double-sidedness and double-aspectivity of the I,[4] whose active being is differentiated into real and ideal activity. Superficially, it is the contrast between doing (*Tun*), on the one hand, and imaging or "seeing" (*Sehen*) of the doing, on the other hand—of being and knowing. The one, ideal activity is the image (copy) of the other, real activity. Knowing as "ideal" activity follows, and even imitates, doing. The latter is the proper, "real" activity.

But on closer analysis it becomes clear that all acting or doing already presupposes a knowing; only through the latter's provision of some goal or end is acting possible in the first place. And inversely, it becomes clear that knowing already presupposes some doing in the course of which something could first be encountered that could come to be known. Thus doing and knowing presuppose each other mutually, and neither of the two can claim priority over the other. Hence the possibility of each of them remains unexplained.[5]

In his deepened investigation of the apparently circular foundational relationship between the ideal and the real side of the I, Fichte resorts to a generically conceived notion of thinking understood as the activity of determination, more precisely, determining (*Bestimmen*), which essentially involves the presupposition of something determinable (*Bestimmbares*) that is to receive determination (*Bestimmung*). Thinking is, on the one hand, as "real thinking" (*reales Denken*), the determination through thinking of that which is, and, on the other hand, as "ideal thinking" (*ideales Denken*), the determination through thinking of that which ought to be. The former case is that of thinking *qua* knowing (*Erkennen*), the latter case that of thinking *qua* doing, more precisely, of wanting-to-do or willing (*Wollen*). The previously formulated circle in the relation between knowing and doing now takes the form of the mutual requirement of ideal or object-thinking and real or end-thinking.[6] In order to break the circle in the relation between the cognitive and conative basic forms of thinking, Fichte takes recourse to a willing in which the cognition of the willed end and the willing of the cognized end coincide. The willing in question is, as Fichte puts it in reliance on Kant's manner of speech and thinking, "pure willing" (*reines Wollen*), which appears to finite consciousness as "categorical ought" (*kategorisches Sollen*). Fichte stresses the generic function of pure willing, which—unlike in Kant—is not supposed to have a specifically ethical meaning.[7]

Thus, in the *Wissenschaftslehre nova methodo* the twofold nature of the subject (as ideal and real activity) is based on a dual concept of thinking (real and ideal thinking) that in turn is grounded in an originally twofold notion of willing (pure willing), in which willing and ought coincide. The duplicity of the I is pushed ever deeper but persists at every level. Yet it must be kept in mind that all transcendental philosophical thinking about thinking and willing is subject to the conditions of finite, discursive thinking. The double nature of the I as reconstructed in and through philosophical thinking is itself already affected by the basic form of (finite) thinking, according to which all determination (*Bestimmung*) occurs successively and hence in temporal extension. Through the thought of the I's original duplicity, finite thinking seeks to comprehend the original unity of the I, which remains in itself and as such unthinkable, with the most authenticity possible.

In the *Wissenschaftslehre nova methodo,* the striving to comprehend the unity of subjectivity as principle or ground is matched by the search for the unity of what is grounded or rendered possible by this principle. Here, too, philosophical thinking has to take into account a duplicity, namely, the doubling of the concept of world into the *real world* of the known or knowable objects (the world of sense or phenomena) and the *ideal world* of the subjects of willing and acting (the world of spirits or noumena). Fichte reconstructs the unity of the two worlds by resorting to the image of a circular movement of relationships of determination (a fivefold "synthetic periodus") according to which the world of sense and the world of spirits interact with each other.[8] To the duplicity in origin there corresponds a circularity in application.[9]

In the *Wissenschaftslehre nova methodo* the moving force in the interdependent cycling of the two worlds is thinking, more precisely the "synthetic" thinking that determines everything and that also determines itself. According to Fichte, the basic law of such thinking is the "law of reflection concerning opposites" (*Reflexionsgesetz des Entgegensetzens*): all determination through thinking occurs through opposition in thinking; thinking opposes, by way of presupposition (*Voraussetzung*), for purposes of its own activity of determining (*Bestimmen*), namely, as the latter's basis, something not yet determined but determinable (*Bestimmbares*).[10] In synthetic thinking, something determined (*Bestimmtes*) is being thought, and something determinable (*Bestimmbares*) is being added in thought in the process. Fichte speaks of the unarticulated "mass" of the determinable, from which the determining thinking seizes something that is thus determined.[11] The sum total of what is thought(-along) as determinable is the "world" (*Welt*), more precisely, on the one hand, the world of the *real* determinable (world of sense) and, on the other hand, the world of the *ideal* determinable (noumena). In a larger sense, though, both worlds, along with their respective inhabitants, have the status of noumena or products of thoughts.[12]

In the *Wissenschaftslehre nova methodo* Fichte distinguishes between synthetic thinking, which is always the thinking of something determined in and through thinking, and "pure" or "absolute thinking"[13]—thinking as such, prior to its further specification as synthetic thinking. To be sure, pure or absolute thinking is not an actually occurring, separately existing mode of thinking but is the universal *form* or condition of thinking something with the essential feature of self-consciousness.[14] In its subsequent specification to the synthetic thinking of the world of sense and the world of spirits, respectively, original (pure) thinking undergoes temporalization. Following Kant, one might speak of the self-affection of thinking.[15]

It must be stressed that for Fichte even the thinking of the intelligible world or of intelligible being (the thinking of the noumena) underlies the temporalization according to the "laws of thinking."[16] In the *Wissenschaftslehre nova methodo* the noumenal in the proper sense, that which is radically non-sensible, that is, infinite, comes into view only indirectly—in the context of the individuation of reason. Fichte argues that the interpersonal appeal (*Aufforderung:* "summons"), which first induces the employment of reason in an individual being capable of theoretical and practical rationality, remains stuck in the circle of mutual presupposition of such summons between given individuals. Thus the interpersonal enabling of the free employment of reason points back to the trans-personal, supra-individual grounding of reason and freedom in some "higher, incomprehensible being."[17]

In the *Wissenschaftslehre nova methodo* the necessary presupposition of a supra-individual ground of individuality is linked, by way of the "law of reflection concerning opposites," to the notion of "the highest determinable" (*das höchste Bestimmbare*). Fichte's continued efforts at thinking the absolute ground of subjectivity are to be found, first, in the popular, explicitly theistically formulated presentation of the main results and insights of the Jena *Wissenschaftslehre* in *The Vocation of Man* (1800). The "pure will" (*reiner Wille*) is here identified with the infinite divine will.[18] The sustained, speculative treatment of the philosophical task of thinking the absolute ground of subjectivity then forms the key concern of the later presentations of the *Wissenschaftslehre* (since 1801–2).

From the Absolute I to Absolute Being

In the face of the multitude of its presentations, which exceed a dozen versions, Fichte stresses the identical content of the *Wissenschaftslehre.* But it remains problematic how Fichte construes the identical, thoroughgoing core of his transcendental philosophy. The terms and concepts employed in the treatments of the *Wissenschaftslehre* are in constant flux and make it exceedingly difficult to distinguish between the core and the cover and to crack the hard nut of the *Wissenschaftslehre.*

In a first attempt to address this issue, Fichte's choice of title for his enterprise deserves to be considered. The *Wissenschaftslehre* is concerned with knowledge concerning knowledge, with ascertaining the essence of knowledge—and this both with respect to knowledge itself and with respect to that which is known in such knowledge. This might suggest a limitation of the *Wissenschaftslehre* to the cognitive or theoretical, to the exclusion of other modes and aspects of rational subjectivity. But any such limitation is overcome through Fichte's double strategy of understanding thinking in practical terms and understanding willing and acting in intellectual terms. Moreover, the knowledge that concerns the *Wissenschaftslehre* is knowledge regarding knowledge also in the other sense that, for Fichte, all knowledge is self-knowledge.

In the Jena period (1794–99) Fichte had placed egological terms and concepts (*Ich,* "I"; *Nicht-Ich,* "Not-I") at the center of the presentation of the *Wissenschaftslehre.* In his Berlin period (or, more precisely, his Prussian period, 1799–1814),[19] the term and concept of the I loses its center role. Initially, in the *Foundation of the Entire Wissenschaftslehre* (1794–95), the I, in its capacity as absolute I, had functioned as the principle of all knowledge. After 1800, the I provides the form (*Ichform:* "I-form") of knowledge as such. The ground is now no longer identified with the I *qua* absolute I but with something absolute prior to and originally independent of the I (*Seyn,* "Being"; or *Gott,* "God"). By contrast, the I *qua* I-form is the basic mode for the appearance of the absolute, which does not appear itself and as such.

The reclassification of the absolute I from principle or ground to form or mode, together with the dissociation of the absolute itself and as such from the I, are already prepared in the "New Presentation of the *Wissenschaftslehre.*" Thus the "Second Introduction to the *Wissenschaftslehre*" (1797–98) understands the egologically conceived point of departure of the *Wissenschaftslehre* as the mere "form of the I" (*Form des Ich*);[20] and the *Wissenschaftslehre nova methodo* addresses the inconceivable ground of all I-ness by taking recourse to the notion of the extra-individual, "pure" will as the unconditional law of all finite willing.[21]

Hence at the center of the later presentations of the *Wissenschaftslehre* (after 1801–2) there no longer stands the relation between the absolute I and the individual I but the relation of knowledge *qua* absolute knowledge (and knowledge about knowledge) to its ground in absolute being, or in the absolute. Fichte conceives of the basic relation between knowledge and the absolute as "image" (*Bild*). The discrepancy between image and reality here serves to convey the inferiority of knowledge with respect to absolute being. But the conception of knowledge as image also indicates the formative (*bildende*) power of knowledge, its ability to produce images. To be sure, it is not being as such that is rendered in the image-creating activity of knowledge. What is imaged in the image (or shaped in the shaping, as one could say based on Fichte's plastic understanding of "image" as the result of some *Bilden*), is nothing that has any being outside and independent of the image. Yet things may seem different if knowledge is not yet sufficiently enlightened about itself—it may appear as though there were something which subsequently and additionally came to be known (or imaged). But actually there is nothing that has any being of its own outside absolute being and its appearance, knowledge.

In this new line of thought Fichte has turned the desperate realization in the Second Book of *The Vocation of Man*—that all knowledge only goes after images and at most produces images of images[22]—into something affirmative and positive. In and through the nothingness of the images there is supposed to appear the solidity of being. The late *Wissenschaftslehre* reconstructs in insistent monotony the constitution ("genesis") of knowledge and its images in a twofold relation: to the absolute being, which cannot be known, and to what is known but which has no independent being.

Thinking and Willing in the *Transcendental Logic*

In Fichte's late work, there is to be found, in addition to presentations of the *Wissenschaftslehre* proper, an entire body of propaedeutical lectures that introduce in various ways the enterprise of the *Wissenschaftslehre*. If one further takes into account that the *Wissenschaftslehre* in the narrow sense is followed by an applied part, then there emerges the picture of a comprehensive system-cycle from Fichte's final years in Berlin.[23] The works in question had their origin in Fichte's teaching activities at the newly founded university in the Prussian capital. Fichte himself did not see any of these lectures to publication. A number of them have been available since 1834–35 and 1845–46, respectively, in the edition by

Fichte's son, Immanuel Hermann Fichte,[24] and they are all undergoing new publication in the Academy edition of Fichte's works.

The following propaedeutical lectures form part of the Berlin system cycle. They are here arranged in systematic (rather than chronological) order: the *Introductory Lectures into the Wissenschaftslehre* (*Einleitungsvorlesungen in die Wissenschaftslehre*) from 1813,[25] *On the Relation of Logic to Philosophy or Transcendental Logic* (*Über das Verhältniß der Logik zur Philosophie oder transscendentale Logik*) from 1812,[26] and *The Facts of Consciousness* (*Die Thatsachen des Bewußtseins*) from 1813.[27] At the center of the cycle stands the *Wissenschaftslehre* of 1812,[28] followed by *The System of Law* (*Das System der Rechtslehre*) from 1812,[29] the *Doctrine of State, or On the Relation of the Proto-State to the Realm of Reason* (*Staatslehre oder über das Verhältnis der Urstaates zum Vernunftreiche*) from 1813,[30] and *The System of Ethics* (*Das System der Sittenlehre*) from 1812.[31]

The inclusion of polemical and methodological reflection and self-interpretation in the system of the *Wissenschaftslehre* can be traced back to the fragmentary *Attempt at a New Presentation of the Wissenschaftslehre* (*Versuch einer neuen Darstellung der Wissenschaftslehre*) from 1797–98 and the lectures on the *Wissenschaftslehre nova methodo,* on which the former publication is based.[32] But in the propaedeutical lectures from the later Berlin years, the extent of the introductory material increases considerably. The *Wissenschaftslehre* proper now focuses exclusively on the relation between absolute being and absolute knowledge, and reflections that might previously have found their place in the *Wissenschaftslehre* itself are delegated into the huge area of its systematic preliminaries. This is also true of the treatment of thinking and willing, both as regards their individual analyses and the discussion of their systematic connection. The discussions in the *Transcendental Logic* that contain Fichte's late theory of thinking are particularly extensive and illuminating.

The *Transcendental Logic* is concerned with the role of thinking in knowledge.[33] In the context of the late *Wissenschaftslehre,* the latter is understood as the image or appearance of the absolute.[34] Fichte contrasts the merely logical notion of thinking in pure logic with the notion of thinking in transcendental logic. The latter originally links thinking (*Denken*) to intuition (*Anschauung*).[35] Fichte characterizes the formal-logical understanding of thinking as the freely proceeding formation and combination of concepts (*Begriffe*). In contrast to such an external, applicative notion of thinking, he insists on the original, pre-deliberative as well as pre-reflective nature of thinking. The knowledge characterized by such original thinking is no longer the particular propositional "knowledge that p" but the situated, basic, cognitive constitution of finite reason with the essential characteristics of distance from the absolute and immediate being-for-itself.

A central component of the transcendental doctrine of *thinking* is the transcendental doctrine of *intuition*. Fichte insists on the *bound* character (*Beschränktheit:* "limitedness") of thinking in relation to the pre-given contents of the formative activity of thinking. To be sure, the facticity of intuition is subject to a detailed "genetic" reconstruction, in which intuition is shown to be a clandestinely operative activity of "seeing the image into place" (*Hinschauen*). But still there remains the irreducible givennness of intuition within a "system of limitability" (*System der Begränzbarkeit*)[36] that cannot be dissolved entirely into functions of thinking. The exact relation between the *content* of the image given in and as intuition, on the one hand, and the *form* or *shape* of the image established through thinking, on the other hand, is that of "subsumption."[37] Fichte here resorts to traditional logical terminology in order to designate a state of affairs—the relation between intuiting and thinking—which logic as such (pure, formal logic) does not even take into account. The choice of terminology follows Kant's account of the a priori relation of the forms of thinking to intuition in the schematism of the pure concepts of the understanding, which is also presented as a relation of subsumption between concept and intuition.[38]

The subsumption of content under form that brings about the image occurs originally; all content is always already taken up into the form of the image. But the content of the image, which is presupposed in all formative thinking, is by no means an amorphous mass. Rather it already contains formations, which then guide the original thinking in its determining, forming activity. Throughout Fichte maintains the irreducible facticity of the content of the image.

Fichte conveys the original relation of thinking to intuition, in particular the dependence of thinking on pre-given original image-contents, through the notion of "understanding thinking" (*verstehendes Denken*).[39] The basic form of the understanding is the conceptual grasp of intuition. Thus, the understanding operates subsequently and imitatively in relation to some, already-determined intuition that forms and informs the thinking of the understanding or the understanding thinking. In its capacity as material for the understanding-reproducing activity of thinking, the intuition is already akin to thinking and is to be regarded as proto-intellectual. Understanding thinking presupposes a (proto-)intellectual-intuitive activity of determination. Intuition (*Anschauung*) as seeing-into-place (*Hinschauung*) is proto-thinking. Here, too, there is the precedent of Kant joining radically or originally joining thinking (or thinkability) and intuition in the notion of "formal intuition" (*formale Anschauung*).[40] Only in the original connection of thinking and intuiting by means of the image-forming activity of understanding does there come about an I in the complete sense of self-conscious knowledge or self-knowledge.[41] Accordingly, the I is as much a thinking I as it is an intuiting I. Moreover, intuiting and thinking are intimately interwoven in the I. The I thinks itself as intuiting and intuits itself as thinking. By contrast, the moment or aspect of immediate self-awareness that underlies the notion of the I represents a merely formal, not independent conception of the I, which Fichte also terms "intellectual intuition" (*intellektuelle Anschauung*).

The precedence of intuition over thinking in original knowledge (i.e., in the origin of knowledge), together with the resultative rather than originary nature of the I, places Fichte's *Transcendental Logic* in sharp opposition to the view of "common logic" (*gemeine Logik*) regarding the independence of pure thinking in the formal spontaneous activity of the "I think" (*ich denke*). Accordingly, Fichte emends the Kantian formula of apperception, "I think," into the gnomic phrase "knowledge thinks" (*das Wissen denkt*).[42] Fichte explicitly denies the independent occurrence of pure thinking: "There is no pure thinking; rather, all that thinking does is understand [something pre-given]."[43]

In the *Transcendental Logic* the necessary reliance of thinking on intuiting receives systematic consideration in the work's detailed doctrine of sensibility (*Sinnlichkeit*). Fichte incorporates a transcendental *aesthetic* into the structure of his transcendental *logic*. Here are to be found deductions of sense, space, and time as well as those of further structural specifications of the intuiting or seeing-into-place that is presupposed by all thinking. Yet in Fichte's understanding, the facticity of the intuitive image-content does not refer to some extra-subjective reality. Unlike Kant, who traces sensuous or sensory determination back to an affection through "things in themselves," the facticity countenanced in the *Transcendental Logic* is *intra*-subjective, albeit *extra*-intellectual: "Seeing-into-place out of oneself; not receiving, receptivity or such . . . nothing foreign enters into it [the appearance]."[44] Moreover, it has to be kept in mind that for Fichte sensory intuition also always contains the formal element of intellectual intuition. In Fichte the dissociation of original intuition from subsequent, reflective, discursive thinking goes together with the integration of original, pre-discursive thinking into intuition under the guise of *intellectual* intuition: "The original intuition . . . is factical and intellectual."[45]

The reconceptualization of the functions of intuition and thinking in the *Transcendental Logic* also affects the relation between thinking and willing in Fichte's late work. The *Transcendental Logic* discusses willing in the context of the universal "genetic form" (*genetische Form*) of nature through which the speculative relation between principle or ground (*Prinzip*) and principled or grounded (*Prinzipiiertes*) takes on the intuitive, intuitable form of "movement" (*Bewegung*). At the summit of the manifold processes of movement that make up nature lies willing, in which the concept functions as the ground of some movement and is at once, immediately and intellectually, so intuited.[46] Willing is the concept rendered factical, or, as Fichte puts it, "the concept that is fact" (*Begriff, der Faktum ist*).[47] Hence willing—and along with willing the concept that governs it—is assigned to the domain of facts. Willing is here not opposed to natural being as some independent, autonomous, self-determining activity but is integrated into nature as part of the latter's "life" (*Leben*).

In the *Wissenschaftslehre nova methodo* and in book 3 of *The Vocation of Man* Fichte had stressed that the will belongs to intelligible, rather than to sensible or sensuous being; he had even represented the absolute as "infinite will" (*unendlicher Wille*). Now, in the *Transcendental Logic,* he stresses the naturalness of willing. Like everything that is without being the absolute itself, willing is appearance. But in the realm of appearance there is no true, ultimate ground, not even in the case of the apparently absolutely self-grounded willing that manifests itself in the categorical "I will." As he did previously with respect to the "I think," Fichte now replaces the "I will" (*ich will*) through a neutral, impersonal notion: "I deny you entirely this, that *you* will."[48] This suggests an emendation of the "I will" into "the will wills." The impersonification of thinking and willing in Fichte's late work foreshadows and prepares the de-potentiation of subjectivity in Schopenhauer, Nietzsche, and Heidegger.[49]

Yet rather than simply viewing the difference in the treatment of thinking and willing between the Jena Fichte and the Fichte of the later Berlin years as a turning away from a noumenalism regarding thinking and willing toward their naturalization and irrationalization, one would have to consider carefully the change in meaning which Fichte's notion of nature underwent during that same period of time. The nature among which Fichte includes even the facticity of thinking and willing in the *Transcendental Logic* is not opposed to the spiritual but is itself of a spiritual, noumenal nature—as the "formal image of the absolute appearance" (*formales Bild der absoluten Erscheinung*).[50]

Thinking and Willing in *The System of Ethics* of 1812

The systematic assimilation of thinking to intuition in the *Transcendental Logic* is matched by the systematic assimilation of willing to some end or goal in *The System of Ethics* of 1812. In both cases, intuition as seeing-into-place (*Hinschauung*) of the object and envisioning of the end (*Erschauung*), respectively, provides the material for the activity in question. In the one case—thinking—the activity is that of the theoretical or cognitive determination of the object; in the other case—that of willing—the activity is that of practical or volontative self-determination, or more precisely, of self-determination to the practical determination of the object.

The System of Ethics of 1812, too, is articulated in the horizon of the concept of image to be found in the later *Wissenschaftslehre*. To be sure, ethics, as applied philosophy that starts from presuppositions that it takes for granted and does not itself establish, leaves out of consideration the relation of the image to absolute being, which is at most mentioned in passing. Yet in Fichte, ethics has a special place among the applied philosophical sciences. In this discipline philosophical reflection gets considerably closer to the core concern of the *Wissenschaftslehre* proper, namely, the comprehension of being as appearance-image of the absolute, than is the case in the philosophical science of nature (*Naturlehre*) or the philosophical doctrine of right (*Rechtslehre*). In Fichte's system of the philosophical sciences, ethics ranks immediately below the doctrine of religion (*Religionslehre*). Fichte even surmises that in ethics "an entirely new light is cast on the truths of the *Wissenschaftslehre*"[51]

The object of *The System of Ethics* as the latter's uncircumventable fact is the basic practical relation between concept and world (or being): "The concept is ground of the world, along with the absolute consciousness that this is the case."[52] Fichte here joins the causality of the concept immediately and originally with the consciousness of it or its "reflex" (*Reflex*). More closely considered, the self-knowledge of the concept regarding the latter's causality is a case of immediate, non-sensory self-intuition or intellectual intuition.[53]

The absolute, intimate, original togetherness of doing and knowing, of acting and seeing the acting, of the real and the ideal is the exclusive mark of I-hood or self-consciousness. But Fichte warns against hastening to declare practical consciousness and its causality to be an accomplishment of the I. He cautions:"What if not the I had consciousness but consciousness had the I?"[54] For the late Fichte, the concept first takes up the "form of consciousness" (*Form des Bewußtseins*) and not vice versa; under the form of consciousness the concept, then, appears in the "form of the I" (*Form eines Ich*).[55] The concept of concept that is operative here is not that of the logical product formed in free reflection but the notion of the concept as the basic appearance of the absolute. By entering into the form of consciousness or self-consciousness, the concept receives "life" (*Leben*),[56] and inversely thereby life becomes comprehending (*begreifend*). Consciousness thus offers the form of life, which is then filled with content by the concept.

Without the determination through the concept, consciousness would only be "formal and free life" (*formales und freies Leben*),[57] some potentiality without a measure for its actualization. The concept conveys to the mere form of practical, free consciousness the "absolute content" (*absoluter Inhalt*), that is, the content determined with reference to the absolute. In Fichte's late *System of Ethics* the concrescence of being *qua* concept and life *qua* consciousness leads to an anti-formalist, decidedly material conception of ethical life (*Sittlichkeit*).[58] To be sure, as the philosophical *theory* of practical consciousness, *The System of Ethics* is not able to specify of its own the content of the ethically relevant concept or concepts, but has to refer everyone to his or her own ethical consciousness or conscience.[59]

For Fichte, the concept that materially underlies the formal life of consciousness must be considered an appearance of the absolute; it therefore has the character of an image (of the absolute). But the image is not the afterimage (*Nachbild*) of something real of which it, as it were, provided the copy; rather, it is the fore-image (*Vorbild*) of something yet to be realized.[60] Through its practical causality under the form of consciousness, the concept transforms itself from a "pure concept" (*reiner Begriff*) that subsists in a self-sufficient "world of images" (*Bilderwelt*)[61] of the purely spiritual or noumenal world into an "objective concept" (*objektiver Begriff*) in the real world: "In consciousness the pure concept becomes the ground of the objective concept."[62] Fichte also speaks of the "deposition" (*Absetzung*) of the ideal being (pure concept) in the real being (objective concept) and links the depository activity with the purpository activity or the purpose of the concept (*Absehen* and *Absicht,* respectively).[63]

Fichte summarizes the interplay of concept and consciousness in practical causality in the schema of a twofold "transition" (*Übergang*), comprising five members.[64] Both transitions are immediately or intellectually intuited. For one, there is the *subjective* transition from the concept as ideal, pure, self-sufficient image to the function of the concept as ground of being in consciousness; the concept here becomes the concept of an end or purpose. Fichte also speaks of the self-determination of the concept in consciousness, but stresses that the self-initiated production of determination concerns only the *form* of the concept, while its *content* is absolutely presupposed (and pre-given) in all activity of determination. The second, *objective* transition involving practical causality consists in the concept exercising its grounding function in the proper, real production of the purpose or end. Moreover, the subjective and the objective transition are in turn related to each other as ground and consequent. As the fifth member of the transitional structure, the latter assures the overall cohesion of practical consciousness.

Thus Fichte distinguishes clearly between the original, ideal concept and its two-phased realization, first through absolute self-determination to potentiality-for-grounding, and second through the actualization of the potentiality for grounding to the (practical) determination of something other. The synthesis of the ideal concept with radical self-determination, as required for practical causality, lies in the will as the "faculty of absolute self-determination with reference to a concept."[65] According to Fichte, willing as such consists in the formal moment of self-determination to taking up the concept into practical consciousness. The content here is not bound to the will but originates in the concept, and hence ultimately in absolute being.

The concept as such possesses no influence on the formation of the willing. For there to be efficacy of the concept *qua* content on the self-determining willing, the "mediating concept of the ought, of absolute determination"[66] has to be inserted. The ought provides the motivation or "motion" (*Motion*) required for all willing.[67] Yet the ought and its motivating force do not belong to the concept itself but only to the form of the latter's entrance into consciousness. The ought is a necessary but not deducible or "factical" component of the form of the I or the I-form (*Ich-form*) that the concept assumes. Hence Fichte can say "that the I must find itself as willing entirely and absolutely because it stands under an ought."[68]

Thus Fichte limits the space of willing in a twofold manner, and this in complete agreement with Kant: materially, willing is limited through the concept; and formally, it is limited through the ought. The remaining moment of freedom in willing consists in the (free) inclusion of the ought into the ground of willing: not only to will *what* ought to be, but to will it *because* it ought to be. Thereby the position of willing in relation to the concept in *The System of Ethics* of 1812 structurally resembles the position of thinking in relation to intuition in the *Transcendental Logic.* In both cases the exercise of some activity (thinking and willing, respectively) is subject to the guidance through contents (intuition and concept, respectively) which provide the factical presuppositions of the activity in question but which also only enter into consciousness through the exercise of that activity. As conditions of the possibility of the sensory or ethical content of consciousness, thinking and willing in late Fichte are the forms of receptivity for absolute being in finite consciousness. In the Fichte of the late Berlin years, the spontaneity of thinking and willing to be found in the Fichte of the Jena period (and in Kant) has been turned into transcendental *aisthesis.*

Notes

1. Work on this essay was supported by a University Faculty Scholarship from the University of Iowa and was carried out at the Obermann Center for Advanced

Studies at the University of Iowa and at the Department of Philosophy of the University of Munich.

2. Fichte himself only published two introductions and the first chapter of the *Attempt at a New Presentation of the Wissenschaftslehre* (1797–98; *Versuch einer neuen Darstellung der Wissenschaftslehre*); see *GA* 1.4:183–281. The publication of the remainder of the *New Presentation* was first prevented by the outbreak of the Atheism Controversy in 1798 and subsequently rendered obsolete by Fichte's further development of the *Wissenschaftslehre* after 1800. So far the following student transcripts of the lectures on the *Wissenschaftslehre nova methodo* are known and available: Johann Gottlieb Fichte, *Nachgelassene Schriften,* vol. 2, ed. Hans Jacob (Berlin: Junker und Dünnhaupt, 1937), 341–612, repr. in *GA* 4.2:17–267; and *WLNM* (1994).

3. *WLNM* (1994), 185. All translations are by the author. Neither of the two late works discussed in sections 3 and 4 is available in English translation. On the "duplicity of the mind," see also *WLNM* (1994), 184, 189, 209, 211–12, 222, 227, 234. For a detailed examination of the relation between thinking and willing in the Jena *Wissenschaftslehre* in general and the *Wissenschaftslehre nova methodo* in particular, see Günter Zöller, *Fichte's Transcendental Philosophy: The Original Duplicity of Intelligence and Will* (Cambridge and New York: Cambridge University Press, 1998).

4. See *WLNM* (1994), 211.

5. See *WLNM* (1994), 191.

6. See *WLNM* (1994), 138.

7. See *WLNM* (1994), 143.

8. See *WLNM* (1994), 190ff., esp. 195 and 215ff., esp. 238–39.

9. See *WLNM* (1994), 207, 227.

10. See *WLNM* (1994), 38.

11. See *WLNM* (1994), 149, 177, 179.

12. On the noumenalism in the second Jena *Wissenschaftslehre,* see Günter Zöller, "Geist oder Gespenst: Fichtes Noumenalismus in der *Wissenschaftslehre nova methodo,*" *Fichte-Studien* 12 (1997): 297–306.

13. *WLNM* (1994), 222.

14. See *WLNM* (1994), 183–84.

15. See Immanuel Kant, *Critique of Pure Reason,* B 66–69. Here and elsewhere references to the *Critique of Pure Reason* employ the pagination of its second and first edition (indicated by "B" and "A," respectively), which is included in all modern English translations of the work.

16. *WLNM* (1994), 153.

17. *WLNM* (1994), 178. In the corresponding passage of the Halle transcript of the *Wissenschaftslehre nova methodo* (*GA* 4.2:176), Fichte refers to the corollaries to section 3 of the *Foundation of Natural Law* (*Grundlage des Naturrechts*), in which the same line of thought is found. See *GA* 1.3:347–48. On the theory of interpersonality of the early Fichte, see Günter Zöller, "Leib, Materie und gemeinsames Wollen als Anwendungsbedingungen des Rechts," in *Fichtes Grundlage des Naturrechts,* ed. Jean Christophe Merle (Berlin: Akademie, 2001), 97–111. On the relation between an individual and a supra-individual conception of reason in Fichte, see Günter Zöller, "Die Individualität des Ich in Fichtes zweiter Jenaer Wissenschaftslehre (1796–99)," *Revue Internationale de Philosophie* 206 (1998): 641–63.

18. See *GA* 1.6:292.

19. Erlangen, where Fichte taught at the university in the summer semester of 1805, was Prussian at the time, as was Königsberg (today's Kaliningrad), where Fichte taught at the university in the summer semester of 1807.

20. *GA* 1.4:266 (section 11).

21. See *WLNM* (1994), 169, 176.

22. See *GA* 1.6:248ff.

23. For a detailed discussion of Fichte's late Berlin system cycle, see Peter Baumanns, *J. G. Fichte: Kritische Gesamtdarstellung seiner Philosophie* (Freiburg and Munich: Alber, 1990), 296–442; Günter Zöller, "Leben und Wissen: Der Stand der Wissenschaftslehre beim letzten Fichte," in *Der transzendentalphilosophische Zugang zur Wirklichkeit: Beiträge aus der aktuellen Fichte-Forschung,* ed. Erich Fuchs, Marco Ivaldo, and Giovanni Moretto (Stuttgart-Bad Cannstatt: Frommann-Holzboog, 2001), 307–30; and Günter Zöller, " 'On revient toujours . . .': Die transzendentale Theorie des Wissens beim letzten Fichte," *Fichte-Studien* 20 (2003): 253–66.

24. *Johann Gottlieb Fichtes nachgelassene Werke,* ed. Immanuel Hermann Fichte, 3 vols. (Bonn: Adolph-Marcus, 1834–35); and *Fichtes sämmtliche Werke,* ed. Immanuel Hermann Fichte, 8 vols. (Berlin: Veit, 1845–46). Integrated reprint as *Fichtes Werke,* ed. Immanuel Hermann Fichte, 11 vols. (Berlin: De Gruyter, 1971), vols. 9–11 and 1–8, respectively. (These works are cited in abbreviated form as *NW, SW,* and *FW,* respectively.)

25. *NW* 1; *FW* 9:1–102.

26. *NW* 1; *FW* 9:103–400. A new edition of Fichte's *Über das Verhältniß der Logik zur Philosophie oder transscendentale Logik* after the original manuscript was prepared by Reinhard Lauth and Peter K. Schneider, with the collaboration of Kurt Hiller (Hamburg: Meiner, 1982).

27. *NW* 1; *FW* 9:401–574.

28. *NW* 2; *FW* 10:315–492.

29. *NW* 2; *FW* 10:493–642.

30. *SW* 4; *FW* 4:367–600.

31. *NW* 3; *FW* 11:1–118.

32. See *GA* 1.4:186–270; and *WLNM* (1994), 3–25.

33. See *TL,* 137.

34. See *TL,* 42.

35. See *TL,* 252–53.

36. *TL,* 136.

37. *TL,* 31ff.

38. See Kant, *Critique of Pure Reason,* A 137 / B 176, A 147 / B 187.

39. See *TL,* 149: "[There is] no pure thinking, but only an understanding. . . . A synthesis of the thinking with an intuiting that posits a fact." (*[Es gibt] Kein reines Denken, sondern nur ein Verstehen. . . . Synthesis des Denkens mit einem Faktum setzenden Anschauen.*)

40. See Kant, *Critique of Pure Reason,* B 160n.

41. *TL,* 110: "The I-form itself is derivative" (*Die Ichform selbst ist abgeleitet*).

42. *TL,* 17, 19, 27, 34, 124.

43. *TL,* 142; see also *TL,* 149–50 ("es wird nicht rein gedacht: sondern es wird durch das Denken nur verstanden").

44. *TL,* 157 ("Hinschauen aus sich; nicht etwa Empfangen, Receptivität u. dgl. . . . kein Fremdes kommt in sie [die Erscheinung] herein").

45. *TL*, 151 ("Die ursprüngliche Anschauung . . . ist faktisch und intellectuell").

46. *TL*, 224.

47. *TL*, 224.

48. *TL*, 225 ("ich läugne dir auch dies ganz ab, daß du willst").

49. On the origin of Schopenhauer's conception of the will in Fichte, see Günter Zöller, "Kichtenhauer: Der Schritt von der *Wissenschaftslehre* zur *Welt als Wille und Vorstellung*," in *Die Ethik Arthur Schopenhauers im Kontext des Deutschen Idealismus (Fichte /Schelling)*, ed. Lore Hühn, with the assistance of Phillip Schwab (Würzburg: Ergon, 2006).

50. *TL*, 225. See also *TL*, 254: "The appearance is appearance of being, of what is truly absolute, that which is beyond all appearance, and independent of the appearance" (*Die Erscheinung ist Erscheinung des Seyns, des wahren absoluten, das da ist jenseits aller Erscheinung, u. unabhängig von der Erscheinung*).

51. *FW* 11; *NW* 3:8 ("ein ganz neues Licht auf Wahrheiten der allgemeinen W.-L. fiele").

52. *FW* 11; *NW* 3:3 ("der Begriff ist Grund der Welt, mit dem absoluten Bewußtsein, daß er es sei").

53. See *FW* 11; *NW* 3:9.

54. *FW* 11; *NW* 3:11 ("Wie, wenn nicht das Ich Bewußtsein, sondern das Bewußtsein das Ich hätte?").

55. *FW* 11; *NW* 3:11.

56. See *FW* 11; *NW* 3:12–13. On the concept of life in Fichte, see Wolfgang Schrader, *Empirisches und absolutes Ich: Zur Geschichte des Begriffs Leben in der Philosophie J. G. Fichtes* (Stuttgart-Bad Cannstatt: Frommann-Holzboog, 1972).

57. *FW* 11; *NW* 3:13.

58. On the foundations of a concrete ethics already in Fichte's earlier ethics, *The System of Ethics* of 1798, see Günter Zöller, "Konkrete Ethik: Universalität und Partikularität in Fichtes *System der Sittenlehre*," in *Ethikbegründungen zwischen Universalismus und Relativismus*, ed. Kristina Engelhard and Dietmar H. Heidemann (Berlin and New York: De Gruyter, 2005), 203–29.

59. See *FW* 11; *NW* 3:25.

60. See *FW* 11; *NW* 3:4.

61. *FW* 11; *NW* 3:5.

62. *FW* 11; *NW* 3:6 ("der reine Begriff wird im Bewußtsein Grund des objektiven Begriffs").

63. See *FW* 11; *NW* 3:22–23.

64. See *FW* 11; *NW* 3:9–10.

65. *FW* 11; *NW* 3:19–20 ("Vermögen der absoluten Selbstbestimmung in Beziehung auf einen Begriff").

66. *FW* 11; *NW* 3:25–26 ("vermittelnder Begriff des Soll, der absoluten Bestimmung").

67. *FW* 11; *NW* 3:26.

68. *FW* 11; *NW* 3:25 ("daß das Ich sich finden müsse as wollend durchaus und schlechthin, weil es soll").

Toward or Away from Schelling? On the Thematic Shift in Fichte's Later Philosophy

Steven Hoeltzel

Some time between the spring of 1799, when he presented the last of his lectures on the *Wissenschaftslehre nova methodo* in Jena, and the end of 1801, when he began a new lecture series on the *Wissenschaftslehre* in Berlin, Fichte seems to have somehow shifted from one theoretical standpoint on the nature of finite intelligence to another, related but importantly distinct philosophical figuration of the free but finite mind. Indeed, some interpreters have deemed this shift sufficiently substantive to mark a division between two different *Wissenschaftslehren:* the doctrine of the Jena period (dominated by an elaborate transcendental egology designed to delineate the cognitive-cum-conative activity-structure of a spontaneously self-enacting subjectivity), and a later, markedly less "egocentric" theory (inaugurated in the *Darstellung der Wissenschaftslehre* of 1801–2 and further unfolded over time) in which systematic centrality is accorded to more broadly epistemological concepts such as "knowledge" (*Wissen*) and "truth" (*Wahrheit*) and, more notably, to the more expansively ontological idea of an "absolute" being (*Seyn* or, in some cases, *Gott*)—a being prior to, more primordial than, and the ultimate originating ground of the being of the finite I as such. Of course, that these ostensibly more traditional epistemological and ontological themes begin to enjoy presentational predominance in Fichte's writings in and after 1800 is indisputable; what is much less clear is the extent to which such pronounced changes in presentation reflect correspondingly sharp shifts in philosophical perspective.

Fichte himself was ever wont to deny any such deep discontinuity. In 1806, for example, he publicly credited the more conspicuous differences between successive presentations of his *Wissenschaftslehre* to the progressive maturation and refinement of a single, essentially unaltered philosophical position that he had first formulated in 1793.[1] Still, as we shall see in more detail below, he also acknowledged that, beginning as early as 1800, he did perform certain conceptually crucial elaborations upon certain initially incomplete or inadequate *philosophical* (not to say pedagogical) elements of the *Wissenschaftslehre*.[2] Still, even while occasionally admitting the need for some such extensions, he consistently maintained that an abiding cluster of commitments comprised the essentially continuous core of the many overt articulations of his system. Indeed, his published insistence on this point in 1806 is noteworthy not because its upshot is unexampled elsewhere in his writings—it is not—but because of the upbraiding that seems to have occasioned it: Schelling's contention, published earlier that year, that Fichte *had* radically revised his philosophical position, and in a manner much indebted to Schelling's work but not openly acknowledged by Fichte to be so.[3]

Schelling's charge, however just or unjust, encapsulates a host of important philosophical, exegetical, and historical issues concerning both the roots and the fruits of Fichte's philosophical growth, at Jena and after Jena. For one, as the preceding may indicate and as what follows should bear out, there is at least some Schellingean savor to the idea, increasingly prominent in Fichte's work from 1800 on, that the I *qua* I is ultimately grounded not in its own unconditioned activity of self-positing but in some "higher, incomprehensible being" of which the individual I is but a finite, finitizing vehicle or manifestation.[4] Schelling had explored such an idea in variously vexing, terse, and tentative formulations as early as 1795 or 1796—this, note, prior to his earliest sustained efforts in *Naturphilosophie*—but shortly thereafter, Fichte had rather forcefully, and publicly, rejected Schelling's speculations as extravagances without explanatory warrant. (I address these matters in a bit more detail below.) Moreover, when in 1806 Schelling charged Fichte with the unacknowledged incorporation into the *Wissenschaftslehre* of distinctly Schellingean ideas, he was not voicing this complaint for the first time. He had raised it already, albeit this time privately, in 1801, near the end of what had become an increasingly fractious epistolary exchange between the two men.[5]

This correspondence commenced shortly after Fichte's departure from Jena in mid-1799, turned openly argumentative toward the end of 1800, crescendoed in contentiousness throughout 1801, and concluded in early 1802.[6] Owing to their philosophical timing and tone, these letters (particularly the later ones) provide us with an often revealing window into the development of both Fichte and Schelling during a crucial and contested phase of Fichte's intellectual evolution especially, and in dialogue with the talented thinker who began as one of his most enthusiastic adherents but quickly became one of his most cutting critics. The exchange ranges over an expansive array of issues; herein I shall address only a certain subset (to my mind, a central segment) thereof. In particular, I shall focus on the basic relationship between finite subjectivity and its ultimate explanatory and existential ground, as this relationship is quarreled over and repeatedly recast in successive phases of Fichte's and Schelling's work through approximately 1800–1801. (Of course, I shall not chart every configuration in which these concepts conspire; instead, I shall selectively survey some especially salient moments in the development of this theoretical theme.)

As I have argued elsewhere, Schelling's earliest writings appear unabashedly Fichtean when in fact they are quite otherwise: Schelling's seeming subscription to Fichte's first principles conceals a conceptually subtle but systematically momentous shift in the philosophical figuration of the ground of finite subjectivity—a development recognized and critiqued by Fichte at the time.[7] Yet, as I shall show herein, Fichte's elaborations upon the *Wissenschaftslehre* shortly after his departure from Jena—most notably, his 1800–1801 contemplation of the completion of his system in a "highest synthesis" of an "intelligible world"—suggest something like a reenactment by Fichte of the same sort of systematic shift that, years earlier, had impelled Schelling in a doctrinal direction distinct from that followed in the early *Wissenschaftslehre*. More specifically, Fichte's reflections on and philosophical figurations of the intelligible world seem to mark the beginning of a turn away from his earlier insistence on the existential and explanatory ultimacy of "the absolute I": a turn in the direction of the systematic affirmation and articulation of the primacy and primordiality of a non-objective, supra-individual, unconditioned ultimate, of which any individuated, world-related subjectivity is but a finite, finitizing expression.

It should be borne in mind, of course, that Fichte continued to be quite critical of Schelling's philosophical *methods* during these pivotal years. And he reaffirmed repeatedly his doctrinal rejection of Schelling's systematic assimilation of finite subjectivity to the outright un- or infra-subjective elements of the natural world. Still, while not at all wishing to downplay their key differences, I intend primarily to focus on some noteworthy convergences underlying the overt conceptual clashes evident in the correspondence and elsewhere—kindred positions adopted, and problems encountered, by Fichte and Schelling in the course of their evolving attempts to discern and disclose the ultimate ground of the finite I.

According to the Schelling of the late 1790s and beyond, the Fichtean I, whose unconditioned but not unlimited activities of self- and world-elaboration comprise the fundament of the *Wissenschaftslehre*, is but a "higher power" of a more primordial potency: a self-originating, self-articulating activity, endlessly spanning an ever-expanding circuit between sheer simplicity and diremptive self-differentiation—but not (that is to say, not initially) a subjectivity *as such,* because not (initially) permeated by self-awareness, of however rudimentary a kind. In Schelling's view, the radically free but ineluctably finite I of the early *Wissenschaftslehre* has theoretically penetrable ontic radices of its own—not in the kind of dull, mechanistic interaction of lifeless materials countenanced by "every chemist and pharmacist"[8]—but in an extra-subjective, unconditioned, and unconscious tangle of self-developing, self-differentiating activity modeled in many ways upon the Fichtean I. As Schelling puts it in a letter of November 19, 1800, the Fichtean finite subject presupposes the existence and activity of "an *ideal-real* . . . only *as* such merely objective and not comprehended in its own intuition. In a word, [this ideal-real] is the same as that which appears in a *higher power* as the I."[9] (Fichte, of course, consistently characterized the I as an "identity" or "immediate unity" of the ideal and real. Indeed, he had insisted on this point in the very letter to which the preceding quotation from Schelling is offered as a response.)[10]

The figuration of the Fichtean I as a comparably late development out of, or on the basis of, some more primordial, self-realizing but not (yet) specifically subjective ground can be found even in Schelling's earliest, most putatively pro-Fichtean publications, well in advance of the sustained work on *Naturphilosophie* that informed his articulation of this idea circa 1800. Beginning in 1794, he openly and ardently aimed at the disclosure of an originary ground (*Urgrund*) of the finite self and its world.[11] Yet while his first published pieces evince quite some enthusiasm for the identification of this *Urgrund* with *das absolute Ich,* the Fichtean facade of these writings actually screens a shift in philosophical foundations.

Fichte's Jena writings figure the absolute I as an integrated, self-articulating complex of intrinsically interrelated activities, one and all simultaneously spontaneous and subject to ineluctable limitations.[12] These manifold a priori activities and limitations are philosophically countenanced insofar as their postulation contributes to an explanation of the basic organizing structures of experience. By contrast, Schelling's early appropriation of Fichte's philosophy focuses first and foremost upon "absolute unconditionality" (*schlechthin Unbedingtheit*) as the definitive mark of the properly foundational, treating this characteristic as essential in more than one sense. First, as Schelling employs these ideas early on (most notably in 1795's *On the I as Principle of Philosophy*), what is conditioned must, as such, be the product of some manner of conditioning by something else, and therefore cannot suffice on its own as a radically original ground of existence or explanation.[13] (At this point it should be recalled that Fichte's doctrine of the *Anstoß* [and, later, the *Aufforderung*] provides the Jena *Wissenschaftslehre* with a way of affirming the "absolute" I's necessary subjection to certain kinds of limitation, while simultaneously and consistently *denying* that the limitations in question ultimately originate in a being other than the I itself.[14] Hence, the "absolute" Fichtean I, while always already a priori agitated by its own intrinsic sensuous and affective modifications, remains effectively unconditioned, insofar as its active-cum-intellectual self-development is in no way the product of any truly "outside" influences. Note also that this idea, which is central to Fichte's overall account of finite subjectivity, receives its earliest systematic articulation in part 3 of Fichte's *Foundation of the Entire Wissenschaftslehre*—a text which Schelling did not read until some time after he composed his own *On the I,* the work whose inspirations and implications did much to define Schelling's intellectual agenda for years thereafter.)[15]

A second and, for present purposes, more important way in which "absolute unconditionality" is essential to the early Schellingean *Urgrund* concerns the manner of Schelling's elaboration upon the latter idea: not via the regressive derivation of additional developments or determinations necessary for the eventuation of experience but, instead, via the deduction, from the concept of absolute unconditionality, of additional abstract predicates purportedly entailed strictly and solely thereby: infinity, simplicity, immutability, and so on.[16] This modus operandi had, among a number of profound implications, the result that the early Schelling was forced to regard the origination and determinacy of finite subjectivity as theoretically unintelligible.[17] Why the self-realizing, seamlessly self-same should unfold into an inwardly articulated, affectively agitated awareness of an environment is, for the Schelling of the mid-1790s, nothing less than the philosophically insoluble "riddle of the world."[18]

All this merits mention here because, as we shall see in more detail below, circa 1800 and 1801 Fichte began to articulate his own evolving position in ways that often appear remarkably reminiscent of these early Schellingean themes. Previously, however, he had explicitly rejected Schelling's initial attempt to found the world-related subject in or upon a non-finite, self-same, supra-individual absolute, something somehow immanent within finite I-hood as such, yet not comprehensibly productive of the latter. As was so often the case, Fichte's objections to Schelling's early procedure were mainly methodological.[19] The core of his criticisms: the fact, conceded by Schelling, that the occurrence of experience is inexplicable on the basis of such "completely free and lawless acting" suffices to show that Schelling's conception of subjectivity's ultimate ground is ill-founded.[20] The existential and explanatory basis of finite I-hood can and should be philosophically figured in ways which intelligibly connect that basis to manifest features of our experience; thus, to the extent that a conception of the absolute fails to fulfill such an explanatory function, that conception is theoretically unwarranted—it is, in a word, "transcendent."[21]

Throughout his writings of the Jena period, quite unlike the early Schelling, Fichte had maintained that philosophy need not postulate any more radical basis for experience than the free but finite, unconditioned but not unlimited self development of the transcendental subject. In 1794, prior to the start of work on the *Foundation,* he pledged to demonstrate systematically that "everything which occurs in our mind can be completely explained and comprehended on the basis of the mind itself."[22] Four years later, with two completed constructions of the system to his credit (and a third, never-to-be-concluded version underway), he continued to contend that "there is no world that subsists on its own. Wherever we look, we see nothing but the reflection of our own inner activity."[23] To be sure, in his lectures on the *Wissenschaftslehre nova methodo,* Fichte had portrayed an initially undifferentiated, "purely spiritual mass" (*eine Maße des rein geistigen*) of supra-individual, intellectual-volitional potency as a presupposition of the original individuation of any I *qua* finite subject.[24] Strictly speaking, however, this "higher, incomprehensible being"[25] is not a necessary ontological commitment of the Jena *Wissenschaftslehre* as such. It is, instead, something necessarily *posited by*—or, better, opposited to—the finite subjectivity whose self-articulation the Jena *Wissenschaftslehre* delineates.

From the finite subject's point of view, "*When* I think and will anything [determinate], what is [correspondingly] determinable appears as something that conditions my thinking and willing, as something 'discovered.'"[26] But this manifestation of the conditioning determinable is not an authentic discovery of something truly transcending the finite I; it is, instead, a reflex of the elementary "law of reflection concerning opposites" (*Reflexiongesetz des Entgegensetzens*).[27] That is to say, it is yet another "reflection" of the "inner activity" of the transcendental subject. The discursive intellect, in cognizing anything as determined or determinate, necessarily "counter-posits" some manner of determinable basis as the intelligible correlate of the determinacy in question. Accordingly, the finite I that thinks and wills its own determinacy *qua* individuated subject does not *intuit* its dependence on, connection to, or egress from any primordial "mass" of spiritual potential;[28] instead, it "*posit*[s] a sphere of rational beings in opposition to [itself]."[29]

Schelling's early project seems to have pivoted—and, in its first formulations, to have foundered—on the problem of understanding how and why determinate, finite subjectivity originally unfolds out of a supra-individual, utterly unconditioned ultimate. But *Naturphilosophie* seemed to offer a way out of this explanatory impasse, and in his correspondence with Fichte, Schelling devoted much energy to its advocacy. The problem with which he had been grappling concerned how to render comprehensible the origin, out of that which is in no strict sense subjective, of the kind of being that just *is* the seeing of a world from a particular vantage point therein and thereupon. His new strategy, prosecuted circa 1797 and thereafter, was to read back into "nature," most primordially considered, abstract anticipations of the self-developing dynamism characteristic of finite subjectivity, as the latter is figured from a Fichtean perspective. (Although I shall drop this device hereafter, I use quotation marks to offset the word "nature" here so as to signal that Schelling's *Naturphilosophie* thematizes the natural in a manner radically removed from our everyday understanding of the physical world. As he eventually would interrogatively press this point against Fichte, "Is it my fault if one attributes to me no concept of nature other than the one used by every chemist and pharmacist?")[30]

The early *Naturphilosophie* rejects the philosophical (not to say the empirical) adequacy of merely mechanistic and objectifying characterizations of the natural, and attempts to find ways of understanding the world in its fundamentality as *natura naturans:* a freedom, life, or spirit, in no sense concretely conscious, actively unfolding according to the same inner principles which eventually inwardly animate subjectivity as such: "The system of nature is at the same time the system of our mind."[31] Natural objects (*natura naturata*) of even the most rudimentary sort are thus regarded not as conglomerations of lifeless "stuff" but as instantaneous arrestations of interplaying and opposed forces: the same restless, originally unaware freedom, life, or spirit that eventually elaborates itself into articulate awareness, first congealing into objectivity in only its own most unevolved manifestations.[32] From this intellectual vantage point, of course, the *Wissenschaftslehre* is a merely one-sided and comparably ill-founded philosophical system: it is the merely "formal" and not the "material proof" of idealism;[33] it must either disclose the real, extra-subjective ground of subjectivity or else remain eternally immured within the I.[34]

Fichte's letters to Schelling are replete with rejections, most of them methodologically motivated, of the latter's evolving enterprise. More pertinent for our present purposes, however, is a series of passages wherein Fichte begins to mark out a substantive shift in his own theoretical thematization of the I, a turn toward sustained speculation on the unconditioned, extrapersonal being necessarily cognized as the basis out of which the finite subject unfolds and upon which it ineluctably depends.[35] Speculations of this sort seem central to later versions of the

Wissenschaftslehre—as they had been, albeit not in exactly the same way, in Schelling's thinking ever since 1795.

In his December 27, 1800, letter to Schelling, in what appears to be the expression of a very broad kind of agreement, Fichte credits Schelling with having rightly detected a deficit in the Jena *Wissenschaftslehre*'s philosophical figuration of finite subjectivity. Insufficient attention, Fichte indicates, had previously been paid to the problem of understanding the finite subject's relation to the radically non-finite, supra-individual source posited as the ground of its being. Because this letter sounds several of the central themes of our discussion, it is worth quoting here at some length. According to Fichte, Schelling's supplementation of the Fichtean theory of subjectivity with purportedly more primordial principles is a project premised on the acknowledged need to

> *further expand* transcendental philosophy *in its very principles,* a task that no doubt is urgent at the present time. I have not yet had time to systematically work out these expanded principles; the clearest indications of such a project can be found in the third book of my *Vocation of Man*. . . . In a word, what is missing is a *transcendental system of the intelligible world.* [translation modified]

Immediately following this passage, in a simultaneously conciliatory and critical spirit, Fichte limns the general contours that such a system should take (supposing that said system is constructed in a methodologically responsible manner, by way of implied contrast with Schelling's):

> I can only agree with your claim that the *individuum* is a higher power of nature, under the condition that I posit nature not just as phenomenon (and as such clearly engendered by the finite intellect, therefore not engendering it), but that I find *something that is intelligible in nature* of which, in a *general* sense, the individuum is the lower power; however, in relation to *something* within the intelligible (that which is only *determinable*), the *individuum* is the higher power (the determined). It is in this system of the intelligible alone that we can understand each other and agree.

These lines clearly recall Fichte's treatment in the *Wissenschaftslehre nova methodo* of finite subjectivity's presupposition of some "higher, incomprehensible being" of a specifically spiritual sort.[36] *Qua* finite, the I is a "lower power" of a spiritual potency figured as originally unconditioned by the limitations definitive of discursivity (that is, by the specific sensory and affective givens to which the spontaneity of thinking and willing, in us, is lashed). *Qua* individuated, on the other hand, the I is a "higher power" or later development of the latter potency figured as sheer, supra-individual potential for concrete subjective specification. Still, these passages point beyond Fichte's earlier efforts, too, in their acknowledgment of an as-yet unsatisfied need to bring the *Wissenschaftslehre* to culmination in the systematic survey of a supra-individual, intelligible order of being. (Though Fichte initially portrayed this project as one requiring a radical revision of basic principles, this clearly was not his considered position on the systematic import of the task at hand. In a letter composed some months after the one cited above, he pointedly proclaims that the *Wissenschaftslehre* is "not at all lacking in principles, but rather in completion, for the highest synthesis, the synthesis of the spiritual world, has not yet been carried out.")[37]

For preliminary indications of the shape such a synthesis should take, Fichte first refers Schelling to book 3 of *The Vocation of Man* and particularly, one presumes, to the narrator's extended meditation on the "sublime living will, which no name can name and no concept encompass": the purest rational willing, understood as the unconditioned origination of a universal law of freedom; pure spirit, figured as freed from the limiting conditions definitive of and pursuant to the discursive nature of the finite I.[38] Two features of this text are particularly pertinent for present purposes—although both are somewhat screened by Fichte's unsystematic and popularized presentation. First, the intellectual approach to this "absolutely unconditioned being"[39] proceeds in a manner much akin to that adopted by Schelling in his 1795 reflections *On the I;* accordingly, it leads to a depiction of the supra-individual basis of finite subjectivity that is in several ways strikingly similar to Schelling's 1795–96 version thereof (prior to his first sustained efforts in *Naturphilosophie*). Second, and as a result of the foregoing, Fichte finds himself facing an in-principle obstruction to any exhaustive explanation of the existence of the finite I—essentially the same obstacle that had blocked Schelling's earliest efforts.

In *On the I,* Schelling had figured the unconditioned ground of finite subjectivity first by pinpointing a self-realizing structure in some sense immanent to the being of the finite subject as such,[40] and then by thinking that structure as radically bereft of any finitizing limitations. So construed, the unconditioned as such "contains all being, all reality."[41] It is infinite, the one and only unconditional, of which everything that is, is "merely" a modification.[42] It is the immanent cause of everything that is, and the sole occupant of the supersensuous world.[43] Compare some of Fichte's key conclusions, which are clearly arrived at in the same way: the "absolutely unconditioned being" is just "reason itself, if reason is conceived purely and independently"; as such, it is the only being that immediately and solely inhabits a purely spiritual order.[44] It is the one "true and imperishable" infinite, the source of "our true original component, the ground and stuff of our whole life."[45] Indeed, "only reason is; infinite reason in itself, and finite reason in it and through it"; as the enabler of the *Anstoß* or *Aufforderung* that spurs or summons the finite I to self-articulation and self-apprehension, it is "the creator of the world" immanent to the community of finite minds.[46]

(There are, of course, important differences between Fichte's and Schelling's respective renderings of finite subjectivity's unconditioned ground. For example, the specifically ethical and trans-personal dimensions of Fichte's figuration of the "sublime living will" are like nothing found in Schelling's early work. Of primary concern herein, however, are a set of broadly ontological and explanatory issues which I do not think are materially affected by such dissimilarities.)

Given all that has so far been said—and in light of the repeated references in book 3 of *The Vocation of Man* to the ultimate incomprehensibility of the infinite[47]—it is perhaps not so surprising that Fichte arrived, circa 1800, at a conclusion much like the one drawn by Schelling in 1795–96. Finite subjectivity, as such, depends upon the existence and efficacy of an ultimate, unconditioned being, a being of which the finite subject as such is but an individuated expression; yet the manner in which and the reason for which finite subjectivity arises on the basis of the originally unconditioned ultimate is unfathomable to the finite intellect. In a letter written to Schelling on the last day of May 1801, Fichte consolidates and conveys, in more technical terminology, the conclusions to which he had come:

> The *Wissenschaftslehre* . . . *presents the universal consciousness of the entire spiritual world as such,* and it is itself this consciousness. Each individuum is a *particular perspective* of this system on the basis of an individual ground [*Grundpunkt*] but this ground is *impenetrable,* that is, = X, to the *Wissenschaftslehre,* which is itself science, that is, penetration of universal consciousness.

In other words, the *Wissenschaftslehre* charts the basic structures and tendencies constitutive of finite subjectivity as such ("universal consciousness"), but it cannot provide a complete and systematic genetic account of any *actual,* individual occurrence of the "collapsing of subject-objectivity" wherein an individuated instance of the generic structure of finite self-apprehension originally opens up.[48] Philosophy's aspiration to ultimate understanding is thus thwarted by the existence and determinacy of even a single individuated *Grundpunkt*—a structure of subjectivity whose appellation aptly connotes the contraction into a finitizing focus of an initially universal, founding ultimate (*Grund*), while simultaneously suggesting the resultant "point of departure" that serves as a basis for further finite self-elaboration.

To take with proper seriousness the being of finite subjectivity, as that which just *is* interested openness upon an environing world, and to wonder how the world could come to contain this kind of being, is to open up a deep and demanding field for philosophical investigation. When, circa 1796, Schelling realized that he could not make intelligible the unfolding of finite subjectivity out of the unconditioned ultimate *as* he understood the latter at the time, he was quick to effect a radical reconceptualization of the problem: maintaining his basic commitment to the spontaneity and self-transparency of the subjective as such, he began to search for ways of re-understanding the unconditioned ultimate such that sentient self-awareness could be seen as a natural outgrowth thereof—as, evidently, it is. However admittedly obscure and apparently unwarranted his efforts on that score, we ought to acknowledge the import of their aim: to make good philosophical sense of the origination of finite subjectivity in, and out of, what originally exists but is as such unaware.

How would Fichte go on to deal with the explanatory lacuna apparently opened up in the course of his own evolving reflections on the relation between the finite I and its supra-individual ground? Given the ways in which his methodological standards and explanatory aims always differed from Schelling's (and I have said little about these here, preferring instead to mark out some key conceptual kinships), Fichte clearly could not embrace anything quite like Schelling's *Naturphilosophie*. More to the point, however, Fichte seems finally to have felt no philosophical need for such measures, preferring instead to see the necessity of the absolute's cleavage and contraction into a community of finite foci, not as a knot to be unraveled intellectually, but as an indisputable lesson taught us by life.[49]

Notes

1. See Fichte's 1806 preface to *Anweisung zum seligen Leben*, in *GA* 1.9:47.

2. See, for example, Fichte's December 27, 1800, letter to Schelling (more about which below). For further bibliographical details on the Fichte-Schelling correspondence, see note 6.

3. F. W. J. Schelling, *Darlegung des wahren Verhältnisses der Naturphilosophie zu der verbesserten Fichtesen Lehre*.

4. *WLNM* (1994), 178; *FTP*, 352.

5. I refer here to Schelling's October 3, 1801, letter to Fichte, which shall be cited in more detail in what follows. For additional bibliographical information on the Fichte-Schelling correspondence, see note 6.

6. The aforementioned sustained exchange was preceded by a single letter from Schelling to Fichte, September 26, 1794. All of the letters are compiled in *GA* 3; they are also in Johann Gottlieb Fichte, *Briefwechsel,* ed. Hans Schulz (Hildesheim: Georg Olms, 1967). At this writing, only selected portions of the correspondence have been translated into English; see especially *Theory as Practice: A Critical Anthology of Early German Romantic Writings,* trans. and ed. Jochen Schulte-Sasse et al. (Minneapolis: University of Minnesota Press, 1997), 73–90. This edition contains translations of most of the epistolary material cited herein. In what follows, I cite the letters by their dates and quote from the translations in *Theory as Practice,* noting my own emendations to the translations where they occur.

7. See Steven Hoeltzel, "Idealism and the Ground of Explanation: Fichte and Schelling, 1794–1797," in *New Essays on Fichte's Later Jena Wissenschaftslehre,* ed. Daniel Breazeale and Tom Rockmore (Evanston: Northwestern University Press, 2002), 261–78.

8. Schelling to Fichte, October 3, 1801.

9. Schelling to Fichte, October 3, 1801.

10. Fichte to Schelling, November 15, 1800. See also *WLNM* (1994), 182ff.; *FTP,* 359ff.; and compare *WLNM* (1994), 200; *FTP,* 396.

11. See F. W. J. Schelling, *On the Possibility of a Form of All Philosophy,* in vol. 1 of Friedrich Wilhelm Joseph Schelling, *Sämmtliche Werke,* ed. K. F. A. Schelling (Stuttgart and Augsburg: J. G. Cotta, 1856–61). English translation in F. W. J. Schelling, *The Unconditional in Human Knowledge: Four Early Essays (1794–1796),* trans. and ed. Fritz Marti (Lewisburg: Bucknell University Press, 1980). This 1794 essay by Schelling echoes Fichte's early radicalization of Reinhold and the doctrine of *das Ich,* and in a manner that displays considerable indebtedness to the following works by Fichte: the *Aenesidemus* review, *Concerning the Concept of the Wissenschaftslehre,* and part 1 (at least) of the *Grundlage.* Schelling's essay concludes with a glowing endorsement of the *Wissenschaftslehre,* but it would not be long before he radically revised his estimation of the stature and scope of Fichte's philosophical system.

12. See Günter Zöller, *Fichte's Transcendental Philosophy: The Original Duplicity of Intelligence and Will* (Cambridge: Cambridge University Press, 1998).

13. See Schelling, *Sämmtliche Werke,* 1:177ff.; Schelling, *Unconditional in Human Knowledge,* 82ff.

14. See Daniel Breazeale, "Check or Checkmate? On the Finitude of the Fichtean Self," in *The Modern Subject: Classical German Idealist Conceptions of the Self,* ed. Karl Ameriks and Dieter Sturma (Albany: State University of New York Press, 1995).

15. See Schelling's letter to Niethammer, January 22, 1796, in *Materialen zu Schellings philosophischen Anfängen* (Frankfurt: Suhrkamp, 1975), 139–42.

16. Schelling, *Sämmtliche Werke,* 1:177ff.; Schelling, *Unconditional in Human Knowledge,* 82ff. See also Ingtraud Görland, *Die Entwicklung der Frühphilosophie Schellings in der Auseinandersetzung mit Fichte* (Frankfurt: Klostermann, 1973).

17. For more detail on Schelling's early divergence from Fichte, see Hoeltzel, "Idealism and the Ground of Explanation."

18. The phrase is from Schelling's 1795–96 *Philosophical Letters on Dogmatism and*

Criticism; see Schelling, *Sämmtliche Werke,* 1:310ff.; Schelling, *Unconditional in Human Knowledge,* 173ff.

19. See the [First] "Introduction" (1797) to the *Attempt at a New Presentation of the Wissenschaftslehre,* in *GA* 1.4:183–281; English translation in *IWL,* 7–35. Although the issues it raises cannot detain us herein, it is instructive to compare Schelling's 1797 *Treatise Explicating the Idealism in the Wissenschaftslehre,* in Schelling, *Sämmtliche Werke,* 1:345–452. English translation in F. W. J. Schelling, *Idealism and the Endgame of Theory: Three Essays by F. W. J. Schelling,* trans. and ed. Thomas Pfau (Albany: State University of New York Press, 1994), 61–138.

20. See *GA* 1.4:200ff.; *IWL,* 26ff. The cited phrase occurs at *GA* 1.4:200; *IWL,* 27.

21. *GA* 1.4:200; *IWL,* 27. Again, for more detail on this and related points, see Hoeltzel, "Idealism and the Ground of Explanation." Note also that the "First Introduction" contains criticisms of Schelling on a number of issues not dealt with herein. In this connection, see Daniel Breazeale's "Editor's Introduction" to *IWL;* see also Reinhard Lauth, *Die Enstehung von Schellings Identitätphilosophie in der Auseinandersetzung mit Fichtes Wissenschaftslehre* (Freiburg: Alber, 1975).

22. From the *Aenesidemus* review: Schelling, *Sämmtliche Werke,* 1:13; English translation in *EPW,* 69.

23. From "On the Basis of Our Belief in a Divine Governance of the World," in *GA* 1.5:350; *IWL,* 145. (See also Fichte's footnote to this passage.)

24. *WLNM* (1994), 149; *FTP,* 301–2.

25. *WLNM* (1994), 178; *FTP,* 352.

26. *WLNM* (1994), 147; *FTP,* 298.

27. *WLNM* (1994), 38; *FTP,* 125 (translation modified).

28. See *WLNM* (1994), 151; *FTP,* 304–5.

29. *WLNM* (1994), 149; *FTP,* 302 (emphasis added).

30. Schelling to Fichte, October 3, 1801.

31. Schelling, *Sämmtliche Werke,* 2:39; English translation in Schelling, *Ideas for a Philosophy of Nature,* trans. Errol Harris and Peter Heath (New York: Cambridge University Press, 1988), 30.

32. For some helpful recent discussion of these topics, see Dale Snow, *Schelling and the End of Idealism* (Albany: State University of New York Press, 1996); see also Andrew Bowie, *Schelling and Modern European Philosophy: An Introduction* (New York: Routledge, 1993).

33. Schelling to Fichte, November 19, 1800.

34. Schelling to Fichte, October 3, 1801.

35. I do not mean to suggest that this alteration is entirely unprepared by Fichte's earlier work. In his invocation of "eine Maße des rein geisigen" in the *Wissenschaftslehre nova methodo,* for example, we certainly find an anticipatory echo of this idea (*WLNM* [1994], 149; *FTP,* 302). Such notions are not really the central foci of sustained attention, however, until at least 1800.

36. *WLNM* (1994), 178; *FTP,* 352. Recall the closing paragraphs of the first section of this chapter; see also Zöller, *Fichte's Transcendental Philosophy,* pt. 4.

37. Fichte to Schelling, May 31–August 7, 1801 (translation modified).

38. The cited phrase occurs at *GA* 1.6:296; English translation in *VM,* 111. My

paraphrase ranges over material found throughout book 3 of Fichte's text and concentrates especially on the last two main subsections thereof.

39. *GA* 1.6:284; *VM*, 99.

40. See Schelling, *Sämmtliche Werke,* 1:167; Schelling, *Unconditional in Human Knowledge*, 75.

41. Schelling, *Sämmtliche Werke,* 1:186; Schelling, *Unconditional in Human Knowledge,* 89.

42. Schelling, *Sämmtliche Werke,* 1:192–93; Schelling, *Unconditional in Human Knowledge,* 92–93.

43. Schelling, *Sämmtliche Werke,* 1:195–96, 202; Schelling, *Unconditional in Human Knowledge,* 95–96, 100.

44. *GA* 1.6:284–85; *VM,* 99.

45. *GA* 1.6:293; *VM,* 107–8.

46. *GA* 1.6:296; *VM,* 110–11.

47. See, for example, *GA* 1.6:297; *VM,* 112.

48. Fichte to Schelling, May 31–August 7, 1801.

49. This is an important theme in the *Wissenschaftslehre* of 1812; see Johannes Brachtendorf's contribution to this volume. The present chapter is a revised version of remarks presented at the fifth biennial meeting of the North American Fichte Society. For stimulating questions and helpful suggestions, I am indebted to numerous conference participants.

Fichte's Reaction to Schelling's Identity Philosophy in 1806

Michael Vater

When Fichte was about to embark on lectures at Erlangen in the summer of 1806, he wrote to various state ministers promising a publication that would address the contemporary state of philosophy in southern Germany and file an "author's reprimand" against Schelling for the theft of his *Wissenschaftslehre*. By the time Fichte assembled the piece late in the spring of 1807 (in part from existing manuscripts), his wife was reporting to him that Schelling was circulating reports that he had come around and embraced *Naturphilosophie* as his own.[1] Fichte sent the piece to the publisher Reimer to serve as an introduction to a longer piece that never appeared: *Toward a History of the Scientific Spirit at the Beginning of the Nineteenth Century*. Fichte's son published a somewhat truncated version after his death under the title *Report on the Concept of the Wissenschaftslehre and Its Current Reception*. This piece has three major parts: (1) remarks on the *Wissenschaftslehre* and its early critics; (2) remarks on contemporary literature directed against Jacobi; and (3) a semi-detailed, sometimes vitriolic repudiation of Schelling's philosophy of identity. I shall focus on the first and third elements in this chapter, for, despite the first section's general tone and its refusal to name names, it certainly has Schelling in view, among others, when it indicts those who have misunderstood Fichte's living philosophy for thirteen years and turned its rational maxims into a system of "reflection."[2]

Fichte begins his *Report on the Concept of the Wissenschaftslehre* by noting that human cognition of truth is often distorted by its starting point, the natural form of consciousness. Operating through its own hidden laws, natural consciousness or reflection interposes itself between us and the truth we would know. This distortion can only be removed by a full exploration of cognition, one that displays all its modes and their origin from knowledge's own inner laws. Kant took it as his task to expose the full panoply of reason's errors by systematically displaying them—metaphysical realism and idealism alike—

as modifications of the one truth. *Wissenschaftslehre* or "transcendental philosophy" improves upon Kant by demonstrating that what he left as separate branches of reason—theoretical, practical, and reflectively judging reason—are one knowledge.[3] It thus equally suspends and nullifies all the products of knowledge's basic law: "reflection," or reduction to finite terms.

Fichte goes on to argue, however, that the reception of *Wissenschaftslehre* has been skewed by distrust, infected by the suspicion that the disease it diagnosed is not yet cured. Some have argued that *Wissenschaftslehre* is false because it leaves some sort of "reality" as a residue, and these same critics cannot conceive "reality" any way other than reflectively, namely, as a finite or empirical object, or a finite subject, or indeed a subject-object. If *Wissenschaftslehre* proved that "reflection" in all its forms utterly lacks reality, contends Fichte, the public has responded by supposing there was something wrong with the proof, since it annihilated the "reality" that the public could not help but imagine was the only possible reality.[4] What the critics were unable to comprehend was the simple fact that thinking is *seeing,* not reflecting. *Wissenschaftslehre* is a painting meant for the light of the eyes, but its critics have only fumbled with it in the dark and then pronounced they have felt the usual objects or stuff signified by the forms of reflective consciousness.[5] Fichte's light imagery is new to his public pronouncements, but the contrast he draws here between *Seyn* and *Sehen* goes back to the fundamental conflict between Fichte and his presumed disciple that the early *Fichte-Schelling Correspondence* documents.[6]

Fichte concludes this short exposition of the fundamental misunderstanding with a reminder that he has often promised to bring out new versions of *Wissenschaftslehre.* The old exposition was adequate, he now reasons, though a new one would serve to make it more familiar. The essence of the older version was this: the absolute form of reflection or finite *I-hood* is the root of all knowledge; everything that arises in consciousness can be explained from it alone. The rest of *Wissenschaftslehre* is but the exhaustive elaboration of this reflective (or dualistic) form inside the one prototype or "absolute synthesis": the reciprocal determination of substance and causality. Readers will not find anything new or different in present or future clarifications of *Wissenschaftslehre,* asserts Fichte.[7] When one compares this short statement to the various versions of the Jena *Wissenschaftslehre,* this text appears curious in its lack of reference to act, agility, spontaneity, or to seeing behind the primary form of reflection. Absent this element of seeing, agility, or spontaneity, one is hard-pressed to find the difference between *Wissenschaftslehre* and Reinhold's "elemental philosophy."

This general discussion of the failure of the philosophic public to understand the premises of *Wissenschaftslehre* and to inwardly reproduce them is followed by an independently composed, short section titled "Preliminary

Discussion." Fichte here makes his point in a purely systematic way that a pure philosophy of being is unacceptable and that the only conceptually acceptable alternative is to adopt *Wissenschaftslehre*'s postulation of consciousness as the living absolute.[8] One is forced by the almost universal parlance of the time to talk of "being," complains Fichte, by which the objectivists mean something that is simply one, self-enclosed, identical—in short, *dead*. Once one has seen the problematic character of simple being, one must adopt a different, but nonetheless monolithic, perspective. *Wissenschaftslehre* accordingly adopts *positive being* or *life* as its original ground and attempts to move in the "immediate life of the absolute."[9] Only in this way will one ever connect to the absolute the sort of being that is ours, namely, conscious life. Fichte's argument unfolds as follows: since "we *are* consciousness," we can alternately say, since "consciousness exists." But we must connect our form of life with this absolute life in such a way that we see that there are not two versions of life, "plain life" and, alongside that, "conscious life." We must adopt the view that there can be but *one life*, that it is the absolute which immediately lives in us, and that it can exist in no other way than in conscious beings like ourselves. If we do this, we have introduced the absolute into the form of I-hood. All that remains is to see what follows in us from and in consciousness, and to separate that from concrete (or "formed," i.e., embodied) life, and we shall complete the project of casting *Wissenschaftslehre* into the shape of a *Lebenslehre*, a philosophy of life.[10]

In this section where he most succinctly states his fundamental insight, Fichte insists that the dead being of the objectivists is not original life, but merely the last product of the supersensible life that in us has entered the form of consciousness. It would be truly enlightening if a genuine life-philosophy would tread the path from life to mere being. But to take the opposite path (as Schelling does in his *Naturphilosophie*) is to introduce a perverse mistake and let objectivism or naturalism permeate all parts of one's system. "Even in science one cannot intuit the absolute outside oneself, for this 'outside' is an utter absurdity; rather one must be and live the absolute life in one's own person."[11] From this perspective, every philosophy except the purified Kantianism of *Wissenschaftslehre* is nonsensical and corrupt. Objectivistic philosophies—the outcome of blind "hands-on" materialism devoid of all *Sehen*, all self-intuition—are produced by those who have too little spirit or who lack the ability to envision themselves as free and conscious. Since transcendental philosophy is practical in Kant's sense, one must consciously will oneself into it and will the embodiment of absolute life as consciousness in oneself.

When the reader turns to Fichte's explicit discussion of Schelling in the second part of the second chapter of the *Report on the Concept of the Wissenschaft-*

slehre, entitled "One Example of the Age's Capacity for Philosophic Judgment," there is little more to be learned about the core view of *Wissenschaftslehre,* or even about fundamental errors in Schelling's philosophy. In a sense relevant to Fichte's philosophy, there is much heat and little light to be found here. The basic objection to Schelling's philosophy in 1801–2 is refurbished here: what Schelling has done is to take the watchword of anti-dogmatic philosophy: *that reality is to be sought not in things, but in thinking and the laws of thought,* and turn it into the objection that this philosophy is subjectivism. To turn the transcendental methodology of Kant and *Wissenschaftslehre* into a narrow subjectivism is to repeat the general mistake of the spiritless age, viewing the explanatory *postulates* of transcendental idealism as no better than an apotheosis of the *concrete I* in all its finitude. Schelling's sole originality is to deck out this misunderstanding of contemporary philosophy with the ghostly apparel of Spinoza and Plato. Fichte takes this historicism as evidence of his counterpart's ignorance of what philosophy is and of his natural lack of aptitude for it.[12] Despite the man's natural talents—skill in dialectics, writing ability, social and artistic abilities—he is lacking as a philosopher.

One need not, claims Fichte, resort to a lengthy discussion of Schelling's early works or even to haul the so-called system of identity before any standing literary tribunal to see this. The seemingly so important identity philosophy convicts itself without any lengthy process and without outside help if one but looks at the first few propositions from the 1801 *Exposition of My System.*[13] The first theorem, or rather stipulative definition: "*I call reason, or reason conceived as the absolute indifference of the subjective and the objective, absolute reason,*" posits reason as something dead at the very start, isolated from all the predicates that Schelling nonetheless goes on to apply to it in succeeding theorems. A living reason ought to have posited difference alongside identity at the very first—a point quietly made by Hegel in the *Differenzschrift* and accepted by Schelling in the *Bruno* and subsequent works.[14] The second theorem fares no better: "*There is nothing outside reason; everything has being inside it.*" Schelling argues that if there is anything outside reason, it will either exist independently of reason, contrary to the first theorem, or exist inside reason, contrary to the supposition voiced here. Fichte correctly comments that Schelling did not say what he meant: if anything exists outside reason, it will either be an independent subject or an independent objective; in both cases it will violate the stipulated non-difference of the two in the first theorem. But the only cogent second theorem to follow from Schelling's first would be: "In and for reason is absolutely nothing," since any "something" that might be posited would be either a subject, contrary to the first theorem, or an object, likewise contrary to the stipulation.[15] The only thing logically coherent that could follow upon Schelling's starting point would be silence.

Schelling's third theorem falls prey to similar self-refutation upon examination: "*Reason is simply one and simply self-identical.*" For were this not the case, reason would require another ground. How do we know that reason needs a ground, asks Fichte, or that "ground" is an applicable concept in this case, or (as Schelling further claims) that reason could not be qualitatively selfsame were it not self-grounding? The real follow-up to the first two theorems ought to have been, claims Fichte: "Reason is simply neither one nor self-identical."[16] Had he been reading Schelling's contemporary essays, Fichte would have found Schelling saying much the same thing: "Reason can be described in no one thing; it must describe itself in everything and through everything."[17] Fichte breaks off the analysis of the 1801 *Exposition* with a summary judgment upon one of Schelling's later assertions: that the *qualitative antithesis* between subjectivity and objectivity is suspended by reason and is explicated in philosophical analysis as a mere *quantitative difference,* is impossible if his initial postulates are true: that reason is the absolute indifference of the subjectivity and objectivity, and that there is no being outside reason. Since this difficult contention is the heart of the first version of the identity system, it is disappointing to see Fichte summarily dismiss it and not carefully refute it.[18] Fichte pushes on, however, to a similarly partial critique of Schelling's 1804 *Philosophy and Religion,* calling it Schelling's least-botched essay.

Fichte considers only three passages of this essay, but finds they contain no less than ten "acts of blindness." All of the passages touch on central themes in Schelling's essay, but we can leave two of them aside, conceding that they might cause difficulties: (1) the notion that intellectual intuition is self-constituted (or that its reality can be deduced from its concept); and (2) that a "fall of Ideas" into finite or temporal existence can provide an explanation of individuality or particularity.[19] The point to which Fichte gives his most careful attention is Schelling's move, central to the "real-idealism" of identity philosophy, to posit a *form* of the absolute alongside its *essence,* "form" being synonymous with "expression" or an ideal elaboration of the indifferent togetherness of all subjective and objective factors which the absolute *qua* essence (*Wesen*) contains without distinction. Fichte quotes Schelling: But identically eternal with the simply ideal is the eternal form. That the absolute is the concept of itself is readily intelligible, Fichte concedes, and likewise that it is identically eternal as the absolute itself. But by form, he contends, Schelling means not "concept" but some sort of ideal reproduction of the sensible inside the absolute, hence a *material,* graspable, sensuous form. Fichte is correct on this point, at least in reference to early versions of the identity philosophy, where form simply was posited as a jack-in-the-box in-packing of all that the sensible world displays as differentiated and individual. Fichte notes that in this essay, however, Schelling asks and answers the questions: How do we come to know about this form? How do we participate in it? Schelling's answer is that the concept of the absolute is I-hood, so that every I participates in the absolute's form.[20] This question and its reply look quite idealistic; indeed, they seem to reproduce the very words Fichte used earlier to state the core view of *Wissenschaftslehre.*

At this crucial point, Fichte breaks away from textual analysis and insists that the real philosophical issue remains unstated, and thus untouched: Whence this "form of the absolute"? Why is it introduced? Schelling's use of the concept gives the answer: in order to derive *reality* from the absolute. Schelling's secret thought, contends Fichte, is that *reality exists in itself.* This is his foundation and starting point; only for its sake are the other elements of his system posited, including the absolute and the form of the absolute. Schelling's philosophy is, at bottom, empiricism.[21] As if this were not bad enough, there is an internal incoherence in the idea of the absolute consisting of essence and form. Is it the absolute itself that is form? If so, it would not be itself in the form. Is the absolute, then, an I that is not an I, an identity that is not an identity? While a positive reply would be a superficially satisfactory response here, Fichte refuses this easy solution. Does the absolute subsist wholly and undividedly in the absolute, or not? asks Fichte with great insistence. Schelling refuses the first or positive reply, for he has sunk his own individuality in this absolute and wishes to preserve himself. If he replies that it is the second or negative alternative—*not* subsisting completely and undividedly in its formal expression—then there are two absolutes, one wholly withdrawn from form, another wholly identified with it. That he does not see this is Schelling's tenth blindness.[22] Here again we are compelled to note Fichte's discomfort whenever his analysis of the core postulates of the identity philosophy results in something similar to his own new metaphysics-cum-epistemology of the Berlin *Wissenschaftslehre,* with being on one side, in itself and unrelated to knowing, which from its side is independent or self-subsisting, yet still referred to being. Is the author of the *Report on the Concept of the Wissenschaftslehre* a crypto-realist? Is this critique of Schelling more than tinged with "ontophobia"? At any rate, Fichte soon tires of textual analysis and closes the essay in a cheerless tirade of personal invective, one of the kinder moments of which is the following riposte: "As an artist, I account him one of the greatest bunglers who has ever played with words."[23]

What about Schelling's ongoing reaction to Fichte's philosophy? Other than secondhand accounts, Schelling was familiar only with the sketches of the 1801–2 *Wissenschaftslehre* that Fichte incorporated into the later exchanges of the *Correspondence.* He nonetheless continued the polemics from his side of the fence and in as public a manner as he had in the preface of the 1801 *My System.* Schelling's *On the True Relation Between Nature-Philosophy and the Improved Fichtean Teaching* (1806) is in its opening and concluding pages the mirror image of the one-sided analysis we have just reviewed on Fichte's part.

"Without something that is not divine there can be no *divinization,*" begins Schelling.[24] If Fichte's new principle is that God is all being and that there is no being outside God, then everything in nature is being and is equal to the divine life. Why, then, does Fichte persist in viewing nature as utter non-being?[25] Though Fichte says he wants to include only the living in his philosophy, he still wants to have nature as something that he can work upon and trample underfoot. If the objective world disappears as objective, then so does he as the Promethean subject.[26] Later Schelling argues that if philosophy is supposed to be the science of the divine as the all-positive, then it consists in the scientific cognition of the sole actuality to be found in the actual, that is, the natural, world. "Philosophy is essentially nature philosophy."[27] Fichte's whole depiction of being as a dead, purely objective something is a completely arbitrary view, suggests Schelling, the product of a sensibility infected with empirical subjectivity.[28] What Fichte takes as nature is really nothing for nature philosophy—not because we do not know it, but because we recognize it as a shadow, a reflection, a creature of mere mediated cognition. And what we call nature, says Schelling, Fichte in turn does not recognize. But here the reason is his lack of cognition, unknowing or willful ignorance.[29]

The pursuit of such claims and counterclaims as we have been reviewing will not lead us to wisdom, I am sure. What moral or philosophical consolation can we gather from the unedifying sight of two competent philosophers and former friends bickering in public? There may be a bit of truth on each side. It seems to me that Fichte, despite the choler of his thoughts and the intemperance of some of his words, sees the basic issues and options for transcendental philosophy more clearly than his sometime fellow traveler. The fundamental question is, as Fichte stated it back in 1800, whether *Sehen* or *Seyn,* seeing or being, is more suitable as the conceptual basis for a systematic philosophy that can embrace both theory and praxis. Of course, it is a philosophical option for us to reject this ideal of systematicity or the unity of knowledge as some outdated Enlightenment ideal; we can settle down, as Nietzsche suggested, and get cozy with nihilism until a new idea or an asteroid strikes. If we want to buy into Fichte's starting point, as voiced in the *Report,* and say that Kant began the work of disillusioning consciousness by showing us the "show" of the naturality of commonsense realism but left that work incomplete in that he left theory and practice severed, then we have to take seriously at least the basis of the unedifying dispute we have just reviewed: what can better unify theory and practice, if only in a provisional way, a philosophy that starts with *Seyn* or one that starts with *Sehen*?

Fichte is essentially correct when, in the closing pages of the *Report,* he characterizes Schelling as a materialistic dualist in the mold of Leibniz or (more damningly) as a second Friedrich Nicolai for his belief in the senses and in "common sense."[30] For his part, Schelling is happy to wrap himself in the mantle of Leibniz at this time. He closes an 1805 work on nature philosophy by affirming the necessity of some positive element, not mere privation, that sets individual finite beings, including those of nature, apart from the all-enclosing identity of God by quoting Leibniz's remark: "Were there no monads, Spinoza would be right."[31] Even to cede limited reality to the entities of the perceived worlds which are the objects of natural science is to opt for a world where cognition is more important than action, perception is more important than affect and ought, and theory in some sense floats free from the embedded practical life of the cognizer-agents who do it.

If given the choice, then, between Schelling's nature-philosophical vision and Fichte's moral vitalism, the nod would go to Fichte. Only a philosophy that begins in *seeing* or *showing* can unite the three human worlds left disunited by the Kantian *Critiques.* A philosophy of being can illuminate only the objective pole of our cognition. Only a philosophy that takes seeing seriously (as *feeling,* the embracing category of affect and ought) can begin to take comprehensive account of our tritophrenic human reality: action, affection, and knowing. I cannot deny the difficulty of the task, or the awkwardness of having no framework common to all three, but in the end I must agree with the opening thought of the unknown idealist's first sketch of systematic philosophy: from now on, all philosophy has to be ethics.[32]

Notes

1. *Bericht über den Begriff der Wissenschaftslehre und die bisherigen Schicksale derselben,* in *GA* 2.10. See the editors' introduction at *GA* 2.10:14–18.

2. Though Reinhold is a plausible candidate for one of the critics mentioned here who substitutes imagination or analytic-synthetic consciousness for the *Schauen* on which *Wissenschaftslehre* depends, Fichte denounces these critics in precisely the terms that he and Schelling used against each other in their early private disagreements. Fichte here writes of his critics: "They supposed that this philosophy's failure consisted in the way it presupposed a subjective-objective being, an actual, concretely existing I, as a thing in itself, which failing they proposed to remedy by assuming an objective-objective being in its place, dignified with the name 'the absolute'" (*GA* 2.10:23).

3. *GA* 2.10:21–22.
4. *GA* 2.10:28.
5. *GA* 2.10:26–27.
6. See Fichte to Schelling, May 31–August 7, 1801, in Johann Gottlieb Fichte and Friedrich Joseph Wilhelm Schelling, *Briefwechsel,* ed. Walter Schulz (Suhrkamp: Frankfurt, 1968), 124–25; and Schelling to Fichte, October 3, 1801, in *Briefwechsel,* 133–34.

If in 1806–7 Fichte still characterizes the difference between *Wissenschaftslehre* and its critics as that of idealism and realism (*Sehen* or *Schauen* versus *Seyn*), it is not surprising that he omits to mention the feature new to his theory after 1801: the unexplained relationship of knowing to an external absolute, sometimes called "being," sometimes God. This new transcendent realism, however, is different from the reification of the finite I that early critics misunderstood as the purport of earlier versions *Wissenschaftslehre.* Fichte's own post-1801 realism, however, is as little consistent with transcendental philosophy as was Kant s thing in itself, which was rejected by Fichte at the start of his philosophical career. In Fichte's defense, it can be said that he asserted this ultimate reference of knowing to being without claiming that philosophy, which moves wholly within the sphere of knowing, could do the least thing to clarify or explain it.

Regarding the 1801 *Wissenschaftslehre,* see Michael G. Vater, "The *Wissenschaftslehre* of 1801–02," in *Fichte: Historical Contexts / Contemporary Controversies,* ed. Daniel Breazeale and Tom Rockmore (Atlantic Highlands: Humanities, 1994), 191–210.

7. *GA* 2.10:29. The formula covers the starting point of the Jena systems and the theoretical part of the 1794 *Grundlage,* but it is opaque in its mention of a synthesis of causality and substance and it curiously omits mention of feeling.
8. Here again, one sees no hint here of the transcendent foundation of the Berlin *Wissenschaftslehre.* In this (admittedly) fragmentary text, we seem to be thrown back to the egological idealism of the Jena system.
9. *GA* 2.10:29–30.
10. *GA* 2.10:31.
11. *GA* 2.10:31.
12. *GA* 2.10:44–45.
13. Fichte's choice of target is less than challenging. Schelling was not up to the rigorous standard of geometrical exposition and, in an amateurish way, packed so much content into the first few propositions of the *Darstellung meines Systems der Philosophie* that either they cannot be understood at all without the whole of what follows them (alas, most of the time not following *from* them) or they are subject to the sort of dialectical "unhorsing" that Fichte provides them. For Schelling's first three theorems, see "*Presentation of My System of Philosophy,*" trans. Michael Vater, *Philosophical Forum* 32, no. 4:349–50.
14. *GA* 2.10:46–47.
15. *GA* 2.10:47–48.
16. *GA* 2.10:48–49.
17. F. W. J. Schelling, *Aphorismen zur Einleitung in die Naturphilosophie* (1805), in *Sämmtliche Werke,* ed. K. F. A. Schelling (Stuttgart and Augsburg: J. G. Cotta,

1856–61), 7:146. See also Schelling's *Aphorismen über die Naturphilosophie* (1806), in *Sämmtliche Werke,* 7:231, where he argues that while imagination (and the particular object to which it is adapted) is a back-and-forth activity between opposites such as being and non-being, reason effects their immediate unity.

18. *GA* 2.10:50. See Schelling's *Darstellung meines System,* in *Sämmtliche Werke,* 4:128–32; "*Presentation of My System,*" trans. Vater, 359–61.

19. See *GA* 2.10:52–53 and 58–59, respectively.

20. *GA* 2.10:54–55.

21. *GA* 2.10:55–56.

22. *GA* 2.10:56–57.

23. *GA* 2.10:65.

24. F. W. J. Schelling, *On the True Relation Between Nature-Philosophy and the Improved Fichtean Teaching,* in *Sämmtliche Werke,* 7:12.

25. Schelling, *On the True Relation,* 7:12–13.

26. Schelling, *On the True Relation,* 7:17.

27. Schelling, *On the True Relation,* 7:30.

28. Schelling, *On the True Relation,* 7:80.

29. Schelling, *On the True Relation,* 7:97.

30. *GA* 2.10:61.

31. Schelling, *Aphorismen zur Einleitung,* 7:196.

32. See G. W. F. Hegel, "The Earliest System Programme of German Idealism," trans. H. S. Harris, in *The Hegel Reader,* ed. Stephen Houlgate (Blackwell: Oxford, 1998), 28.

The Light That Lights the Seeing of the Light: The Second *Wissenschaftslehre* of 1804

George J. Seidel

It was fortunate that I had earlier worked on Fichte's 1806 *Anweisung zum seligen Leben,*[1] for which the *Zweiter Vortrag* of the *Wissenschftslehre* of 1804 might be seen as the theoretical preparation. Though it would doubtless be more accurate to look upon the 1806 *Anweisung* as, instead, the popular presentation of the 1804 lecture series.

The *Wissenschaftslehren* after 1800 must be seen in context. They occur after the celebrated Atheism Controversy with its, for Fichte, unpleasant outcome. A philosopher like Fichte could have two reactions to a charge of atheism. The knee-jerk reaction would be to claim that he had simply been misunderstood, or that his presentation had not been sufficiently clear. More sober reflection, however, could lead to the gnawing suspicion that there might be some truth to the accusation. But the accusation simply could not be true, since, as Fichte insists at the end of the second *Wissenschaftslehre* of 1804, his philosophy is fully consistent with Christianity and with Christian belief.[2] Or as he will say later in the *Anweisung,* the *Wissenschaftslehre* is the metaphysical truth of which the Christ of Christianity is the reality.[3]

An initial reading of the second *Wissenschaftslehre* of 1804 may lead one to wonder if it has anything at all to do with Fichte's earlier effort. But it does, in spite of its very different orientation and language. For example, from the *Wissenschaftslehre* of 1794 one might conclude that it is the third fundamental principle—the finitely posited self with its finitely opposited non-self—that is at the basis of the system: "The *form* of the system depends upon the highest synthesis."[4] On the other hand, in the 1804 work, Fichte characterizes the task of philosophy as the presentation (*Darstellung*) of the Absolute (*WZV,* 8), which would appear to emphasize the first fundamental principle. However, in the earlier *Wissenschaftslehre* he had also added: "That there should be a system at all depends upon the absolute thesis," which would indicate the overriding importance of the first fundamental principle. Just before this he had said that while the necessity for the joining of the two principles rests immediately on the third principle, the necessity for joining them at all depends on the first.[5] Still, the emphasis in the earlier work appears to be upon the third fundamental principle, since it is the finite self that posits the absolute self; whereas in the later *Wissenschaftslehre,* the shift is clearly toward the absolute and its presentation.

In 1804 Fichte continues to insist that his system is still essentially Kantian (*WZV,* 18); Kant's thing-in-itself is contained in the tiny word *Ich* (10–12). However, the appearance (*Erscheinung*) is no longer simply Kant's "phenomenon" but is, rather, Kant's sensible and supersensible combined (29). The "That" (*Daß*)—the appearance of knowledge expressed in an external existence, *Dasein,* as factical—which must appear, must necessarily appear from somewhere (the *terminus a quo* of Absolute being, *Sein*), and appear immediately as Both (*Beides*) the changeable and the unchangeable (26). Matters have clearly shifted to the absolute In-itself. Also, in this work Fichte draws a distinction between (divine) being (*Sein*) and factical existence (*Dasein*), a distinction, borrowed likely from Schelling, whose meaning will become even more explicit in the 1806 *Anweisung.*[6]

The Absolute is a point of unity. However, Fichte maintains that his system is unlike that of Spinoza, in that while the latter begins with a unity, he has no way of getting to a many or conversely from the many to a unity (*WZV,* 33–34, 55). Fichte characterizes Spinoza's system as lacking an organic unity; it is essentially mechanical, a substance that is lifeless (*Sein ohne Leben;* 35, 76). There is a related criticism of Schelling. Being and thought, subject and object, are indeed joined together in the appearance (*Erscheinung;* 17)—their disjunction an illusion (*Schein;* 45). Nevertheless, any *Indifferenz,* as with Schelling's philosophy of identity, always implies *Differenz* (140–42). This is in accordance with one of the two basic principles of German idealism enunciated in the earlier *Wissenschaftslehre:* namely, that there is no unity without a prior difference, just as there is no difference without a prior unity.[7]

For the unchangeable to make itself obvious (*einleuchten*), says Fichte, it must appear in the changeable (*WZV,* 36). This becomes a midpoint (*Mittelpunkt*) of pure light. In the bearer of this light, the light in its origin (*Ursprünglichkeit*) and absolute character (*Qualität*) is by no means immediately given, but only mediately in the proxy (*Stellvertreter*) and copy (*Abbilde*) of itself (39–40). There is a glimpse (*Einsicht*) of this original and absolute light in the representative or proxy, since it is both emanent (external) and immanent (self-contained; 53). As he indicates later, it is "emanent," formally emanent, in the sense that it appears in an external form (*Äusserlichkeit;* 260). It is "immanent" in that it represents a living self-contained image (*in sich geschlossenes Bild;* 249–50). This light, then, is the appearance (*Erscheinung*) of the appearance from the appearance. It is an image of the light without being a copy of the copied (66–67).

In other words, Fichte's notion of image (*Bild*) should not be read after the fashion of Plato's image, reflecting the image of the idea. For Fichte, in this appearance there is the inner life of the original appearance (*Urerscheinung*). Further, in the contemplation (*Betrachtung*) of this light, the light reveals itself (*WZV,* 65). We become en-lightened; the light is also in us (67–68). The externally existent light is as one with the Absolute, eternally equal with it (78). Thus, the light exists in two modalities (*Weisen*): the inner life of light, which is unseen, and the outer (95). There is an absolute relation between the copy and its image, and vice versa (85); the distinction between the inner and the outer lies only in the viewpoint of factical existence (99). In the light we see the light, both lights. Further, by virtue of the two basic principles of German idealism, these two lights are both the same and not the same. There is the light that appears and the light that does not appear, with the light that does not appear appearing in the light that does.

In all this there is something of Hegel's speculative Good Friday. Fichte speaks of this self-contained, externally existent light, one and equal with the absolute and original light, as the graveyard of the concept (*Grabstätte des Begriffs; WZV,* 81), since the (absolute) In-itself (*Ansich*) is independent of every saying, thinking, and intuiting. Thought denies to itself the thought of the In-itself (121–22). Fichte speaks of a projection through a cleft or opening (148) as contrary to reason (*projectio per hiatum irrationalem;* 157–64). It is both incomprehensible and inexplicable because it is both in itself and not in itself (147), since it is given over to human weakness (*Gebrechen*) and becomes the repository of death (*Lager des Todes*) as a consequence of this projection through the cleft or hiatus (144).

There is a significant difference in the direction of the projection in the 1804 *Wissenschaftslehre* from that of 1794. In the earlier *Wissenschaftslehre,* it is the finite self that projects the infinite or absolute self. Here the projection is from the other direction, since Fichte begins with the Absolute In-itself. He attempts to finesse this difference by insisting that this "construction" (*constructio:* "what is put together," "joined together") is the embodied (*versinnlichte*), purely understood (*intelligirte*) meaning of the In-itself (*WZV,* 147). It is self-contained light, a self closed in upon itself in its unchangeableness, a light that goes into itself (155–56). Thus, when Fichte speaks of the source of the factical as consciousness (137), it may sound like the oppositing of the non-self in virtue of the finite self's positing of the infinite or ideal self of the earlier *Wissenschaftslehre.* However, he maintains that the In-itself is already "constructed" (145); indeed, it represents a self-construction (162). Later he will speak of it as a post-construction (*Nachconstruction*) of an original pre-construction (*Vorconstruction;* 245). The factical Dasein is the first fully self-made reality. It is the self-creator of its own being (*Selbstschöpfer seines Seins;* 168).

The absolute In-itself reveals itself as the source of the light, which bears within itself the character of a higher realism whose self-produced life, with the light joined to it, illuminates that first reality (*Realismus*) derived from the In-itself (*WZV,* 128). That self-produced life is one with, and inseparable from, the absolute and original life, and the light also proceeds (*geht auf*) from the absolute self-construction just as this emerges from the absolute light as well. It is "self-produced" in that it constructs itself by itself (*es construirte sich selber durch sich selbst;* 124).

It is perilous for philosophers to play with light. They can be blinded or burned. When Plato urges ascending from the cave, beyond the fire burning at the mouth of the cave, and going out into the blinding sunlight and, finally, looking at the sun itself (i.e., the Good) as the cause of all that exists and of all that would be seen, he envisions a cause that is both separate and distinct from its seen effects (see *Republic* 516b-c). When the Neoplatonist Plotinus uses the sun as an analogy for the One (alias the Good), that which proceeds from the One is distinct, though not separate, from its source, just as the sunlight is distinct, though not separate, from the sun. However, the light that proceeds from the sun is a lesser reality than the sun. The product is necessarily less than the producer (*Enneads* 5.1.6). Fichte's light is neither Plato's Good nor is it a lesser reality than the absolute In-itself source of the light. Fichte does not want to be blinded. He has already been burned. Rather, the light is equal with the light source and represents a self-produced life with the light joined to it, illuminating all that is derived from the In-itself (*WZV,* 128). The light Fichte is playing with is that of the prologue to the Gospel of John, the true light that was already in the world, since everything came to be from, by, and through it; and this light is also the Through (*Durch*), that through which all those coming into the world would be enlightened (105–7; compare John 1:4–10). In the light lighting the light we see the light.

Two things remain constant in the *Wissenschaftslehre* of 1804. First, being is still posited being (*WZV,* 13), and there is still the *Sollen* of Fichte's moral idealism. At the end of the work, for example, Fichte will speak of the sensible world as the sphere of ought-governed action (283). Being, however, is here understood verbally (*verbaliter;* 166), as the absolute life of a self-contained I (153): where there is being (*das Seyn*) there is the I (*das Ich*), and where the I, being. Nevertheless, activity has been shifted from the positing finite consciousness in the 1794 *Wisenschaftslehre* to the Absolute self in the 1804 work.

Thus, through an original (genetic) penetration (*Einsicht*) of life and self there is the basic source and ground of all clarity. But while objective, it is unnoticed (*WZV*, 153). The light is an absolute qualitative unity, though a hidden one (231). Still, although the light is essentially one, there is a double genesis or origin. There is the absolute origin, which exists as a simple fact without any possible further external ground (*Sein* as absolute *Nichtgenesis*). But there is also a light that is absolutely self-originating, an origin that is a self-origin (*Sichgenesis;* 227–31), granted an invisible origination (238). An absolute "what" is given, not its "how" (163). It is because this represents the primal self-made person ("What am I, after all, but that into which I make myself?")[8] that Fichte can refer to this as a new and higher idealism (183).

Second, there remains the moral idealism of the ought (*Soll;* see *WZV*, 175 ff.). However, in accordance with the self-origination of the light, as in itself, by itself, from itself, and through itself (180), if the light ought to be (*soll*), and if it is an absolute From (*Von*), so must (*muß*) it be (211). The light splits into a duality through this absolute "ought"; Fichte insists that there is no philosophy of this, only of the I (188–89). Contained in this shift from an "ought," from an absolute From, to a "must," is the shift from ethics to religion. Still, while Fichte may speak of this "ought" as the confirmed standpoint of religion as faith, the God of this religion is still, basically, the God of the moral law (282), a law (*Gesetz*) that posits (*setzt*) itself in us (250). It may be a higher idealism, by virtue of this shift from the ethical to the religious, but nonetheless it remains a higher *moral* idealism.

There is no light without creation, so creation is inseparable from the light, thus only is it (creation) through and in the light. The absolute light represents an absolute From (*WZV*, 196–97). Every From, as origin, posits light, as the light posits the origin or genesis. The appearance (*Erscheinung*) of the light derives from the light (199–200).[9] The absolute From, which Fichte terms a primal From (*Urvon*) or primal light (*Urlicht*), is presupposed. The From, then, is the pure, absolute, immediate unity. But there is also a self-positing of this *Urlicht*. The first creation derives from here; and with a split in this *Urlicht* one gets the second creation (*Nacherschaffung*). This appearance is itself an origin or genesis (206–7, 210). This is not a simple From, but, as he says, a From in the From and a From of the From (*Von im Von, und Von des Von;* 221). Again, there is here a double genesis or origination. In Fichte, as is typical in German idealism generally, a close connection is drawn between creation and incarnation.

In addition to the absolute self-contained light that cannot come out of itself (*WZV*, 160) and the self-created, yet hidden, light that is the revealing and externalizing of God (172), there is also the absolute light that we ourselves are, and it we. There is a genesis or origin here as well.[10] There is the positing of an absolute being of knowledge in knowledge, which here is not "irrational" (217). However, although Fichte may speak of the understanding and reason as one, there is no insight into the essence of reason (the Logos?) without presupposing the understanding as absolute; and, on the other hand, no insight into the essence of the understanding without its absolute denial by reason (218–19). (Again, Hegel's speculative Good Friday?) Thus, when I say something (*prädicere*) about the light, the light says something about itself, it predicates itself (240). This does not mean that we do the construction; rather, it constructs itself before us and is posited in us (247). The insight of (or into) the origin is the factical *Dasein*, the appearing of the absolute knowing in us; *Dasein* has its ground in an absolute purpose that it should be absolute knowledge, by virtue of knowing the absolute image. This *is* life (253–55).

There thus exists a penetrating seeing, which, as independent, posits an absolute being, the description of a self-contained certitude (*WZV*, 266). It represents a seeing of the seeing (*Sehen des Sehens;* 268) of the light.[11] Reason is the ground of its intrinsic (*innerlich*) living and acting existence (*Dasein;* 270); reason itself is immediately and simply ground of an existence, its existence, as a pure absolute fact. And we are ourselves reason (272) in that we see this light. This reason appears as the ground or cause of its own existence, of its objectivity, for itself, and herein rests its original life (275). It is in this sense that Fichte can speak of the theory of reason (*Vernunftlehre*) as the first and most important part of the *Wissenschaftslehre* (268–69), for in it, in this penetrating seeing, we see the light through a pure absolute fact (272). It is in the light that we see the light.

At the very beginning of the 1804 lectures Fichte asks the question: what are we seeking when we seek the truth? Characteristic of the philosophies of the nineteenth and twentieth centuries, the question is indicative of philosophy's heightened self-awareness, a consciousness of what one is doing when one does philosophy. In the 1804 lectures, the answer given is, I think, essentially that of Hegel at the end of the *Phenomenology of Spirit*, namely that religion, above all Christianity, is the content of which philosophy is the form. As Fichte says, the inner essence of knowledge (*Wissen*) can be expressed only in the concept (*Begriff*), indeed in a primal concept (*Urbegriff; WZV*, 92). However, Hegel would, I am sure, still find Fichte's "concept" deficient. For Hegel, Fichte's I is an empty, lifeless thinking, a self merely "reflecting itself into itself." This self, this absolute self may be subject, but it is not substance. It would not represent a shape (*Gestalt*) freed from its appearance in consciousness. Hence, it would not yet be Spirit. It would not yet be the absolute knowing (*absolutes Wissen*) of a certainty brought to the In-and-for-itself of Truth, the comprehensive knowing that would know itself in the form or shape of Spirit.[12]

Hegel did not read the work we have been dealing with here. He was unaware of what Fichte had to say about "emanence," the externalization (*Äusserung*) of the light, in the *Wissenschaftslehre* of 1804. The lectures were given privately to a small circle at a private dwelling in Berlin. Nevertheless, Hegel did read the popular presentation of this work in the 1806 *Anweisung*, a work which, unfortunately, overly emphasizes the appearance aspect of the Logos of the prologue to the fourth Gospel, but does not emphasize its emanence aspect. There is, indeed, another serious defect in Fichte's reflections. He did not read far enough into John's Gospel. He failed to get to the central notion of Spirit. This means that he also failed to elaborate a theory of community, and develop the kind of social theory that could have provided the basis for his political interests and concerns.

Further, although I have my doubts that Heidegger read much of the later Fichte, he would have found in Fichte's identification of *Sein* with God, as in the philosophy of Hegel, an example of *Onto-Theo-Logie*,[13] and would insist on the need to get God out of metaphysics, as Being out of theology. In other words, he would fault Fichte with the same charge that he does Hegel.

Fichte likely falls into another Hegelian trap, namely that of a pistol-shot Absolute.[14] For in the 1804 second set of lectures on the *Wissenschaftslehre*, Fichte simply begins with the Absolute and with *Absolutes Wissen*. He does not travel the long road that it takes to get to the concept or *Begriff*. True thoughts, thoughts concerning the truth, and scientific insight can be won only through the work of the concept, a working out of the concept, the for-itself of self-certainty worked out in the in-itself of reality.[15] In the end, Hegel would say that Fichte avoids the *Mühe der Wissenschaft*, the arduous task of science.

Notes

1. G. J. Seidel, "The Atheism Controversy of 1799 and the Christology of Fichte's *Anweisung zum seligen Leben* of 1806," in *New Perspectives on Fichte*, ed. Tom Rockmore and Daniel Breazeale, 143–51 (New York: Humanities, 1995).

2. *WZV*, 255.

3. *SW* 5:542; see also *SW* 5:570.

4. *SW* 1:115.

5. *SW* 1:115.

6. As I have indicated earlier, Fichte most likely gets this distinction between being (*Seyn,* God the Father) and factical existence (*Daseyn,* the Christ, God the Son) from Schelling's *Vom Ich als Prinzip* of 1795. See Rockmore and Breazeale, eds., *New Perspectives on Fichte,* 146n21.

7. *SW* 1:111. The Christological significance of the word *Erscheinung* will become even clearer in the *Anweisung.*

8. *SW* 4:227.

9. Fichte had earlier spoken of this appearance as the revelation and externality of God: "Die Erscheinung, die hier in ihrem höchsten Punkte als innerlich genetische Construction des Absoluten erfasst ist, als die Offenbarung und Äusserung Gottes" (*WZV,* 172).

10. "Wir sind selber das absolute Licht, und das absolute Licht wir, und es ist hier selbst Genesis" (*WZV,* 214–15).

11. This is a theme that will be taken up later in the *Wissenschaftslehre* of 1812, as pointed out by Johannes Brachtendorf, *Fichtes Lehre vom Sein* (Paderborn: Schöningh, 1995), 296.

12. G. W. F. Hegel, *Phenomenology of Spirit,* trans. A. V. Miller (Oxford: Clarendon, 1977), 483, 485, and 489ff.

13. Martin Heidegger, *Identität und Differenz* (Pfullingen: Neske, 1957), 56–57.

14. Hegel, *Phenomenology of Spirit,* 15–16.

15. Hegel, *Phenomenology of Spirit,* 43.

After Jena: Fichte's *Religionslehre*

Yolanda Estes

Introduction

In the winter of 1805–6, Fichte delivered a series of lectures titled *Die Anweisung zum seligen Leben oder auch der Religionslehre* (henceforth, *Religionslehre*). In the "Preface" to the *Religionslehre,* he asserts:

> These lectures . . . are entirely the result of my unremitting development—during the past six or seven years of more leisure and greater maturity—of a philosophical view that came to me thirteen years ago. Although I hope a good many things might have changed in me, no part of this view itself has changed since that time.[1]

Despite this assertion, the tone and language in Fichte's *Religionslehre* seem to disown his early philosophy of religion. The *Religionslehre* appears to reject the modest task of "explaining the system of representations accompanied by a feeling of necessity," which he specified in the early philosophy.[2] Indeed, a first reading of the *Religionslehre* might lead one to believe that Fichte replaced the doctrine of infinite striving with the doctrine of the Absolute. Christoph Asmuth asks:

> Could this Fichte, who was forced to leave Jena under scandalous circumstances, now have changed from Saul to Paul? Could the atheist Fichte now—seven or eight years later—have been transformed into a believing Christian, into an exegete of the holy scripture, into a preacher of the gospel?[3]

Is the *Religionslehre,* which Fritz Medicus describes as "eines der reifsten und tiefsten Werke der gesamten Literatur der Menschheit," a monstrous hybrid that combines the worst features of dogmatic theology, fanatical mysticism, and absolute idealism?[4] In this essay, I shall argue for the relatively controversial position that Fichte's *Religionslehre* reflects no profound departure from his early philosophy of religion or, at least, that it signifies no "repudiation" of the ideas of God, religion, and philosophy expressed in his early works, such as "Über den Grund unseres Glaubens an eine göttliche Weltregierung" (1798), "Aus einem Privatschreiben" (1800), *Die Bestimmung des Menschen* (1800), or the lectures on the *Wissenschaftslehre nova methodo* (1796–98).[5] More specifically, I maintain that the *Religionslehre* clarifies some important distinctions between Fichte's concepts of morality and religion, but it reveals fewer and less significant changes in his concepts of God and philosophy. My essay assumes the structure described below.

In the first section ("A Popular Presentation of an Empirical Guide to Blessedness"), I describe the *Religionslehre* as a popular presentation of an empirical (or practical) account of blessedness.[6] In the second section ("Morality and Religion in the *Religionslehre*"), I compare this account of blessedness to Fichte's "Über den Grund unseres Glaubens an eine göttliche Weltregierung," "Aus einem Privatschreiben," and *Die Bestimmung des Menschen.* I indicate significant changes in Fichte's understanding of morality and religion, but I suggest that these changes reinforce rather than undermine his early philosophy. In the third section ("A Popular Presentation of a Transcendental Philosophy of Religion"), I describe the *Religionslehre* as a popular presentation of a transcendental philosophy of religion based on the principles of the *Wissenschaftslehre.* In the fourth section ("Philosophy and God in the *Religionslehre*"), I compare this philosophy to the *Wissenschaftslehre nova methodo,* arguing that the *Religionslehre* remains consistent with Fichte's concepts of God and philosophy during the Jena period. In the concluding section, I explain briefly that the *Religionslehre* does not represent dogmatic theology, mysticism, or absolute idealism.

A Popular Presentation of an Empirical Guide to Blessedness

The *Religionslehre* contains a guide to blessedness, because it teaches the way to a blessed life. It is empirical, or practical, insofar as it speaks to the empirical individual at the standpoint of life. It is a popular presentation, because it illustrates the truth without the mediation of argument and without deriving or demonstrating anything.[7] In the *Religionslehre,* Fichte leads the listener (or reader) to understand (*verstanden*) the conclusions that he (Fichte) has already demonstrated to himself.[8]

In the *Religionslehre,* Fichte claims that life consists in the original duality of a self-conscious I, which strives to unite its divided, finite consciousness with the eternal—*Sein*—or God. This drive is man's fundamental interest or love. Love consists in self-satisfaction, self-enjoyment, and blessedness; and thus true life, love, and blessedness are the same.[9] Each individual life obtains its unique character by virtue of its love or interest.

> Show me what you truly love—what you seek and strive for with all your desire in hope of finding true enjoyment of yourself—and you have thereby revealed your life to me. As you love, so you live. This very love is simply your life and the root, the seat, and the middle point of your life.[10]

If true life is satisfied and blessed, then most human beings would only appear to be alive. A truly blessed life would be a self-sufficient whole in which every moment possessed its own perfection, but most lives involve an ever-changing cycle in which one moment consumes the preceding moment. The reason for this feeling of unease in time is that blessedness depends on "Liebe, Streben, Trieb" for unification with the eternal.[11] Although this drive dominates all human life, some individuals feel it without understanding or satisfying it, because they seek happiness in the sensible world, which is the only reality they perceive.[12]

Eventually such individuals despair.[13] They perhaps renounce happiness and denigrate all striving as "Treiben im Nichts, um das Nichts."[14] Their despondency leads some to scorn the present world and to console themselves with images of a "future world" in which they expect to satisfy their sensible desires.[15] Others try to earn happiness through "virtuous" action, failing to grasp: "Die Seligkeit erwerben können wir nicht, unser Elend aber abzuwerfen vermögen wir, worauf sogleich durch sich selber die Seligkeit an desselben Stelle treten wird."[16]

In other words, misery is a deprivation of clear consciousness, which requires "klare und lebendige Denken," "Ernst," or "Tiefsinn."[17] Consciousness consists in thinking, so individuals who do not truly think do not truly live.[18] Any aspect of life that does not enter a *particular* individual's *consciousness* plays no role in *that* individual's *life*. No individual finds itself dirempted from life entirely, but sensibility obscures the undeveloped subject's view of itself and the world.

The individual perceives and enjoys itself and the world through the objects of its love, which its drives and interests determine. At the lowest level of conscious development, the individual loves itself and believes in its personal, individual freedom, but the objects in which the individual seeks its satisfaction establish the nature of its self-love.[19] At the level of sensibility, the sensuous individual's self-love expresses itself as desire for particular sensible objects. When the sensuous individual enjoys the desired objects, it feels itself to be free, but the sensuous gratification is never forthcoming, so the individual seeks new, different, and better objects; and its own nature changes with every passing desire. The sensuous individual finds itself as dependent and dissipated—unfree and unhappy—because it disperses its thinking and energy among a multitude of things that fail to satisfy its needs.

Sensibility negates itself by destroying the individual's interest in itself and the world. At the level of legality, love of law replaces sensuous self-love.[20] The stoic individual submits itself to an ethical law in an attempt to become self-sufficient. Although the individual escapes sensuous desires and compulsions, the resulting sense of freedom is merely negative, empty, and formal, because its freedom consists in its ability to obey or disobey the law.[21] The stoic individual acts only to avoid self-condemnation, but its activity provides no positive gratification. Indeed, every personal inclination threatens the stoic individual's freedom, so it renounces happiness.

The stoic individual determines itself in opposition to its inclinations. To the extent that it resists desire, it feels free, but its freedom is aimless. The law and the individual will coincide in the stoic's act of self-determination. Nonetheless, insofar as it chooses freely to obey the law, it holds forth the possibility of opposing the law and thus, the law appears as an external will. The stoic individual adopts an indifferent attitude to the external will, which is the source of a categorical imperative.[22]

By determining its will according to a categorical imperative, the stoic individual renounces its individual, personal will and thus, higher morality replaces legality. At the level of higher morality, the moral individual views its individuality as an expression of the external will—a pure will—which it adopts as its own and loves as itself. Immediate consciousness reveals to each moral individual a vocation wherein the divine will, the individual will, and desire coincide.[23] Hence, the moral subject's fundamental command is: "Wolle sein . . . was du sein sollst, was du sein kannst, und was du eben darum sein willst."[24]

Although the moral individual's freedom and desire coincide in its inner intelligible willing, it wants its will to be efficacious in the sensible world. To the extent that this produces an outer sensible result, it feels contented, but it feels failure as an affront to its freedom and as a frustration of its desire. Nonetheless, this feeling of limitation compels the moral individual to reflect on itself and thereby, to clarify its intelligible goal.[25] Insofar as the moral individual recognizes that its goal consists in developing the intelligible world, it believes that its willing succeeds. Moral willing implies this belief and the concomitant belief in the sensible sphere of free activity. Self-conscious faith in the ultimate success of intelligible willing distinguishes the level of religion from morality.

The moral-religious individual views the sensible world and its own personality as means to a life of faith in action. It strives within the world without needing to change the world, because faith reveals a new intelligible world within the sensible world.[26] The moral-religious individual recognizes that the outer result of its willing depends partly on other individuals' freedom, which it ought not to thwart, and thus, it wills a sensible result conditionally as a temporal manifestation of the divine life. It promotes others' freedom, because its ultimate task is to cultivate freedom in itself and others. The moral-religious individual acts in the sensible world, but it loves the intelligible world, or namely, freedom itself.

According to Fichte, this love creates the concept of God; and the human subject is God insofar as it lives in this love. Without love, the human subject cannot act morally, because the intelligible world does not exist for it. Without moral action, there is no God. Moral activity is itself complete and thus, despite individual failure and death, the religious subject believes in its fellow men and hopes for their future. It treats others as if they were what they ought to be and as it expects them to become. The moral-religious individual has immediate conviction of its vocation, so it does not fear the future.[27] It devotes itself wholly to its present activity, so it does not mourn the past.

Morality and Religion in the *Religionslehre*

As an empirical account of blessedness, the *Religionslehre* emphasizes human goodness, on the one hand, and human happiness, on the other hand. This dual emphasis constitutes an important change in Fichte's approach to morality and religion, but it enriches rather than undermines his early writings on the subject. In "Über den Grund unseres Glaubens an eine göttliche Weltregierung" and *Die Bestimmung des Menschen,* Fichte rarely addresses happiness. Although happiness is irrelevant from a purely moral perspective, feeling constitutes part of the system of representations accompanied by a sense of necessity, which the philosopher is obliged to comprehend and the moral subject is obliged to master.[28] Consequently, the question of happiness deserves consideration in the context of the philosopher's attempt to understand consciousness and the moral subject's attempt to master itself.

The *Religionslehre* provides an oblique discussion of the unhappiness, or despair, of the moral subject.[29] Fichte's description of the sensible standpoint is a poignant illustration of human beings in a state of moral and emotional peril. The sensuous individual exists in a state of moral catalepsy. To the extent that it is self-conscious, its sensible desires enslave it. Moral despair arises within the standpoints of legality and morality, because the stoic individual and the moral individual are conscious of the tensions between their intelligible freedom and their sensible limitation.

The stoic individual defines freedom as independence. It attempts to preserve its independence by resisting anything that threatens to determine its will and thus, it breaks the hold of sensuous compulsion and becomes aware of itself as an intelligible freedom. Nonetheless, its vain flight from external determination and self-condemnation leaves it opposed to its own desires, to other individuals, and to the ethical law itself. Overcome by moral despair, the stoic individual renounces happiness and submits its individuality to the categorical imperative.

The moral individual's desire, will, and duty coincide in its individual vocation, but it resents its failure to mold the sensible world (and the denizens thereof) in the image of the intelligible. Moral responsibility presupposes guilt for misdeeds and regret for inefficacy.[30] Every moral subject can know and obey the moral law; every moral subject feels shame for past transgressions and present shortcomings.[31] The ethical law remits no wrong, so inconsolable remorse often consumes the moral subject. Overcome by the magnitude of its own inefficacy and culpability, the moral individual succumbs to moral despair, which the ideal of the moral-religious consciousness mitigates.[32]

In "Göttliche Weltregierung" and *Bestimmung des Menschen,* "morality" and "religion" refer to the same beliefs and behaviors. Morality consists in obeying the ethical law, which coincides with implicit belief in a moral world order whereby willing becomes efficacious.[33] Religion consists in cheerfully satisfying duty without regard for the consequences.[34] In the *Religionslehre,* Fichte elevates moral-religious consciousness above moral consciousness. Although the moral individual and the moral-religious individual share identical beliefs and behaviors, the moral-religious individual's belief in the intelligible world constitutes an explicit feature of its consciousness and thus, it views the sensible world, its fellow man, and its own empirical self differently.[35]

In "Aus einem Privatschreiben," Fichte claims that the question of sensible results would never arise if the moral subject were a pure will and thus, not constrained to act in time.[36] The moral subject wills as a supersensible subject in an intelligible world governed by the law of freedom, but it also acts as a sensible subject in an empirical world constituted by *a priori* principles of intuition and cognition. It must think of its intelligible willing as accompanied by a sensible action that initiates a temporal series of causes and effects, but the sensible action and its effects are separable from the intelligible act of willing.[37] The ethical law commands an autonomous determination of the will, which is both the motive and the goal of morality. Preoccupation with the sensible results of moral activity betrays a moral subject's indecisiveness about the nature of morality and doubt about its ability to fulfill its vocation. The moral-religious individual believes that moral willing always succeeds and hence, it renounces sensible results without abdicating its moral vocation.[38]

In the *Bestimmung des Menschen* and the *Wissenschaftslehre nova methodo,* Fichte claims that a summons from another rational being initiates individual ethical consciousness.[39] Each individual must answer the summons that defines its vocation according to its own conscience.[40] To the extent that the moral subject views itself in abstraction from a social context, it falls prey to the vain illusion that the goal of morality depends on its individual will alone. Such a subject fails to grasp that its individuality serves as a means to expand the realm of freedom.[41] This arrogance leads it to devalue others and to despair of its own task.[42] In the *Religionslehre,* Fichte describes the moral-religious individual as conceding its own limitations and deferring to others' freedom, on which its goal depends.[43] Moreover, the moral-religious subject relinquishes its preoccupation with its own past—not simply because it cannot change the past—because the entire constitution of its inner drives and motivations has already been transformed.[44] The consequences of its former sensuous personality become parts of the unique set of obstacles that it is obliged to overcome on its path toward a good will and a good life.[45]

A Popular Presentation of a Transcendental Philosophy of Religion

The *Religionslehre* shows the way to blessedness, but it also contains a popular presentation of Fichte's transcendental philosophy of religion. The latter is transcendental insofar as it relates God to the system of human consciousness and thus, also presents the general principles of the *Wissenschaftslehre.* It is a popular exposition, because it communicates the philosophical conclusion that conscience (and concomitant belief in God) grounds consciousness without demonstrating the details of how a determinable world and a determinate individual arise from God (or *Sein*).[46]

Philosophy attempts to account for experience, which includes both sensations and consciousness of sensations.[47] Although some philosophies try to ground consciousness on sensation, consciousness is never felt sensibly and thus, such philosophies fail to explain experience. As a determination of consciousness, sensation presupposes consciousness. Transcendental philosophy grounds sensation on consciousness. The transcendental philosopher abstracts from sensible consciousness and relates it to an intelligible ground.

Philosophical reflection has no intrinsic limit and thus, yields no ground of consciousness. The transcendental philosopher simply postulates a self-sufficient ground, which Fichte calls *Sein* or God in the *Religionslehre.* Nonetheless, this ground is not immediately present in empirical consciousness. Insofar as *Sein* exists, it is a concept without consciousness. This concept and the actual consciousness that represents it must be mutually dependent and opposed. Consequently, actual consciousness finds itself divided as representing subject and represented object. The existence of *Sein* must be conceived as a pure self-consciousness, but reflection cannot escape consciousness to comprehend the original determination of *Sein* as *Dasein.*

> *Dasein* simply cannot be without finding, grasping, and presupposing itself, inasmuch as self-apprehension is inseparable from its being; and thus, knowledge, through the certainty of its existence, and through its dependence on its existence, is cut off from any possibility of passing beyond itself, or of conceiving, or deriving, itself apart from its existence.[48]

Everything that enters consciousness falls under the laws of cognition. Hence, *Sein* enters consciousness as a concept. Other than the reciprocal opposition of *Sein* (or God) and *Dasein* (or actual consciousness), nothing exists except as a determination of consciousness; thus, actual consciousness is God's existence. The transcendental philosopher must explain the original division of this unity.

Sein and *Dasein* are united, but the laws of thinking require us to conceive of *Sein as Sein* (as something determinable in opposition to a determinate consciousness). This law—the principle of reflective opposition—governs all cognition and generates all division in consciousness. Cognition is discursive and thus, cannot think of anything "in itself" but only in reciprocal opposition to something else. Every object enters consciousness through representation; and thus, when the knowing subject attempts to make itself an object of consciousness, it must grasp itself through representation. The knowing subject grasps itself piecemeal—as a series of acts—because it thinks discursively. Were it able to comprehend itself as a whole, it would grasp God; but consciousness introduces a division between *Sein* and *Dasein.* In thinking *Sein,* consciousness posits it as an independent being, which appears within consciousness as a world.

In self-reflection, the knowing subject observes itself as representation. *Dasein* ought to be something determinate in opposition to the determinable *Sein;* and this "ought" issues from an external will. Hence, God is determined as self-consciousness, or actual freedom. The knowing subject becomes aware of itself as a determinate self-consciousness that stands opposed to something determinable, because in reflection, all knowledge is of the particular. Consciousness appears to itself as a world, which is determined as an infinite manifold in time because reflection is infinite and free.

Actual consciousness is the divine *Dasein,* which grasps itself and becomes self-conscious so that its "being"—*Sein*—becomes a world for it. Consciousness contains nothing but the world, but the immediate divine life is the "being of consciousness" (*Sein des Bewußtseins*), which conditions the possibility of empirical consciousness. Every actual consciousness involves an act of reflection, which divides the world into an infinite multiplicity, of which a finite series enters each actual consciousness. The fundamental form of representation constrains thinking; thus, the world and its counterpart, the divine life, are not reflected upon as wholes.

> This one *Sein* is divided into an unending succession of forms through reflection, which in real consciousness is inseparably united with *Sein.* This division is, as said, something simply original that can never be eliminated or superseded by anything else in real consciousness: so, the real forms, which obtain reality through this division, can only exist in real consciousness.[49]

This original division is ineliminable from actual consciousness. In order to account for sensible consciousness, the transcendental philosopher postulates *Sein* as a mere hypothesis. In reflection, *Sein* is originally divided into *Sein* and *Dasein. Dasein* itself is divided into its appearance as a determinate consciousness and as an infinitely determinable world. Actual consciousness perceives the world from five perspectives: (1) as a sensuous subject, (2) as a juridical subject, (3) as a moral subject, (4) as a religious subject, and (5) as a philosophizing subject.

Philosophy and God in the *Religionslehre*

The *Religionslehre* expands the rudimentary philosophy of religion that Fichte expounded during the Jena period. The concepts of God and philosophy contained in the *Religionslehre* correspond to the concepts of God and philosophy in Fichte's early philosophy of religion. Moreover, the essential principles of the *Religionslehre* overlap with the fundamental principles of the early *Wissenschaftslehre.*[50]

Although philosophy is not necessary for most individuals to attain a blessed state, it serves two main purposes for individual human beings.[51] First, philosophy mitigates the tensions between reason and conscience that distress many individuals.[52] Nonetheless, satisfying this need does not require such an individual to comprehend a rigorous exposition of a philosophical system, because a popular exposition, such as the *Religionslehre,* reconciles knowledge and faith by illustrating their harmony in human consciousness. Second, philosophy is one possible vocation for individuals who have a talent for reflection and a drive for knowledge.[53] Satisfying this need requires abstraction and inner, or intellectual, intuition.[54] The task of philosophical science is to relate sensible consciousness to its ground.[55] The transcendental philosopher abstracts from experience in order to demonstrate the necessary conditions for empirical consciousness, which include space, time, material objects, and individual subjects.[56]

Philosophical reflection has no intrinsic limit, so the philosopher must assume a starting point, or foundation.[57] In the *Wissenschaftslehre nova methodo,* Fichte calls this foundation the pure will. In "Über den Grund unseres Glaubens an eine göttliche Weltregierung" and *Bestimmung des Menschen,* he calls it the moral world order, or God. In the *Religionslehre,* it is God, or *Sein.* The pure will, the moral world order, God, and *Sein* play the same role in Fichte's philosophy.[58] As a concept, each falls under the law of reflective opposition.[59] Due to this law, the concept of a ground gives rise to a division within itself.[60] The transcendental philosopher cannot conceive of pure consciousness except as standing in reciprocal determination with empirical consciousness.[61] Consequently, thinking cannot escape the circle of consciousness to comprehend its ground.[62] Were the philosophizing subject able to comprehend its own consciousness as a whole, it would grasp the Absolute; but it must grasp itself as a series of acts, because it thinks discursively.[63]

Like the *Wissenschaftslehre nova methodo,* the *Religionslehre* culminates in the *synthetic periodum.*[64] *Sein* has the form of an I that is originally determined as individuality.[65] The original determination of the pure will, or *Sein,* is the explanatory ground, or central point, of consciousness, which the transcendental philosopher simply postulates as a hypothesis, or *qualitas occulta;* however, it can only be justified in actual consciousness.[66] In the *Religionslehre* and the *Wissenschaftslehre nova methodo,* Fichte's description of how this intelligible ground appears in empirical consciousness is the same. The reciprocal opposition of *Sein* and *Dasein,* or the pure will and the empirical will, appears as a feeling of desire.[67] A summons, or a feeling of "ought," initiates the individual's awareness of itself as a determinate freedom in a determinable realm of other rational beings.[68] In the *Nova Methodo,* this summons remains a theoretical hypothesis, albeit one that appears to empirical consciousness as the ethical law.[69] In the *Religionslehre,* the *Bestimmung des Menschen,* and "Über den Grund unseres Glaubens an eine göttliche Weltregierung," this hypothesis becomes God.[70]

Fichte offers no substantial alteration of his concept of God in the *Religionslehre*. Considered practically or transcendentally, the concept of God belongs among the "representations accompanied by a sense of necessity" that transcendental philosophy explains.[71] Considered practically, this idea is the object of the empirical subject's belief in a will that issues a categorical imperative.[72] For the empirical subject, God is a subjectively necessary reality that provides the ultimate pre-philosophical justification for the ground of the *Wissenschaftslehre*.[73] Considered transcendentally, this concept is the philosopher's hypothesis of the pure will, which contains its own law and concept of a goal.[74] For the philosopher, God is a "transcendentally objective reality."[75]

In the *Religionslehre* and the *Wissenschaftslehre nova methodo,* God represents the central point, the highest synthesis, and the *Erklärungsgrund* of all consciousness, which is determined by the laws of thinking as individual consciousness and the world.[76] Although God binds all individual I's as one, this unity must be thought discursively as an infinite series of determinate lives and individual conscious subjects.[77] From the practical perspective, this ongoing discursive thinking of God is revealed as an infinite progress (the postulate of immortality).[78] From the perspective of religion particularly, the religious (or blessed) life is simply what the moral-religious individual does.

> In whatever the holy man does, lives, and loves, God appears: no longer hidden by shadows or cloaked in garb but rather in his own, immediate, and efficacious life. The question, which the empty, obscure notion of God cannot answer—What is God?—is answered here. He is whatever his devoted and inspired follower does. Do you want to see God, as he is in himself, face to face? Do not search for him in the clouds. You can find him wherever you are. Just look at his followers' lives and you see him. Give yourself to him and you find him in your own breast.[79]

Conclusion

A comparison of the *Religionslehre* with texts from the Jena period reveals no solid reasons for supposing that Fichte abandoned transcendental idealism and the doctrine of infinite striving for dogmatic theology, fanatical mysticism, or absolute idealism. The *Religionslehre* represents no dogmatic theology, because it presents a theory of God in relation to human consciousness. Immediate consciousness of the ethical law implies belief in freedom and God, which resemble the moral world order and the pure will more closely than a personal, transcendent deity.[80] One must discount

Fichte's explicit rejection of mysticism in order to call the *Religionslehre* "mystical."[81] The *Religionslehre* outlines a theory of consciousness based on the Absolute, but it is not an absolute idealism, because it remains a transcendental and foundational project.[82] Moreover, it expounds no reconciliation of duality but rather the claim that duality is ineliminable.[83] Rather than undermining the notions of infinite striving or human finitude, the *Religionslehre* stresses the interdependence of moral, social, and religious consciousness. Rather than obscuring morality, religion, and philosophy, the *Religionslehre* shows that these are separate activities connected only within the empirical individual who acts, believes, and knows.

Notes

1. *RL,* 3. (All translations of the *Religionslehre* in this chapter are mine.) Compare "Aus einem Privatschreiben," in *GA* 1.6:369–70; in English, *IWL,* 157.

2. *Versuch einer neuen Darstellung der Wissenschaftslehre,* in *GA* 1.4:186; in English, *IWL,* 8.

3. Christoph Asmuth, "Wissenschaft und Religion: Perspektivität und Absolutes in der Philosophie Johann Gottlieb Fichtes," *Fichte-Studien* 8, no. 1 (my translation).

4. F. Medicus, "Preface," in *RL,* iii. See also Heinrich Scholz, "Preface," in *Fichte: Die Anweisung zum seligen Leben* (Wald: Pontifica Universitas Gregoriana, 1966), 12; and Nicolai Hartmann, *Die Philosophie des deutschen Idealismus* (Berlin: De Gruyter, 1974), 3.

5. In this regard, I follow Ives Radrizzani's approach to *Die Bestimmung des Menschen.* Radrizzani says: "No conversion to Jacobi, no romantic mysticism, no recourse to a 'transsubjective basis,' no turning from idealism to realism can be found in the *Vocation of Man;* we discover there instead a living and graphic presentation of the main results of the *Wissenschaftslehre,* as they are exposed particularly in the *Wissenschaftslehre nova methodo*" (Ives Radrizzani, "The Place of the *Vocation of Man* in Fichte's Work," in *New Essays on Fichte's Later Jena Wissenschaftslehre,* ed. Daniel Breazeale and Tom Rockmore [Evanston: Northwestern University Press, 2002], 337). For another discussion of the place of *Die Bestimmung des Menschen* in Fichte's work, see Alexis Philonenko, *L'Oeuvre de Fichte* (Paris: Vrin, 1984), 87.

6. For various interpretations, see Hansjürgen Verweyen, "Introduction," in *ASL;* Edith Düsing, "Sittliches Streben und religiöse Vereinigung: Untersuchungen zu Fichtes später Religionsphilosophie," in *Religionsphilosophie und spekulative Theologie: Der Streit um die Göttlichen Dinge (1799–1812),* ed. W. Jaeschke (Hamburg: Meiner, 1994); Asmuth, "Wissenschaft und Religion," 1–20.

7. For a discussion of the distinction between a popular and a philosophical exposition of truth, see *RL,* 32–33; compare *VM,* 1–2.

8. At the beginning of the *Religionslehre,* Fichte states his intentions to the listener (reader): "Ich ersuche sie bloß, was sie, ohne Zweifel auch ohne meine hilfe, ebensowohl würden haben können, was aber mir nur mit leichterer Mühe zu teil

wird . . . und so trage ich denn Ihnen an, das gemein Verständliche, zum Guten und Schönen und Ewigen Führende, was bei meinen spekulativen Arbeiten abfallen wird, hier Ihnen mitzuteilen, so gut ich es habe, und es mitzuteilen verstehe" (*RL,* 25). See also *RL,* 32.

9. *RL,* 12. Nonetheless, to the extent that life is unblessed—and an admixture of death and life—it is incomplete, apparent life, which only exists because it participates in true life (*RL,* 12; see also *RL,* 151). Compare: "Only in love is there life" (*VM,* 24–25).

10. *RL,* 13. Compare: "Whatever you perceive as a consequence of these boundaries possesses reality, the only kind of reality that pertains to you or exists for you" (*IWL,* 150; "Über den Grund unseres Glaubens an eine göttliche Weltregierung" [1798], in *GA* 1.5:353]). See also *WLNM* (1982), 144–45; *Wissenschaftslehre nova methodo,* in *GA* 4.2:136; in English, *FTP,* 294–95.

11. *RL,* 16.

12. *RL,* 17–18; compare *VM,* 78–79.

13. The following passage illustrates the sensuous subject's state of mind: "So sehnen sie, und änstigen, ihr Leben hin; in jeder Lage, in der sie sich befinden, denkend, wenn es nur *anders* mit ihnen werden möchte, so würde ihnen *besser* werden, und nachdem es anders geworden ist, sich doch nicht besser befindend; an jeder Stelle, an der sie stehen, meinend, wenn sie nur dort, auf der Anhöhe, die ihr Auge faßt, angelangt sein würden, würde ihre Beängstigun weichen; treu jedoch wiederfindend, auch auf der Anhöhe, ihren alten Kummer" (*RL,* 18).

14. *RL,* 19; compare *VM,* 81.

15. *RL,* 19. Fichte continues: "Und so irret denn der arme Abkömmling der Ewigkeit, verstoßen aus seiner väterlichen Wohnung, immer umgeben von seinem himmlischen Erbteile, nach welchem seine schüchterne Hand zu greifen, bloß sich fürchtet, unstet und flüchtig in der Wüste umher, allenthalben bemüht, sich anzubauen; zum Glück durch den baldigen Einsturtz jeder seiner Hütten erinnert, daß er nirgends Ruhe finden wird, als in seines Vaters Hause."

16. *RL,* 22. On true life as a moral choice, see also *VM,* 99.

17. *RL,* 21–22.

18. *RL,* 42.

19. *RL,* 126. On interest as a defining feature of individual life, see *VM,* 73. On the self-love of "the good," see *VM,* 84–85.

20. On rights, duties, and the standpoint of legality, see *VM,* 78–79.

21. The inherent flaw of this type of spiritual life is that it fails to rise to the level of true spirituality. The stoic individual rejects a capricious God who rewards obedience with sensible pleasures. Moreover, the stoic individual rejects any form of religion and love that depends on sensibility. Stoicism annihilates error without grasping the truth.

22. *RL,* 130. Compare: "It appears to come from a rational being outside of us" (*FTP,* 353; *WLNM* [1982], 178). See also *VM,* 80.

23. *RL,* 144; compare *VM,* 90.

24. *RL,* 146; see also *RL,* 145.

25. *RL,* 146–47; see also *RL,* 141–42.

26. *RL,* 136–37. On the intelligible world revealed to consciousness, see *VM,* 80–81; "Über den Grund," in *GA* 1.5:351; in English, *IWL,* 146–47.

27. *RL,* 162. On the infallibility of conscience, see *VM,* 75.

28. On the theoretical task to comprehend one's drives, see *VM,* 73.

29. Compare *RL,* 144 and *VM,* 90. Obviously, happiness cannot serve as a moral goal or motivation in Fichte's philosophy, and hence any discussion of happiness in his philosophy refers to something else. Philosophers such as Hegel have often objected to the futility, the rigor, and the slavishness of the doctrine of infinite striving. The obvious reply to such philosophers is that morality is not concerned with happiness. However, such an answer perhaps allows Fichte too easy an escape. Indeed, Fichte himself seems to give such objections a more serious consideration and answer in the *Religionslehre.* Morality is not concerned with happiness, but happiness concerns the moral subject *qua* sensible subject and hence concerns the philosopher as well.

30. *VM,* 18–19. Fichte continues: "I want to do everything for the best; want to feel glad about myself when I have done well, and sad about myself when I have done badly. And even this sadness is to be sweet to me, for it is an interest in myself and a pledge of future improvement. Only in love is there life; without it there is death and annihilation" (*VM,* 24).

31. Compare *RL,* 162 and *VM,* 75. On Fichte's claim, "I can because I ought," see "Über den Grund," in *GA* 1.5:352–53; in English, *IWL,* 148–49.

32. Fichte's concluding discussion in the *Religionslehre* indicates that the moral-religious subject is an ideal (*RL,* 174–78). His use of Schiller's "Das Ideal und Das Leben" supports this interpretation as well.

33. On the moral world order, see *VM,* 104–5.

34. "Über den Grund," in *GA* 1.5:354; in English, *IWL,* 150.

35. *RL,* 147–48; compare *VM,* 102–3.

36. "Aus einem Privatschreiben," in *GA* 1.6:384; in English, *IWL,* 172.

37. *VM,* 94–96; "Aus einem Privatschreiben," in *GA* 1.6:181–84; in English, *IWL,* 169–73.

38. *RL,* 136–37.

39. *VM,* 76–77 and 118–20. Compare *WLNM* (1982), 177–78; *Wissenschaftslehre nova methodo,* in *GA* 4.2:177–78; in English, *FTP,* 352.

40. *WLNM* (1982), 241; *Wissenschaftslehre nova methodo,* in *GA* 4.2:263; in English, *FTP,* 469.

41. *RL,* 149; see also *Das System der Sittenlehre,* in *GA* 1.5:230.

42. *VM,* 116–17.

43. *RL,* 148–49.

44. *RL,* 163. See also *RL,* 19, 22, 42–43, and 54; and *VM,* 99 and 102.

45. This aspect of moral consciousness is a very serious issue in Fichte's ethics and philosophy of religion, and thus it merits a more detailed account than I can offer here. I am grateful to Stephen Houlgate for helping to clarify this problem during our discussion at the conference on "Philosophy and Religion in German Idealism" sponsored by the Center for German Idealism, Catholic University, Nijmegen, Netherlands, January 2000.

46. *RL,* 83; compare *VM,* 99.

47. *RL,* 44. Compare *WLNM* (1982), 42; *Wissenschaftslehre nova methodo,* in *GA* 4.2:39; in English, *FTP,* 132.

48. *RL,* 53.

49. *RL,* 70.

50. *RL,* 20 and 41.

51. *RL,* 20 and 41. Fichte is not entirely consistent in this claim. He also suggests that full moral-religious consciousness depends on philosophy (*RL,* 28). Christoph Asmuth suggests the latter interpretation in "Wissenschaft und Religion."

52. Compare *RL,* 61–62 and *WLNM* (1982), 6–7; in English, *FTP,* 81. See also *RL,* 71 and *VM,* 26–27.

53. *VM,* 114–15.

54. *RL,* 51; see also *Wissenschaftslehre nova methodo,* in *GA* 4.2:38.

55. *RL,* 49.

56. *RL,* 70–71.

57. *RL,* 49. Compare *WLNM* (1982), 143; *Wissenschaftslehre nova methodo,* in *GA* 4.2:135; in English, *FTP,* 293; *VM,* 71; "Über den Grund," in *GA* 1.5:350n and 351; in English, *IWL,* 145–46n and 147.

58. On the moral world order as the absolute starting point of objective cognition, see "Über den Grund," in *GA* 1.5:354–55; in English, *IWL,* 151. On *Sein,* the pure will, and the moral world order, see *VM,* 99. On God as the pure will, or the divine will, and its connection to the *Aufforderung,* see *VM,* 107–11.

59. In the *Religionslehre,* this principle acquires a new name—the *Prinzip der Spaltung* or *Prinzip der Mannigfaltigkeit*—but serves the same function.

60. *RL,* 66–67.

61. *RL,* 52. On the law of reflective opposition, see *VM,* 70 and *WLNM* (1982), 38; in English, *FTP,* 125.

62. *RL,* 52. Compare: "This is impossible" (*FTP,* 413–14; *WLNM* [1982], 208).

63. *RL,* 64. Compare *WLNM* (1982), 67; *Wissenschaftslehre nova methodo,* in *GA* 4.2:61; in English, *FTP,* 173. See also *Grundlage der gesamten Wissenschaftslehre* (1794–95), in *GA* 1.2:275.

64. *RL,* 124 and *WLNM* (1982), 188; *Wissenschaftslehre nova methodo,* in *GA* 4.2:191; in English, *FTP,* 371. See also *WLNM* (1982), 216 and 219; in English, *FTP,* 427–28 and 434.

65. *RL,* 142.

66. Compare *RL,* 120 and *WLNM* (1982), 144; *Wissenschaftslehre nova methodo,* in *GA* 4.2:135; in English, *FTP,* 293–94. Compare also *RL,* 124 and *WLNM* (1982), 188; *Wissenschaftslehre nova methodo,* in *GA* 4.2:191; in English, *FTP,* 371.

67. Compare *RL,* 126 and *WLNM* (1982), 145; *Wissenschaftslehre nova methodo,* in *GA* 4.2:136; in English, *FTP,* 295. See also *WLNM* (1982), 189; *Wissenschaftslehre nova methodo,* in *GA* 4.2:192; in English, *FTP,* 373.

68. Compare *RL,* 129 and *WLNM* (1982), 145; *Wissenschaftslehre nova methodo,* in *GA* 4.2:136; in English, *FTP,* 295.

69. *WLNM* (1982), 143 and 151.

70. The scope of this essay precludes a thorough discussion of the relation between the original determination of the pure will and moral-religious conscious-

ness. For a more detailed account, see my "Intellectual Intuition, the Pure Will, and the Categorical Imperative in the Later Jena *Wissenschaftslehre*," in Breazeale and Rockmore, eds., *New Essays on Fichte's Later Jena Wissenschaftslehre*, 209–25.

71. *WLNM* (1982), 22; *Wissenschaftslehre nova methodo*, in *GA* 4.2:25; in English, *FTP*, 102. Compare: "We thus could express the task of philosophy in different words as follows: Philosophy has to display the basis or foundation of all experience" (*IWL*, 8; *Versuch einer neuen Darstellung der Wissenschaftslehre*, in *GA* 1.4:186).

72. *RL*, 66. On the "ought" as a command issuing from the pure will, see *WLNM* (1982), 144; *Wissenschaftslehre nova methodo*, in *GA* 4.2:136; in English, *FTP*, 294.

73. *WLNM* (1982), 145–47; *Wissenschaftslehre nova methodo*, in *GA* 4.2:137–39; in English, *FTP*, 295–98.

74. *RL*, 66.

75. *WLNM* (1982), 106–7; *Wissenschaftslehre nova methodo*, in *GA* 4.2:96–98 and 172; in English, *FTP*, 230–32. Compare *RL*, 120. On the difference between a "necessary belief" and a "pious wish," see "Über den Grund," in *GA* 1.5:348; in English, *IWL*, 144. On the necessity of an intelligible world, see *Versuch einer neuen Darstellung der Wissenschaftslehre*, in *GA* 1.4:210n; in English, *IWL*, 38n.

76. *RL*, 144. Compare *WLNM* (1982), 67 and 144–45; *Wissenschaftslehre nova methodo*, in *GA* 4.2:61–62 and 135–37; in English, *FTP*, 174 and 293–95. See also *VM*, 116; *RL*, 68. Compare: "The empirical will is derived from the pure will and all other objects are derived from the object of the pure will" (*FTP*, 293; *WLNM* [1982], 143).

77. *RL*, 20 and 68. Compare *WLNM* (1982), 213 and 423; in English, *FTP*, 422–24. See also *Wissenschaftslehre nova methodo*, in *GA* 4.2:230–31; in English, *FTP*, 451–53; and "Aus einem Privatschreiben," in *GA* 1.6:384; in English, *IWL*, 172–73.

78. On the objective reality of immortality, see *WLNM* (1982), 22–24; *Wissenschaftslehre nova methodo*, in *GA* 4.2:25–26; in English, *FTP*, 102–4. On immortality and heaven, see *VM*, 94 and 99–100.

79. *RL*, 83. Compare "Über den Grund," in *GA* 1.5:354; in English, *IWL*, 150.

80. *RL*, 66 and 130–34. Compare *VM*, 110; "Über den Grund," in *GA* 1.5:349 and 355; in English, *IWL*, 144–45 and 151–52; "Aus einem Privatschreiben," in *GA* 1.6:412–13; in English, *IWL*, 179–80. On the impossibility of God as a person or intellect, see *VM*, 112; "Über den Grund," in *GA* 1.5:349; in English, *IWL*, 145. For clarification of this point, see "Aus einem Privatschreiben," in *GA* 1.6:372–74, 386–88, and 379–80; in English, *IWL*, 160–61, 174–75, and 167–69.

81. *RL*, 37–41. Nonetheless, for a fine, sensitive mystical interpretation of the *Religionslehre*, see Anthony N. Perovich, Jr., "Fichte and the Typology of Mysticism," in *Fichte: Historical Contexts/Contemporary Controversies*, ed. Daniel Breazeale and Tom Rockmore (Atlantic Highlands: Humanities, 1994), 128–41.

82. *RL*, 71.

83. *RL*, 12–13, 17–18, and 68. On the original duality of pure willing and on the absolute "X" that grounds consciousness, see *WLNM* (1982), 213; *Wissenschaftslehre nova methodo*, in *GA* 4.2:230–31; in English, *FTP*, 423. See also *VM*, 107–11.

Fichte's Conception of the System of Philosophy in *Die Anweisung zum seligen Leben*

Ernst-Otto Onnasch

It is certainly true that in past and current research, Fichte's *Anweisung zum seligen Leben oder auch die Religionslehre* (*Guide to the Blessed Life, or the Doctrine of Religion*), published in 1806, has not received the attention it deserves.[1] One of the major reasons for this might be that Fichte himself labeled it a popular work, implying that it is of no major interest for professional philosophers. At least Schelling and Hegel took it thus. In his lectures on the history of philosophy, Hegel harshly criticizes Fichte's popular work in general and the *Anweisung* in particular. Since almost all the books Fichte published after 1800 are of a popular nature, Hegel's criticism is mainly directed at Fichte's later work. In his courses on the history of philosophy Hegel described Fichte's "popular works" as being "without any philosophic interest" because they only suit "a general public."[2] Since not all of Hegel's lectures on the history of philosophy have been published, it is not clear in which course or courses these remarks have been made. In the new edition of the 1825–26 lectures,[3] however, Hegel does not even mention any of Fichte's so-called popular works. Moreover, the quite important distinction Hegel made earlier between Fichte's popular philosophy and his speculative philosophy is absent.[4] The rather mild and factual tone of Hegel's remarks on the late Fichte in the 1825–26 course stands in sharp contrast to the harsh and condemnatory tone in the influential second printing of these lectures contained in the *Freundesvereinsausgabe*. Here the popular nature of Fichte's later writings is defined by Hegel as an attempt to force the readers to understand.[5] Actually, this definition of "popular" is taken from the subtitle of Fichte's *Sonnenklarer Bericht an das größere Publikum über das eigentliche Wesen der neuesten Philosophie: Ein Versuch, die Leser zum Verstehen zu zwingen* (*A Crystal Clear Report to the General Public Concerning the Actual Essence of the Newest Philosophy:*

An Attempt to Force the Reader to Understand), published in 1801.[6] Of course, Hegel certainly did not think Fichte had succeeded or would ever succeed with such an enforcement on his readers.

Schelling, on the other hand, discusses Fichte's *Anweisung* quite extensively in his *Darlegung des wahren Verhältnisses der Naturphilosophie zu der verbesserten fichteschen Lehre* (1806).[7] He declares the *Anweisung* to be the third in the triad of Fichte's popular works consisting of *Die Grundzüge des gegenwärtigen Zeitalters* and *Vorlesungen über das Wesen des Gelehrten.*[8] This triad is compared with the three parts of Dante's *Divine Comedy;* in this respect the *Anweisung* is associated with paradise, though it is in fact—as Schelling critically remarks—everything but a paradise, for Fichte turns the "vivid being" (*das lebendige Seyn*) into death.[9] Schelling also implicitly charges Fichte with Spinozism by stating that if "religion is to see everything in God and thus be equal to the life of God, then the absolute consciousness [*Bewußtseyn*] is the true principle of irreligion, of everything malicious [*Argen*] and undivine in man."[10] Some years later Schelling not only accuses Fichte of having plagiarized his ideas, but also of having stolen the title for the *Anweisung* from a phrase in *Philosophie und Religion* (1804).[11] As is clear from the above, Schelling's criticism is directed against the actual arguments of the *Anweisung,* whereas Hegel dismisses Fichte's popular works as philosophically uninteresting altogether. This different perception might be due to the fact that Schelling, indeed, owes more to Fichte than Hegel does.

Hegel, as we have seen, focuses on the popular status of the *Anweisung,* implying that it does not attain the strict scientific standard of the *Wissenschaftslehre.* However, this criticism is rather *gratuite,* since Fichte himself explicitly distinguishes his popular philosophy from his scientific philosophy, that is, his scientific program of the *Wissenschaftslehre.* He calls the lectures of the *Anweisung* "popular." Indeed, but all the same, they are the "brightest spot of light" that a popular rendering of philosophy can possibly reach.[12] This gives rise to the question of what Fichte had in mind by a popular rendering of his own scientific program.

If we look at Fichte's use of the term *popular* in his writings, it is apparent that it was frequently employed in order to criticize other philosophical standpoints, for example, the then-influential *Popularphilosophie,* but also the frequent attempts made to popularize the rather difficult Kantian philosophy, which Fichte reckoned to be exclusively his task. But the expression also occurs when he tries to explain something from a commonsense point of view. Within such contexts, "popular" implies using materialized pure concepts and ordinary language, but also tracing philosophical problems down to the realm of common consciousness or common experience. Fichte might feel the need for the latter due to the influence of Friedrich Niethammer; we will come back to this. In contrast, the contrary term *un-*

popular is used by Fichte to characterize his own transcendental idealism or scientific-philosophical endeavor as represented in the *Wissenschaftslehre.*[13]

According to Fichte, a popular account of his philosophy must be possible, for otherwise nobody would be able to climb to the highest standpoint of thought and autonomy of spirit (*Geist*), which is explicated by the *Wissenschaftslehre.* Everyone needs, in other words, to be directed toward this highest standpoint, which we "own" but are generally not conscious of. The idea of publishing a popular account of the *Wissenschaftslehre* is first mentioned by Fichte in a letter to his publisher Friedrich Cotta in December 1797.[14] In this letter "popular" indicates something meant for a wider audience or readership, an audience not able to comprehend the rather difficult philosophy of that time, especially Kantian philosophy. With this background, it is not surprising that Fichte states that "every true philosophy, as I think, might be popular philosophy; whereas scholarly philosophy is a cobweb and the fly netted by it loses its blood and life."[15] This quote clarifies the distinction between "popular" and scholarly philosophy with regard to Fichte's transcendental idealism. Only the latter can truly be called popular, since only here is the popular rendering based on a scientific philosophical investigation called *Wissenschaftslehre.* Indeed, as Fichte points out, the popular account of scientific philosophy is at bottom the same as the scientific account, with the difference lying in the method of demonstration: "In my scientific philosophical lectures I proclaim the same . . . only furnished by quite different proofs."[16]

It must also be mentioned that Fichte notices that any popular account of a scientific investigation is bound to the Zeitgeist, which means that any such account will become outdated (although, of course, the central doctrines of the *Wissenschaftslehre* remain untouched).[17] Even if the Zeitgeist "is not as fast as the annual book fairs," Fichte himself hereby delivers an argument for the widespread neglect of his later, popular renderings of his philosophy. Indeed, soon after the *Atheismusstreit* Fichte would only publish popular works (his *Antwortschreiben an Herrn Prof. Reinhold* [spring 1801] was his last scientific publication). Around 1800 Fichte became convinced of the impossibility of conveying the content of the *Wissenschaftslehre* by means of written texts. As a consequence, he quickly lost his influence on the philosophical debate; and the philosophical world started doubting whether Fichte could keep up with the new tendencies in the debate, mainly brought in by Schelling and Hegel. Fichte's opponents had an easy target because in his popular writings he often left his theses unsubstantiated and unexplained, while difficult questions were not addressed or resolved.

In the fifth lecture of the *Anweisung* Fichte brings forth a doctrine of the five standpoints or, as he also calls them, the five ways to view the world.

Within this doctrine religion is the fourth and thus the second highest standpoint. The final and highest standpoint belongs to science and is occupied by the *Wissenschaftslehre.* In the *Anweisung* these five standpoints are elaborated quite extensively. Considering the popular status of this book, it is worth noticing that we can find similar versions of this doctrine in some of Fichte's scientific works, for instance in the second presentation of the 1804 *Wissenschaftslehre.*[18] This indicates the systematic importance of this doctrine. Indeed, in a manuscript from 1807, Fichte points out that in order to resolve the initial question of the *Wissenschaftslehre,* it is necessary to describe the principle and its division into a fivefold infinity corresponding to the five standpoints or ways of viewing the world.[19] We may ask ourselves why the doctrine of standpoints unfolded in the *Anweisung* is part of a popular account. Before we can go into this question, we first need to outline the philosophical problem considered in the *Anweisung.*

The lectures of the *Anweisung* deal, indeed, with an issue of great systematic relevance. At stake is the question of how the pure being—that is, the unity of God—can be present in the manifold of the world and thus in our representation [*Vorstellung*] of this world. As we have already indicated, this question expresses one of Fichte's most important concerns in the years following his Jena period. At this point we can only hint obliquely at the origin of this problem. Most likely it is the result of discussions about the first published *Wissenschaftslehre* (1794–95) with Niethammer and Friedrich Hölderlin (if not directly with the latter, then indirectly via Niethammer). Already in the mid-1790s, Hölderlin is aware of the problem that Fichte in his *Wissenschaftslehre* deals illegitimately with self-consciousness as an identical proposition, "I am I" (thus two identical I-subjects), whereas this proposition involves an I-subject opposed to an I-object; and these are not two identical but differing and also distinguishable terms. This leads Hölderlin to criticize Fichte's account of self-consciousness in the *Wissenschaftslehre* as being something primary and initial in the process of deduction. In his famous philosophical fragment "Seyn, Urtheil und Modalität"[20] (probably 1795; "Being, Judgment and Modality"), Hölderlin distinguishes two levels: first *one* being, and second an initial bifurcation (*Ur-Theilung*) of this being into the self-consciousness of the I, so that the assembling of an I-subject and an I-object is *not* primordial, as Fichte argues in his *Wissenschaftslehre* 1794–95. In Hölderlin's fragment, "being" takes the role of the primordial moment presupposed by self-consciousness which is the source for the differentiation of being into an I-subject opposed to an I-object. It is most likely that Fichte knew about this criticism of his conception of self-consciousness in the *Wissenschaftslehre* 1794–95, for in the fifth paragraph of that work difference is introduced in the absolute I.[21] This introduction does not seem to be caused by any reasons relating to the development of the argument in this paragraph. In any case, Fichte just touches the issue here, and there is no elaboration of it. However, if indeed an influence of Hölderlin's argument can be supposed for the Jena *Wissenschaftslehre,* Fichte obviously did not care too much about it, most likely because it was not forwarded publicly. But this would change soon. The proceedings of the *Atheismusstreit* pointed out some severe systematic problems within Fichte's systematic philosophy, problems that have some resemblance to the problems Hölderlin mentioned.

One of the most influential criticisms during the *Atheismusstreit* followed from an obvious misinterpretation of the systematic status of the absolute I in the *Wissenschaftslehre* 1794–95, which consisted in its identification with God—that is, with the pure and absolute being or unity of God. This misinterpretation was widespread, notwithstanding the flood of offensive and sometimes mocking publications that Fichte wrote in order to correct this misinterpretation of his *Wissenschaftslehre.* Under the pressing conditions during the *Atheismusstreit,* it is not surprising that Fichte did not succeed in dealing systematically with the difference between the absolute unity of being and its self-conscious representation. After finally being discharged as a professor at Jena, Fichte obviously found the necessary time to deal with this problem in a more appropriate way.

In looking back on his philosophical conduct of the past years, Fichte remarks in 1804 that his main concern had been the initial unity of being and its representation in self-consciousness. Against the backdrop of Hölderlin's critique, Fichte's astonishing answer is that this initial unity is beyond and thus independent of its division [*Spaltung*] into being and consciousness. In religious terms this unity is portrayed by the Logos of John the Evangelist; in philosophical terms it is reason [*Vernunft*] or knowledge [*Wissen*] (not to be identified with conscious knowledge). Thus, the system that has this unity as its subject is consequently called "Wissenschaftslehre, logologia."[22] To represent this unity takes, as Fichte points out, an extensive and long preparation under the guidance of the most abstract speculation. The *Wissenschaftslehre* thus presupposes, as it seems, an introduction or preparation. Indeed, in the introductions of the *Wissenschaftslehre* in the *Philosophisches Journal,* appearing in 1797, Fichte departs from our everyday sense of consciousness to show that the I must be an immediate, self-intuiting activity. Here once again Fichte appears to formulate an answer to Niethammer's earlier criticism of the *Wissenschaftslehre,* namely, that the starting point of a scientific-philosophical investigation must be something beyond denial, even for the skeptical philosopher (according to Niethammer, this must be our common understanding and more precisely the fact of experience). In any case, with this new approach Fichte openly distances himself from the Reinholdean *Grundsatzphilosophie*. This does not entail denying that philosophy is not scientific and accordingly based on a principle, but rather involves the claim that such a principle must be searched for by a more or less tentative investigation based on common understanding. This new approach is documented by a letter from early 1801 where Fichte states that his first published *Wissenschaftslehre* "bears too many traces of the period in which it was written," hinting at the *Grundsatzphilosophie* that was in vogue during that time.[23] In the following years, the new approach for finding the starting point of speculative philosophy becomes an integral part of all new versions of the *Wissenschaftslehre*. The second rendering of the 1804 *Wissenschaftslehre*, for example, starts explicitly with an introduction and a propaedeutics.

The new versions of the *Wissenschaftslehre*, as presented in Fichte's lectures after 1800, deal explicitly with the problem of how, if there is only *one* unity and thus nothing that can be brought into position to differentiate this initial unity, this initial unity can be divided and differentiated into multiple subordinated principles. This is also the problem in the *Anweisung*. If, as Fichte points out here, "being as such [*an sich*] must be the very one, immutable and unchanging," the question becomes urgent "from where mutability and changeability, which real consciousness finds in that being, enters that same being."[24] According to the first 1804 course of his *Wissenschaftslehre*, the most difficult to *find*—note: *not* to grasp, that is, immediately accessed—is, indeed, the clear "intelligating insight" [*intelligirende Einsicht*] into the basic principle of the *Wissenschaftslehre*, serving the disjunction of the one without losing the absolute unity of this principle.[25] It is apparent that the principle for the division of the one will also provide the bridge to derive the relative from the absolute and vice versa. Fichte's solution to the problem is that the differentiating and dividing principle comes into action because there is consciousness. Consciousness provides a pure—indicated by the neologism "intelligiren" that we have tried to translate by "intelligating"—principle dividing the absolute unity of being. Obviously Fichte hints at something belonging to the very root of consciousness; in his *Diarium* he speaks of the "true, ultimate root of the apperception."[26] One of Fichte's main concerns has been, as he has stated many times, to elucidate Kant's unity of transcendental apperception which he reckons to be the starting point of all versions of the *Wissenschaftslehre*.[27]

This important principle of Kant's critical philosophy has been put under systematic pressure since the writings of Reinhold from the late 1780s and early 1790s. Following Reinhold, Fichte too—explicitly since the "Second Introduction" (1797)—becomes openly critical of the way Kant presents the unity of apperception in his first *Critique.* His main argument against Kant's account is that this unity is elaborated in its solution and not in its particular fundamental being. In other words, Kant did not describe this unity scientifically.

With regard to Fichte, we must keep in mind that the dividing principle cannot be part of a unity; rather, it is introduced with the fact of consciousness. As a consequence, there are actually two basic principles. First there is the pure unity of being and secondly the unity of consciousness. The latter must be understood as initially divided in its unity, since it is also the principle of division as such. The unity of initial being is thus opposed to the unity of consciousness, which opposition is only possible because consciousness itself is in its unity divided into the *two* terms *being* and *consciousness.* This structure reminds us of Hegel's speculative proposition of the "unity of unity and difference." It is due to the principle provided by consciousness that there is division at all, since it is the very essence of consciousness to be divided and to divide, but also to hold the division unified in itself by its initial operation. Within the unity of being and consciousness, being is divided by consciousness into a manifold being in consciousness, since there can be a manifold only in consciousness. The question at stake is how the unity of being, as it is for itself, can be represented by the unity of being and consciousness, whereby consciousness embodies division into the two poles of an I-subject and an I-object, but also the unity of both in a representation. We will come back to this when we elucidate the same problem with regard to the *Anweisung.*

In contrast to the *Wissenschaftslehre,* the initial account of division in the first lectures of the *Anweisung* is not developed on the basis of consciousness, but on the basis of the concept of love [*Liebe*]. Although Fichte is not very explicit about this, it is likely that an exposition of the initial division on the basis of what is contained in the meaning of love must be seen in relation to the Christian, that is, religious, understanding of it. Like consciousness, love too expresses a relation of difference, namely that between the lover and the beloved, which cannot be reduced to another (we will not go into problems concerned with love for oneself). The Christian understanding of the concept of love is connected to unity and difference in its own way, as love is provided by the one God through his revelation, whereas the relation of difference is established by Jesus Christ on earth. Fichte's use of "love" rather than "consciousness" as the dividing moment must have a different result with regard to the division itself. This becomes quite clear in the *Anweisung* when Fichte defines the difference between religion and science with regard to the fundamental question of how unity can be in the manifold.

According to the *Anweisung*, religion provides only one of the ways in which we can find unity in the manifold of the world. The difference between religion and science—that is, *Wissenschaftslehre*—is formulated in this way, that is, "science goes beyond the insight supported by religion *that* the entire manifold as such is founded in and can be reduced to the one." In contrast to religion, science has as its task to elucidate "the insight of the *how* of this coherence," namely that between the manifold and the one. Thus science renders "genetically what according to religion is merely an absolute factum. Although this factum in religion can be an imperturbable belief, science sublates all belief by transforming it into inspection [*Schauen*]."[28] So there are two different and well-defined tasks for religion on the one hand and science on the other hand, for religion supports *that* and science *how* the manifold is founded in the one. This reminds us of Kant's distinction between a metaphysical and a transcendental exposition of concepts. The exposition of a concept is metaphysical when it "contains that which exhibits the concept *as given* a priori."[29] Such a metaphysical explanation involves some circularity, since it explains what is always already presupposed for the act of that very same exposition. If we apply the rather technical sense of Kant's definition to the issue brought forward by the *Anweisung*, we can say that for the employment of "love" for initial division, we always already perform what we know about this concept when we try to explain it. To put it differently, religious belief on the one hand supports the insight into the unity of the manifold in God, although this unity on the other hand is always given with the mere fact of this very same religious belief. Against the backdrop of the metaphysical explanation we might be justified in the conclusion that the systematic status of the *Anweisung*—being a doctrine of religion—can thus, in Kant's terminology, be characterized as *metaphysical*. The sixth lecture provides a justification for this interpretation, since here Fichte states simply that only metaphysics blesses.[30] And if we recall the task of *Anweisung*, namely to guide us toward a blessed life, this task can be characterized as a metaphysical task. In the appendix to the sixth lecture, Fichte gives an account of the notion "metaphysical." Metaphysical is what follows necessarily and can be derived [*ableiten*] from a higher law.[31] What is metaphysical should therefore not be taken as a factum, as Fichte clarifies; obviously because the employed concept of love can be explained on a more principled level than that provided by religion. Indeed, the metaphysical account of the *Anweisung* finds its ground in a higher principle, as the doctrine of standpoints makes clear. In other words, the doctrine of religion put forward by the *Anweisung* finds its ground in the *Wissenschaftslehre*.

By contrast, the transcendental exposition is described by Kant as "the explanation of a concept as a principle from which insight into the possibility of other synthetic a priori cognitions can be gained."[32] Such an explanation incorporates the question as to the *how*. With regard to the *Anweisung*, the question is *how* the manifold can possibly be founded in the one. An explanation of this *how* surpasses the means of the *Anweisung* since, in short, religion is not able to explain what religion is. In this respect it is correct that Fichte does not inquire in what way and by what right the *Anweisung* is entitled to use the concept of love for explaining the initial division and its unity. Insofar as we are correct in characterizing the *Anweisung* with regard to its method as a metaphysical approach, it also presupposes a critique or a transcendental approach, since otherwise the whole exercise would merely produce some form of popular dogmatism. Such a critique or transcendental approach would have to examine our entitlement to use (initial) concepts like those derived from religion, that is, love. In the 1794 *Begriffsschrift* (*Concerning the Concept of the Wissenschaftslehre*) Fichte clarifies this by stating: "Metaphysics explains the ordinary point of view, and metaphysics is itself explained by critique."[33]

One might be somewhat surprised that Fichte, in the second lecture of the *Anweisung*, develops an argument for the possibility of "a popular account of the deepest truth." This gives rise to the question of why a scientific account of truth, that is, one beyond the religious account, would still be necessary at all. As we already know from the *Offenbarungsschrift*, Fichte held the conviction that religious and thus moral truth cannot possibly be the exclusive domain of religion, since one would never be able to *prove* this, if reason itself did not possess this truth from the very beginning. Accordingly, in this lecture Fichte argues that if the scientific philosophical understanding [*Einsicht*] had never existed, Jesus, his apostles, or anyone else for that matter, even philosophers, would not have been able to gain such understanding.[34] But what grants the accessibility of this understanding? Definitely not philosophy, as every philosopher will agree that it is not by philosophy that understanding is gained. The deepest truth and insight into the unity in the manifold prevailed in all ages (that is, more precisely, all ages after Christ), although often hidden, unappreciated, or persecuted. And indeed, there have been many attempts in the past to derive that truth by means of a philosophical endeavor, but Fichte holds the *Wissenschaftslehre* to be the very first attempt which is capable of success. Religion obviously makes us aware of the initial principles, although it is not able to account for this other than metaphysically. Thus it is the task of the *Anweisung* to bring contemporary mankind to the standpoint from which the insight can be gained that the deepest truths must and can be made clear on the bases of a scientific philosophical discourse. Religion not founded by such a discourse holds the serious danger of leading into some kind of dogmatism, and history shows us, indeed, that this happened more than once.

Love, the important methodological principle of the first lectures of the *Anweisung*, can prevent us from falling back into such a dogmatism and false metaphysics. Indeed, the Christian understanding of love imposes on us a moral duty to prevent religious truths from such a relapse into dogmatism. Based on an understanding of love inspired by Christianity, we can argue that this love obliges us to seek a scientific justification of our religious beliefs that are assumed for the concept of love. Fichte claims, indeed, that the principles of religion can and also must be derived from those of the *Wissenschaftslehre*,[35] not as a result of this science, but because it follows from the *moral duty* of a Christian-inspired understanding of love. Thus, Fichte does not argue on the basis of science for the need to surpass the standpoint of religion by a higher (and in this case, highest) standpoint of science. On the contrary, "the demand to realize the science in us and in others belongs to the sphere of higher morality [*höhere Sittlichkeit*]."[36] A moral claim contained in Christian religion demands us to realize science. Of course, the legitimacy of this claim is ultimately grounded in science, although it is also clear that we have no immediate access to that science, for we have to be brought to this standpoint via morality and religion.

Higher morality is the third of the five standpoints, preceding the standpoints of religion and science. This third standpoint of higher morality expresses a law for the spiritual world, namely a creative [*schaffende*] law characterized as the ability to bring about something new, that is, something that was not available before. It is important to notice that this law is not creative in the sense of ex nihilo. It rather supplies some resting or inactive forces with new life by virtue of its creative abilities. These resting forces are identified with the solidified activity and life of God, to which we have no direct access; our access to God's life is by virtue of the *image* of this life and activity. Therefore, as Fichte puts it, the creative law of higher morality strives for "the *qualitative* and *real* idea,"[37] an idea that is defined as the exteriorization of God's inner essence.[38] With this in mind, we can understand that the end of higher morality is to form mankind according to its destination, namely, to approach as closely as possible the image of the divine inner essence. If we compare the Kantian perspective on the moral law, which holds the destination of mankind postponed in time and place, to the Fichtean account, we see that although the *final* destination of mankind is not realized, there is nonetheless a *real* blessed life under the conditions of *this world* shown to be possible; moreover, this forming of mankind according to its destination has *real* results *here* and *now* when the creative powers of the law of higher morality bring to life (some of) the ideas of the solidified exteriorization of God's inner essence. But the next question immediately presents itself: what can account for the content of these ideas, and moreover for their divine content? As an *image* of God's life and activity, these ideas have lost the immediate divine content. The problem formulated here is therefore not trivial, because the idea in the Fichtean perspective is not qualified through a speculative logic as an idea with absolute content. Before we can go into this question, we need to shed some light on the way Fichte introduces the five standpoints in the *Anweisung*.

In the third and especially in the fourth lecture of the *Anweisung*, Fichte endeavors to *show* his audience how the one and unchanging being converts into a manifold and changing being. At stake is how changeability and conversion which consciousness finds in being enter that very same being. As we have seen above this is a similar question to the one Hölderlin addressed to the Jena *Wissenschaftslehre*. Fichte's solution, though, is somewhat different from the one Hölderlin seems to present in his brief sketch. Fichte argues roughly as follows.[39] If there is, as is indeed the case, one unchanging being, knowledge of this being is involved, because knowledge entails a proposition, expressing that "being is." Without implying anything about the content of being, the form of being is expressed by the proposition "being is." The unity of being unites being *and* the faculty that divides being in order to be able to form any proposition. In short, to state that there is only one being involves to begin with and *for us* that being and consciousness, which brings division in order to form a proposition from a unity of different terms, namely "being" and "consciousness." It is thus by means of reflection executed by consciousness that there is division at all. The very fact of this division is truly initial and neither dissolvable within real consciousness nor replaceable by something else. It is "reality," a "fact of consciousness"[40] or the "initial root of life"[41] which we cannot possibly derive from anywhere; we can only, as Fichte puts it, live [*leben*] and experience [*erleben*] it.[42]

However, it is because of consciousness and its operation by reflection that there is difference in the one being. Actually we can register two divisions. First, there is a division of the divine being within consciousness. This division results in an infinitely changeable world by the forms of reflection; more precisely, it is a classification with regard to the object which brings about the diversity of objects. The second division is intimately coupled with the first and divides the world in five ways to view the world;[43] this division causes a classification in the "viewpoint of the object,"[44] leading to the five standpoints according to which the one enduring world is viewed and understood.

If we take a closer look at the principle of this division, it is immediately clear that it is not the same as the activity performed by the being of God; and Fichte is fully aware of this, as he remarks: "The principle of the division cannot be part of the activity of the divine being, but must be outside of it; that is, however, in such a way that this outside clearly is associated immediately with this living act and necessarily follows from this act."[45] We see Fichte struggling to connect this principle to and distinguish it from the activity of divine being. He has, on the one hand, to distinguish it, since otherwise conscious activity would—with regard to its principle—be the same as divine activity, which is unacceptable, at least because this would lead to the same accusations Fichte had to face during the *Atheismusstreit.* On the other hand, he has to connect them because the result of the division of being must be a result that comes from the activity of that being itself; otherwise the world cannot be a result of God, but would be a result of our reflection. The absence of the latter connection could be, of course, easily linked with the viewpoint of Kantian philosophy, according to which we comprehend the world according to the principles we impose on it, that is, the world is as we comprehend or know the world. It seems obvious that Fichte tries to overcome this viewpoint. That he does so is inevitable, if we remember his point of departure, namely clarifying Kant's principle of the transcendental apperception.

Fichte's fundamental thought is that the unity of being and consciousness is divided by reflection, which has two results, namely the world and the way it is viewed. Both the world and the structures according to which the world is viewed have their being in their joint being with consciousness. Therefore we can never have the world without a viewpoint and vice versa. But what happens when the viewpoint manages to take a stand that merges with the dividing reflection and thus reflects the being itself? This is, indeed, the case within the fifth standpoint expressed by the *Wissenschaftslehre.* Here a unity is reflected within itself, which, because there is reflection, necessarily involves difference, although this difference is necessarily absent on the level of that unity as it is for itself, namely the absolute divine being. But if there is no difference within the pure unity, overreaching both being and consciousness, the principle of division consequently does not follow from that absolute unity. The principle of division is thus stated and not derived from absolute being. The task must be to abolish, in a scientific undertaking, this division so that we eventually end up with pure being. Such a procedure is necessary because otherwise there would be two relatively independent principles (namely, being and division by consciousness), with the result that the *Wissenschaftslehre* would lack unity itself. This abolition determines the method of the *Wissenschaftslehre* 1794–95, where the negativity introduced on the level of the second *Grundsatz* is or at least should be abolished by the exercise of the deduction carried out within the *Wissenschaftslehre*, so that its starting point—absolute being—is, at the end of the whole undertaking confirmed to be the comprehensive content of the reflecting I.

However, with regard to the later versions of the *Wissenschaftslehre,* this cannot be the method followed because, as we have seen, Fichte has by then come to think of the unity of pure being or God as itself representing a pre-reflexive or even trans-reflexive structure that is only *mirrored* by the being that is in unity with consciousness (Fichte speaks in this respect of an image). Contrary to the first published version of the *Wissenschaftslehre,* the later versions—in principle—never result in the absolute unity preceding every division, for it is impossible to abolish the difference implied by consciousness and its reflecting operation. Moreover, there is no connection between the fundamental law of reflection (namely, division) and absolute being and therefore the division is a result of a principle different from the one supported by pure and absolute being itself. For the explanation of the *how* of the division, represented by the *Wissenschaftslehre,* the *that* of this division is merely presupposed, for it does not have its ground in pure being, but in consciousness. The principles of the scientific system therefore suffer from a lack of critique. Of course, Fichte claims to deduce the principles of the several doctrines of spirit [*Geisteslehren*], like religion and morality, from the principles of the *Wissenschaftslehre,* but insofar as the whole system is an explanation—although a scientific one—of the functions performed by consciousness, there is no scientific justification for the initial act of division performed by consciousness, since it is not grounded in the one highest principle of absolute or pure being. If, therefore, it is not proven that the reflection of consciousness exercises the very same activity that pure being exercises in order to exteriorize itself as the ideas, the system based on this activity does not supply the proof that its principle exhaustively explains absolute and pure being. The idea as an exteriorization of absolute being only reflects the *formal structure* of the absolute, while the content of this idea draws back on a mere fact of division performed by consciousness. Both exteriorization and reflection perform the same activity only ideally. The *how* of this performance is inexplicable. Therefore the later versions of the *Wissenschaftslehre* are metaphysical and in the end lead to some form of dogmatism. The only way out of this problem is an idealism that manages to show that the universal is the specific, or that the idea is also the real content of all being. This outlines an idealism as it is unfolded by Hegel, who blamed Fichte's speculative philosophy for being dogmatic.

Notes

1. There is an old English edition of the *Anweisung* edited and translated by William Smith in *The Popular Works of Johann Gottlieb Fichte,* 2 vols. (London: Chapman, 1848–49 [repr. London: Thoemmes, 1999], 2:291–496. Here the title of Fichte's book is translated as *The Way Towards the Blessed Life,* which is, in my opinion, a less proper translation of the German noun *Anweisung.*

2. See G. W. F. Hegel, *Lectures on the History of Philosophy,* ed. E. S. Haldane and F. H. Simson (London, 1892–96), 3:506.

3. G. W. F. Hegel, *Vorlesungen über die Geschichte der Philosophie,* ed. P. Garniron and W. Jaeschke, vols. 6–8 (Hamburg, 1994–96).

4. Hegel, *Vorlesungen,* 8:480.

5. Hegel, *Vorlesungen,* 8:521, although not as clearly stated as in the first edition of these lectures by Michelet.

6. Unfortunately, the English translation of this book, *A Crystal Clear Report to the General Public Concerning the Actual Essence of the Newest Philosophy: An Attempt to Force the Reader to Understand,* trans. John Botterman and William Rash, ed. Ernst Behler (New York: Continuum, 1987), is not always reliable.

7. See F. W. J. Schelling, *Sämmtliche Werke,* ed. K. F. A. Schelling (Stuttgart and Augsburg: J. G. Cotta, 1856–61), 7:1–126. (This work is cited by series, volume, and page number in these notes.)

8. See Schelling, *Sämmtliche Werke,* 7:24–25n.

9. Schelling, *Sämmtliche Werke,* 7:88.

10. Schelling, *Sämmtliche Werke,* 7:88.

11. For this phrase, see Schelling, *Sämmtliche Werke,* 6:17. For the accusation of plagiarism, see 2.1:465.

12. *GA* 1.9:47.

13. See *Grundlage der gesamten Wissenschaftslehre,* in *GA* 1.2:383; and *Sonnenklarer Bericht,* in *GA* 1.7:185.

14. See *GA* 3.3:103: "Das grössere Publikum, das der Autorität nicht mehr glaubt, und der Philosophie in ihrer gegenwärtigen Gestalt unfähig ist, bedarf eines Buches, in welchem ihm, ohne den künstlichen Apparat des Systems, allgemein verständlich, und so, daß auch sein Geschmak angezogen werde, die Resultate der neuern Philosophie vorgetragen werden. Ich habe den künftigen Sommer, für welchen ich schon jezt die Aussetzung meiner Vorlesungen angekündigt, und den ich deshalb auf dem Lande zubringen werde, der Ausarbeitung eines solchen Buchs bestimmt." The first result of this plan seems to have been *Die Bestimmung des Menschen* (1800); in English, *VOM.* With a somewhat different orientation, the idea of an introduction to the *Wissenschaftslehre* is already present in Jena. Fichte's lectures on logic and metaphysics based on Ernst Platner's *Philosophische Aphorismen* are announced as a "popular propaedeutics" (*GA* 3.2:418) or "popular introduction . . . to the entire philosophy" (*GA* 2.4:9).

15. *GA* 1.6:142: "Aber jede ächte Philosophie, dünkt mich, sey Popular-Philosophie; die Schul-Philosophie aber ein Spinnengewebe: die arme Fliege, die es umstrickt, verliert Blut und Leben."

16. See *GA* 1.8:276: "Ich trage in wissenschaftlich-philosophischen Vorlesungen dasselbe vor [as in his scientific writings and lectures]; aber ich versehe es mit ganz andern Beweisen."

17. See *GA* 1.8:278.

18. *GA* 2.8:416–20; *FW* 10:312–14.

19. See *Nebenbemerkungen zu 1,* in *GA* 2.10:255.

20. Still quite common is the title "Urtheil und Seyn," of the first publication of the fragment in the Stuttgart edition of *Hölderlins Werke* (Stuttgart, 1961), 4:216–17. (See "On Judgment and Being," in H. S. Harris, *Hegel's Development: Toward the Sunlight 1770–1801* [Oxford: Clarendon, 1972].). This title draws on the wrong arrangement of the two-page manuscript, that is, recto is taken as verso and vice versa; see Michael Franz, "Hölderlins Logik. Zum Grundriß von 'Seyn Urtheil Möglichkeit,'" *Hölderlin-Jahrbuch* 25 (1986–87): 93–124.

21. See mainly *GA* 1.2:405.

22. See Fichte's letter of June 23, 1804, to a certain Appia, in *GA* 3.5:246–47.

23. *GA* 3.6:9: "Meine gedruckte Wißenschaftslehre trägt zu viele Spuren des Zeitraums, in dem sie geschrieben, und der Manier zu philosophiren, der sie der Zeit nach folgte."

24. See *Anweisung zum seligen Leben oder auch die Religionslehre,* in *GA* 1.9:101.

25. The quote is taken from the parallel text of this course provided by the second 1804 course, in *GA* 2.8:242–43n.

26. Johann Gottlieb Fichte, *Ultima Inquirenda: J. G. Fichtes letzte Bearbeitungen der Wissenschaftslehre Ende 1813/Anfang 1814,* ed. Reinhard Lauth (Stuttgart-Bad Cannstatt: Frommann-Holzboog, 2001), 138.

27. See "Zweite Einleitung," in *GA* 1.4:221–29, but also in the late *Wissenschaftslehre* 1811, in *GA* 2.12:381: "Die W.L. ist von der Untersuchung über diese Apperception ausgegangen; und durch die Lösung der Frage, was diese sey, u. warum sie nothwendig sey, entstanden."

28. See *Anweisung zum seligen Leben,* in *GA* 1.9:112; *FW* 5:272: "Sie, die Wissenschaft, geht über die Einsicht, dass schlechthin alles Mannigfaltige in dem Einen gegründet und auf dasselbe zurückzuführen sey, welche schon die Religion gewährt, hinaus zu der Einsicht des Wie dieses Zusammenhanges: und für sie wird genetisch, was für die Religion nur ein absolutes Factum ist. Die Religion ohne Wissenschaft, ist irgendwo ein blosser, demohngeachtet jedoch unerschütterlichen Glaube: die Wissenschaft hebt allen Glauben auf und verwandelt ihn in Schauen."

29. See Immanuel Kant, *Critique of Pure Reason,* ed. and trans. Paul Guyer and Allen W. Wood (Cambridge: Cambridge University Press, 1998), B 38.

30. See *GA* 1.9:122; *FW* 5:485: "Nur das metaphysische . . . macht seelig."

31. See *GA* 1.9:188; *FW* 5:568.

32. See Kant, *Critique of Pure Reason,* B 40.

33. Published in *EPW,* 97; *FW* 1:33.

34. See *GA* 1.9:70: "Ist also die wissenschaftlich philosophische Einsicht nie

vorhanden gewesen; auf welchem Wege ist denn Christus, – oder, falls bei diesem jemand einen wunderbaren, und übernatürlichen Ursprung annimmt, den ich hier nicht bestreiten will, – auf welchem Wege sind denn Christi Apostel, – auf welchem Wege sind denn alle folgenden, die bis auf unsere Zeiten hinab zu dieser Erkenntniß kamen, – zu ihr gekommen?"

35. An attempt at such a deduction can be found in Fichte's lectures *Die Principien der Gottes-, Sitten- und Rechtslehre* (1805).

36. See *GA* 1.9:112; *FW* 5:472–73: "Das gottseelige und seelige Leben ist durch ihn zwar keinesweges bedingt; dennoch aber gehört die Anforderung, diese Wissenschaft in uns, und andern zu realisiren, in das Gebiet der höhern Moralität."

37. See *FW* 5:469: "Es [das Gesetz] strebt an . . . die qualitative und reale Idee selber." What Fichte means by "real idea" he deals with mainly in his lectures *Grundzüge des gegenwärtigen Zeitalters* given in Berlin during winter 1804–5 and in his 1806 *Über das Wesen des Gelehrten, und seine Erscheinungen im Gebiete der Freiheit.*

38. See *FW* 5:526.

39. See *GA* 1.9:101–2.

40. See *Sonnenklarer Bericht,* in *GA* 1.7:204.

41. See *Wissenschaftslehre Königsberg 1807,* in *GA* 2.10:116.

42. See *GA* 1.9:101; for this formula, see also *Wissenschaftslehre 1810,* in *GA* 2.11:603 and 615–16.

43. See *GA* 1.9:102; *FW* 5:460.

44. See *GA* 1.9:102; *FW* 5:460.

45. See *GA* 1.9:95; *FW* 5:540: "Das Princip der Spaltung [kann] nicht unmittelbar in jenem *Akt* des göttlichen Daseyns fallen, sondern es muß *außer denselben* fallen; jedoch also, daß dieses Außer, einleuchte, als unmittelbar, mit jenem lebendigen Akte Verknüpft, und aus ihm nothwendig Folgend."

How Not to Read Fichte's *Anweisung zum seligen Leben* (1806): Against the Mystical Reading

Kevin Zanelotti

Die Anweisung zum seligen Leben, a series of lectures delivered by J. G. Fichte during the 1805–6 winter semester in Berlin, is a work largely ignored by Anglo-American scholarship.[1] Those who do address this work generally exercise one of two interpretive options: (1) a reading negatively contrasting the *Anweisung*'s alleged mystical extravagances with the rigor of the systematic presentations of the *Wissenschaftslehre* (from which, it is claimed, the *Anweisung* is most certainly a departure); or (2) a reading praising the *Anweisung* either because of its development of a Christology bringing to the fore Fichte's religious commitments or because it putatively exhibits mystical sensibilities important in their own right. In the first case, the result has been either a neglect of the *Anweisung*'s claims or a reproach of the same,[2] while in the second case the attention that is directed toward the *Anweisung* distorts its philosophical import. In what follows, I focus on Anthony Perovich's reading of the *Anweisung* as a text purportedly exhibiting mystical sensibilities[3] and argue that the mystical reading of the *Anweisung* is, in fact, a misreading. Such a reading distorts (1) the purpose of the *Anweisung,* (2) the specific claims made therein, (3) the relation of the text to the Jena-period *Wissenschaftslehre* as a whole, and (4) its philosophical significance. Instead, I will argue that the actual aim and significance of the *Anweisung* become clear *only* if the mystical reading is rejected.

I will proceed as follows. First, I will discuss my reasons for focusing on the mystical reading and will offer a conception of mysticism against which we may gauge Perovich's claims (this is necessary since I intend my argument to apply to the mystical reading in general, though for reasons of exposition I focus on Perovich's model example). Then I will discuss Perovich's argument, noting point by point why his reading, and *any* mystical reading in general, must fail. And lastly, I will offer an interpretation of the *Anweisung* that makes sense of the often strange, mystical-sounding language therein.

Why oppose a mystical reading of the *Anweisung*? I do so not from an opposition to mysticism *as such,* but rather from a belief that (1) the mystical reading of the *Anweisung* is quite simply a misreading, and (2) this misreading is in large part responsible for the general neglect and specific reproach that has been the *Anweisung*'s unfortunate *Wirkungsgeschichte.* Even a brief survey of the secondary literature reveals that the mystical reading of the *Anweisung* has attained wide currency. Vaughan, for instance, claims to have discovered an affinity between Fichte and Meister Eckhart,[4] while other scholars have associated Fichte with mystics as diverse as the Buddhist Nishida,[5] the German theosophist Boehme,[6] and the Hindu Ramakrishna.[7] This tendency to characterize the *Anweisung* as a mystical or purely religious text extends to Fichte scholars as well. Seidel, though certainly not claiming Fichte to be a mystic, describes the *Anweisung* as a "high Christology" that both saves Fichte from the accusation of atheism and brings to the fore the centrality of religious commitments in his thought.[8] In more direct fashion, Hunter claims that the *Anweisung* "has a marked tendency to be formulated in terms . . . which are more than suggestive of what seems to be an almost incommunicable, mystical experience."[9] However, perhaps the most articulate recent expression of the mystical reading comes from Anthony Perovich, who quite explicitly claims that the *Anweisung* "is in some sense a mystical text."[10] Such claims may appear credible given the language of Fichte's argument, where, for example, he writes of an "impulse to be united with the imperceptible and transfused therein"[11] and asserts that "blessedness . . . is unwavering repose in the One Eternal" (*WBL,* 303). Indeed, such expressions appear throughout the *Anweisung,* thus giving *prima facie* reasons for subscribing to the mystical reading. I hope to show that a close reading of the *Anweisung* demonstrates the inadequacy of such a reading.

Mysticism is a notoriously difficult phenomenon to define.[12] For my present purposes, however, I need only provide a definition that is as acceptable as possible to the majority of readers and that captures in an analytically useful way some central features of mysticism. As such, I will use the definition of neither an advocate (e.g., Pike[13] or Findlay)[14] nor an opponent (e.g., Katz);[15] rather, I will rely on two conceptions of mysticism that are nearly canonical in the field, namely those of William James and Walter Stace. James lists four characteristics of mystical experience: (1) ineffability, (2) noetic quality, (3) transiency, and (4) passivity.[16] Combining these four features, I characterize mysticism as an experience of union with an Absolute (most typically, God) that transcends sense perception and discursive thought and that involves some or other insight, illumination, or revelation into ultimate reality; furthermore, these experiences are rare (i.e., they are temporary modifications of normal consciousness) and involve one's being overcome by some "greater power." Mystical experience may include other characteristics (e.g., a sense of oneness with the world or reality, a sense of timelessness, etc.), but James's four "marks" capture the relevant structural features. Stace offers a further aid in classification via his distinction between introvertive and extrovertive forms of mysticism. Extrovertive mysticism refers to those states in which unity with the Absolute is perceived in and through the multiplicity of worldly things and creatures (i.e., "All is One"). Introvertive mysticism, on the other hand, refers to a state in which there is a unity or oneness with the Absolute from which *all* multiplicity has been excluded (i.e., "The One that is Nothing"). These characteristics, though neither comprehensive nor without shortcomings, capture the salient features of mysticism and will serve as the backdrop against which I will address the question: is Fichte's *Anweisung* a mystical text?

Fichte nowhere claims to have had the kinds of experiences typical of mystics. More importantly, and as I will discuss shortly, Fichte explicitly *denies* that the *Anweisung* is a mystical text. In a work from the same period, *Die Grundzüge des gegenwärtigen Zeitalters* (1806),[17] Fichte devotes an entire chapter to a vigorous attack on mysticism. Yet Perovich is correct in noting that a text may be termed "mystical" even if the author makes no claim of himself having such experiences.[18] Such experiential bases (i.e., an author writing based *entirely* on her own mystical experiences) pertain only to one kind of text, one which can be called "mystical" in a strong sense. However, a text can be mystical in a weaker sense, namely, if it lays no claim to an experiential basis but rather aims merely to recall or illustrate certain aspects of other experiential mystics. Perovich is not concerned with arguing that Fichte is a mystic of the stronger sort (though he alludes to evidence that Fichte did indeed have such direct experiences).[19] He instead argues that Fichte's *Anweisung* makes use of language and ideas that are characteristic of weaker versions of mysticism. This is, admittedly, a more moderate (and thus more defensible) claim than simply asserting that Fichte is a mystic in the strong sense of the word.

What is Perovich's evidence for this claim? First, he offers an argument by association, noting that throughout the literature on mysticism—from Eckhart and Boehme to Sankara and Dogen—Fichte has been associated repeatedly with various mystics.[20] However, this manner of argument proves little, and thus Perovich notes that he is not concerned with such comparative studies but, rather, with locating Fichte's "place in the general terrain of mystical phenomena."[21] With this in mind, Perovich notes that mystical states typically involve some form of union between the human and the divine, and that Fichte often writes of just such a union. Perovich sees this "union" in Fichte's claim that "in this love [between God and a human], Being and Existence, God and Man, are One; wholly transfused and lost in each other" (*WBL*, 465). Perovich presents this claim (and others like it in the *Anweisung*) as evidence for his conclusion, namely, "that Fichte's statements recall such claims [of mystics] is beyond question."[22] It is interesting that Perovich reaches this conclusion without attempting to account for such statements in a non-mystical way. With his brief survey of such claims, Perovich thinks that he has established that Fichte is a mystic of the weaker sort, with the only remaining question concerning what kind of weak mysticism we find in the *Anweisung*. Indeed, Perovich moves quite quickly to this very topic, importing Stace's distinction between introvertive and extrovertive mysticism in an attempt to further "typify" Fichte's putative mysticism.

Continuing his argument, Perovich writes that "there are good reasons for regarding Fichte's mysticism as introvertive rather than extrovertive."[23] First, as Perovich correctly notes, Fichte discusses union solely in terms of a union with God, *not* mere things. Second, this union is based on love (*Liebe*), where Fichte explicitly refers to the two exclusive possibilities of either loving the world of sense or loving the supersensible (i.e., God). Thus, the prerequisite for extrovertive mysticism, namely, a union with All (supersensible *and* sensible), is not present in Fichte's case. Key for Perovich's argument is Fichte's claim that union *as such* is possible only with God and not with the sensible world: "We cannot . . . be dominated by a love of the world, for the world does not allow itself to be loved."[24] Perovich follows Fichte in postulating union with God as being possible, and then notes that for this union to occur it must occur in love, which by definition excludes everything but God from the relationship. Fichte is thus, on this reading, an introvertive mystic. But, continuing the attempt to classify his putative mysticism, what kind of introvertive mystic is Fichte? The remainder of Perovich's paper is concerned with this question, which reveals a problem that I will call "the antinomy of typology."

Once Fichte is classified as an introvertive mystic, a "typology of mysticism" seems to demand a further classification, namely between monistic and theistic forms of introvertive mysticism.[25] Theistic introvertive mysticism is dualistic in that a distinct nonspatial and nontemporal "object" (the Absolute) is posited as one pole of the relation while the other is the self (this union, typically characterized in terms of love, is exclusive of all other things and entities). In contrast, monistic introvertive mysticism involves an undifferentiated unity and is virtually indistinguishable from pantheism.[26] The antinomial nature of this typology arises with the realization that we seem to be faced with reasons that support both the theistic and the monistic interpretation, yet each position excludes the other. Perovich notes that "Fichte's text offers passage after passage that supports this [monistic] reading,"[27] referring in particular to passages that assert the unity of the self and God through a love that breaks down any distinction between the two.[28] Yet there are also passages that seem to support a theistic interpretation that maintains the separateness of God and self.[29] There are two points that I must note regarding this antinomy: (1) Perovich "solves" it by putting into question the very distinction between monistic and theistic introvertive mysticism, arguing that a mystical text such as the *Anweisung* demonstrates that any attempt to offer a "typology of mysticism" is highly problematic (if not doomed outright);[30] and (2) Perovich identifies Fichte's "negative theology" as the reason for the failure of the distinction.

Regarding the last point, Perovich offers an argument for the rational acceptance of mystical claims. He claims that this argument follows from Fichte's putative negative theology, and his reasoning is illustrative of important aspects of the mystical reading. First, there is the question of how we can "know" (in some, not necessarily conceptual, sense) of God if, following Fichte's negative theology, God surpasses our cognitive powers. Perovich answers in a typically mystical way, claiming that "only in love do we achieve an unfalsified grasp of God."[31] Perovich nowhere addresses the problem of how a person can grasp God if both self and God are, in fact, "wholly transfused and lost in each other" (*WBL,* 132). Yet even if this contradiction is suppressed, there is still the problem of accounting in some meaningful way for the "grasp" one can have of God in mystical experience. In more of an evasion than an answer, Perovich notes that mystical claims can have meaning and a ground of justification because of the empirical fact that mystics understand one another.[32] From this claim, Perovich suggests that we can find evidence for the rationality and coherence of Fichte's alleged mysticism if we can find comparable passages in the writings of other mystics. As an example of this manner of justification, Perovich refers to certain parallels between the *Anweisung* and the claims of the Greek Orthodox mystic Gregory Palamas: for example, both claim that God in his essence is unknowable and that God is both identical to yet distinct from the Existence that is God's manifestation (or emanation). Perovich concludes that such resemblances "are sufficiently impressive to encourage us to be respectful even where we are necessarily uncomprehending."[33] That is, and given Perovich's earlier claims regarding Fichte's mysticism, though the nature of mysticism is such that it eludes our grasp, family resemblances among mystics such as Fichte and Gregory Palamas somehow enrich our appreciation and understanding of mysticism *überhaupt.*

What are we to make of Perovich's claims? There are, I think, two questions that must be addressed: (1) is there actually overt evidence of mysticism in Fichte's text? and (2) is there covert evidence of mysticism in that text? These are, as Perovich notes, distinct questions, for it is possible that a writer may overtly criticize and deny being a mystic and yet still make use of mystical language, imagery, and claims. Indeed, Perovich's notion of a weak sense of mysticism captures just this possibility. We thus must let the text speak for itself, independent of the author's claims regarding his own intentions. This is important, for, as mentioned previously, Fichte quite explicitly remarks in both the *Anweisung* and the *Grundzüge* that he is *not* a mystic and that mysticism is opposed in its essence to the spirit of the *Wissenschaftslehre*. Thus, if Perovich's mystical reading is warranted, it must either show that Fichte's rejection of mysticism does not extend to mysticism *überhaupt* but rather to a specific, deviant form of mysticism or that Fichte covertly assents to what he overtly denies.

In lectures 2 and 5 of the *Anweisung*, Fichte discusses the charge that the doctrine he espouses therein is mysticism. Recall that the *Anweisung* is a "popular" work designed for a philosophically unsophisticated audience. It is a popular communication of some central notions of the scientific presentation of the *Wissenschaftslehre*. Popular opposition to the scientific discourse is to be expected, since it takes place on a level utterly dissimilar to and *abstracted from* that of everyday life. Fichte recognized that philosophy is an exceedingly artificial enterprise whose connection with everyday life is as an *explanans* to an *explanandum*. Yet there is another impediment to a reception of the popular presentation, namely, a hesitancy toward the apparent "severity" of a doctrine that claims to be the one true doctrine.[34] In addition, the modern tenor of skepticism (particularly regarding all things religious) is a further impediment to the popular presentation. In fact, Fichte claims that the very opposition of the modern (enlightened) age to (unenlightened) fanaticism has itself become a kind of fanaticism. It is in this context that Fichte comments on one of the "odious nicknames" and charges that have been directed at his work, namely, that it is an exercise in "mysticism" (*WBL*, 324).

Fichte clearly locates the substance of this accusation, for his accusers call him a "mystic" *not* because they have a clear idea of what mysticism is but, rather, because it is a *word of reproach*. He then proceeds to examine the reasons that lead his opponents to level the charge of mysticism: namely, they oppose the notion of any supersensible reality and deny the inward independence and creative power of thought. They are, in other words, dogmatists (of the kind referred to in the first and second introductions to the 1797–98 *Versuch einer neuen Darstellung der Wissenschaftslehre*).[35] Indeed, if those are the reasons behind their charge, Fichte can only respond that "we admit the whole accusation, and willingly confess . . . that in this sense of the word our doctrine is indeed mysticism" (*WBL*, 326). Now, this quite clearly is a criticism of "mysticism" to which Perovich's argument can respond, for his interpretation is based on a narrow conception of mysticism. However, the *Anweisung* contains another discussion of mysticism in lecture 5, where Fichte distinguishes between true religion and mysticism. He notes that "the true and real religious life is not alone percipient and contemplative . . . but is essentially active" (*WBL*, 378). The active life should here be understood as the life of moral action. This clearly mitigates against those forms of mysticism that issue in quietism and withdrawal, so we thus have managed to take the first step in critiquing the mystical reading. However, we have as of yet eliminated only *some* forms of mystical readings, for not all mystics advocate quietism and withdrawal.[36]

Fichte also comments on mysticism in the *Grundzüge*, which is something of a companion piece to the *Anweisung*. The scope of my criticism of Perovich's mystical reading enlarges with this work, wherein Fichte notes that mysticism is a phenomenon of the third, and present, age.[37] The present age (nineteenth-century Europe) is characterized as an age of revolt against external sources of authority. It is also an age that embraces sense-experience as the touchstone for truth and meaning. However, this age "bears within its own breast the germs of a reaction against itself" (*CPA*, 123). The phenomenon of mysticism is this germ of resistance, and it is characterized by a reaction against the equally dogmatic standpoint of sense-experience. In this regard, since the present age's embrace of sense-experience occurred as a result of its opposition to the dogma of external authority, and since it merely replaced one dogma with another, mysticism becomes the resistance to any such dogma whatsoever. Mistaking external authority and sense perception for being the only possible explanatory grounds, mysticism posits as its supreme principle precisely what the twin dogmas of external authority and empiricism deem as being most inconsequential; namely, the idea of an incomprehensible and unseen Absolute (*CPA*, 124). Both mysticism and transcendental philosophy thus share an initial similarity in their resolute turn toward thought itself as the supreme principle of experience. However, whereas transcendental philosophy possesses a systematic method, mysticism is at the whim of what Fichte calls the "blind-thinking power" of nature (*CPA*, 128).

What is this "blind-thinking power of nature"? Consider the act of abstraction that in the *Wissenschaftslehre* brackets out the everyday standpoint and initiates a thinking of thought itself. Unlike critical philosophy, which has a fundamental principle to orient this cognition of cognition, mysticism proceeds capriciously. In Kantian terms, mysticism lacks the proper "orientation in thinking." There is thus no intelligible connection between ideas, nor is there clarity in the ideas entertained. Without either a systematic method or a fundamental principle to guide this cognition of cognition, the thinker is left at the whims of her individual temperament, constitution, health, mode of life, and so on. Deep questions regarding Kant's and Fichte's focus on systematic matters remain, but it is at least certain that each thinker conceived of system-construction as a bulwark against mere rhapsodizing, however edifying it might be. It seems absurd to think of a system of mystic thought, where all propositions express some or other mystical phenomenon or insight. The very content of such propositions (ineffability, fusion of differences, etc.) is unsuited to any meaningful kind of systematic connection. After all, systematic interconnection highlights the subordinate and superordinate hierarchies that obtain in a body of propositions, but properties like ineffability make such distinctions impossible. Nor is it likely that propositions expressing mystical phenomena or insights can themselves be situated systematically among other, non-mystical, propositions. If mystical propositions defy our ordinary means of classification—which proceeds by making the distinctions, for example, between species and genera, that are superseded in mystical experience—then how can they be classified as items in any hierarchy? So mystical experiences and propositions expressing the same seem antithetical to the kind of system-building that Kant and Fichte embraced.

Fichte describes mysticism as "a somewhat unusual empirical phenomenon" (*CPA*, 128). His criteria for something counting as mysticism are two: (1) the notion that God, the nature of life, and so on, proceed from an ineffable "inward and mysterious light" (*CPA*, 133); and (2) mysticism is never a moral philosophy and sees religion as the mere deification of nature. He notes that, in the end, mysticism is always a *Naturphilosophie* in which one "listens attentively to the voice of nature thinking within him" (*CPA*, 130). Unlike the *Anweisung*'s discussion of mysticism, it is clear that Fichte intends the discussion of the *Grundzüge* to apply to mysticism *überhaupt*. When considered together, the *Anweisung* and *Grundzüge* offer compelling evidence against Perovich's reading (or *any* mystical reading of the *Anweisung* whatsoever). Yet something more is needed if the present refutation of Perovich's mystical reading is to succeed, for there are indeed mystics who seem to offer a moral philosophy and who do not appear to deify nature.[38] I do think that one could argue against such exceptional cases (showing that they are, as Fichte claims, mere instances of *Naturphilosophie*), but this enterprise is beyond the scope of the present study. However, even if we grant such exceptional cases and admit that

Fichte's refutation of mysticism in these two works may not apply to *all* mystics, we have another resource to complete our refutation of the mystical reading, namely, the content of the *Anweisung* itself. Indeed, I hope to demonstrate that the mystical reading is both unnecessary and a distortion, since Fichte's putatively mystical claims have a distinct non-mystical meaning. I will demonstrate this by offering an interpretation of the *Anweisung* that will place *all* of Fichte's problematic claims therein within a proper systematic context; however, my interpretation will also demonstrate why such claims locate the *Anweisung* beyond the confines of any possible transcendental philosophy.

What is the purpose of the *Anweisung*?[39] We need not speculate, for in the first lecture, Fichte asserts that "I have pledged myself to show you the means by which [the] Blessed Life may be attained and enjoyed" (*WBL,* 308). "You" in this sentence refers not to the professional philosopher, but rather to the common person The *Anweisung* is a work whose target audience is the person immersed in the standpoint of everyday life, and who has an "open and candid mind" and possesses a sense (albeit uncultivated) of his or her spiritual nature (*WBL,* 320). In this regard, in lecture 2 Fichte notes that certain individuals possess a "natural sense of truth" (*WBL,* 320), an inchoate felt recognition of one's status as a free moral agent.[40] This "natural sense" is, I believe, the analogue of the Jena *Wissenschaftslehre*'s notion that idealism is rooted in a lively sense of one's own freedom.[41] It is precisely to such individuals that Fichte addresses the *Anweisung.* Yet, Fichte does not intend to communicate a doctrine per se; nor is his a merely edifying discourse. His aim is not to "communicate such instruction" but, rather, to "awaken a desire to receive it" (*WBL,* 310). Thus, I shall interpret the *Anweisung* as a manual[42] of sorts, one that if followed actively and purposefully by the reader can create in her the conditions necessary for the possibility of attaining the standpoint of philosophy (or, if philosophy proper is not entered into, at least nurturing and enlivening an idealist sensibility within her). When will Fichte consider his communication to be successful? When the reader truly "understands" it, namely, "by everyone who, moved by these discourses, is elevated above the common view of the world" (*WBL,* 318). Fichte wants to aid the reader in elevating herself above the common mode of life wherein dogmatism (i.e., a captivation by and identification with the things of the sensible world) continually threatens the person's felt sense of autonomy; indeed, Fichte hopes to provide the resources for attaining a higher spiritual standpoint toward what he calls "blessedness." The *Anweisung* is, then, therapeutic in nature.

But what is this "blessedness" and "blessed life" (*Seligkeit*)? The notion of the blessed life functions as a regulative ideal in the *Anweisung.* "We cannot win blessedness," Fichte tells us, "but we may cast away our wretchedness" (*WBL*, 308). The *Anweisung* cannot deliver blessedness before the reader (either the actual state or even a determinate concept of the same),[43] but it can—and must, if it is to be successful—provide the occasion for the reader's "casting away" her own wretchedness and turning toward the ground of her moral vocation. This is a turn away from the multiplicity and transiency of the world of the senses and toward the "eternal and unchanging" supersensible foundation of that world.[44] Such a turning seeks to leave behind the merely apparent life of the sensible world and of sensual interests and inclinations: "The True Life loves the One, Unchangeable, and Eternal; the mere Apparent Life attempts to love the transitory and perishable—were that capable of being loved, or could such love uphold itself in being" (*WBL*, 301). Blessedness (and the related terms "love," "true life," etc.) thus involves an orientation away from the multiplicity and ceaseless change of the world of objects and a turn toward the unity and abiding ground of the world; in this regard, Fichte defines blessedness as "the living possession" of the theory we have now set forth [in the *Anweisung*]" (*WBL*, 410). This "living possession" is made possible by the "withdrawal of our mind from the Visible, [in which case] the objects of our former love fade from our view, and gradually disappear, until we regain them clothed with fresh beauty in the aether of the new world that rises before us [the true life of true thought and love]" (*WBL*, 309).

Hunter notes that Fichte's aim in the *Anweisung* is to provide a "phenomenology of love,"[45] but this is only partly correct. Fichte *does* offer a (for lack of a better phrase) "phenomenology of love"; however, this is not in itself the end of the work but, rather, the means toward the true end, namely, nurturing the reader's receptivity toward idealism and philosophy proper. We thus must not fault Fichte for failing to account for certain aspects of human love (e.g., sensual, familial, etc.)[46] when this was not at all his intention. What, then, *is* Fichte's "phenomenology of love"? He notes that a subject can take various standpoints toward her world. These ways of seeing the world correspond to "the five stages and grades of development of the inward spiritual life"[47] (*WBL*, 368). Throughout the *Anweisung,* Fichte writes of love (which he claims is identical with life and blessedness), and we can approach these five stages by focusing on the putative object of their "love" and "enjoyment" (i.e., what is the highest value?).[48] The lower stages place all value in the sensible world, and each successive stage grows in greater approximation to that which is truly of value (i.e., a value that is eternal and unchanging, that ever abides despite the ceaseless change of the sensible world). This "phenomenology of love" is a mechanism by which Fichte hopes to lead the reader from the merely relative values of the sensible world to an absolute ground of value. Thus, Fichte's "phenomenology of love" is in the service of a larger problem, which I call the Problem of the Good.[49]

There is a classic problem in the philosophy of religion, namely the problem of evil. But there is a prior problem that must be addressed before we confront the problem that evil poses for our conception of a meaningful and justifiable world-order. The presence of evil certainly raises many questions, but what are we to make of the presence in our world of values such as goodness, values that appear to be actualized instances of some absolute value? This is the problem of goodness: namely, how and why is goodness actualized in the world? Put differently, is there a supersensible source of value? Or is value a mere standard that we create, a mere projection of our psychological needs and interests? Fichte's aim in the *Anweisung* is to assist the reader in preparing herself (Fichte cannot do it for her) for the standpoint of philosophy by addressing this very problem, a problem whereby dogmatism is quite clearly distinguished from idealism. For the dogmatist (in the *Anweisung,* the person captivated by the merely apparent life), there is no supersensible source of value: the presence of value in the world is a mere accident. By asking the question of the source of value—a question I think is implicit throughout the whole of the *Anweisung*—Fichte sensitizes his reader toward the philosophical standpoint (since merely relative values are found in the former standpoint and one's pre-philosophical commitments to morality and religion demand a non-relative source of value).

A problem for my interpretation remains, namely the problem that, as it stands, my interpretation of the purpose of the *Anweisung* is not at all incompatible with the mystical reading. Indeed, is not a core feature of mysticism the claim that one must give up one's present life (of the senses and of sensual delight) and aspire toward the eternal ground of that life? From Eckhart to Sankara, this distinction between the genuine and the merely apparent life is a seminal motif of mysticism. What I must therefore demonstrate is that (1) the *Anweisung* does not in fact take a mystical form, and (2) the mystical form is itself antithetical to the purpose and claims of that work.

First, does Fichte argue for a kind of direct, immediate experience of union with the Absolute? This is important since it is a defining feature of mysticism. Recall that mystical experiences contain a noetic quality that involves some or other insight, illumination, or revelation into an ultimate reality; and the noetic quality is of a form that transcends the normal perceptual and conceptual bounds of experience. However, Fichte is emphatic that whatever else the "blessed life" may be, it is most surely different in kind from such mystical "knowledge." Fichte is adamant in claiming that we can never escape from the limitations of human thought. He initially defines thought in general as "a certain view of ourselves and of the world" (*WBL*, 306), but his later development of the concept of thought is clearly an idealistic doctrine emphasizing the bounds of possible experience and knowledge. Fichte writes that "knowledge . . . is cut off from all possibility of passing beyond it [knowledge], or of conceiving and tracing itself prior to [its] existence" (*WBL*, 343). Furthermore, the necessary form of all possible knowledge is "image, representation, or conception" (*WBL*, 344). Indeed, it follows from this that our union with God cannot transcend the limits of human knowing: "Only in pure thought can our union with God be recognized" (*WBL*, 345). Such thought must of course prepare itself and orient itself away from the world of sensibility, but, and this is key, it does not thereby acquire some occult access to an otherworldly reality. Instead, it is a *new orientation on the same reality*. "To the outward eye," Fichte notes, "these two opposite modes of life [true and apparent] closely resemble each other; both proceed upon the same common objects, which are perceived by both in the same way; inwardly, however, they are very different" (*WBL*, 346).

The task of human life is a striving to reconcile the contradictions between our perception of reality and pure thought's standpoint toward that same reality (i.e., the contradiction that the everyday standpoint reveals merely relative values but pure thought reveals an absolute value.) This task is described by Fichte as a casting away of our sensual selves and an aspiration toward union with God. However, Fichte is clear in indicating that this is *not* a world-renouncing mystical union, for "even in our union with him [God] he does not become our own being; but he floats before us as something foreign to, and outside of, ourselves, to which we can only devote ourselves, clinging to him with earnest love" (*WBL*, 365). Indeed, it is not that we *lose* one world and gain another but, rather, we gain a new perspective upon that *same* reality: "It [the sensible world] only assumes a new significance" (*WBL*, 365).

I believe that we thus possess compelling reasons for rejecting the mystical reading of the *Anweisung*. First, I have discussed Fichte's explicit remarks concerning mysticism in the *Anweisung* and the *Grundzüge*. This in itself is a powerful reason for rejecting the mystical reading but, as I noted above, it is not conclusive (since there are possible forms of mysticism not captured by Fichte's discussion). Therefore, I have offered an interpretation that exhibits Fichte's intention in the *Anweisung* and the manner in which this intention is incompatible with the mystical reading. Though my interpretation has, I believe, succeeded on one level (refuting the mystical reading), it is not yet complete. As it stands, my interpretation would lead one to believe that the *Anweisung* is merely a reiteration (albeit in vastly different language) of central doctrines of the earlier, Jena-period *Wissenschaftslehre*. However, this would be incorrect. If I have shown why the *Anweisung* is most certainly *not* a mystical text, I must also show why it consistently has been interpreted as such. The reason for this is, I believe, that Fichte has indeed departed from the recognizable domain of transcendental philosophy. This departure from the limits of transcendental philosophy accounts for the mystical-sounding language of the *Anweisung*. These two issues, namely, the departure of Fichte from the earlier *Wissenschaftslehre* and the mystical appearance of the *Anweisung*, are intimately related.

I construe the Jena-period *Wissenschaftslehre* as a system of radical human finitude, a *Strebungsphilosophie* grounded in the free activity of the self as it strives to transform the not-I into the image of the I. This task is infinite, since such a tension between the I and the limitation of the not-I is the necessary condition for the possibility of any human experience whatsoever. Nevertheless, it is the ideal toward which human life must aspire, namely, to have one's head in harmony with one's heart, the harmony of practical and theoretical interests and reason. Daniel Breazeale describes Fichte's philosophy as a "practical (or even 'ethical') foundationalism,"[50] and this is indeed correct. As Breazeale notes, "Fichte's insistence upon the legitimacy . . . of his own foundational project is . . . ultimately based upon an appeal to the categorical character of one's self-awareness as a free agent."[51] Fichte's practical foundationalism requires an understanding of the limitations of theoretical reason, which cannot address questions such as the origin of our freedom or of the world but only the world as it is experienced by a radically finite consciousness. It is precisely at this point that the *Anweisung* departs from the Jena-period *Wissenschaftslehre*. Indeed, the *Anweisung* is in large part an attempt to formulate an *ontology* that can account for what Fichte calls the "transmutation" of the one, unchanging, and ever-abiding Absolute into the multiplicity of experience. Fichte thus addresses what is perhaps *the* problem of philosophy, namely, the problem of the one and the many. In terms of my own interpretation of the *Anweisung*, the problem is this: the experience of consciousness is a factual given, and in this experience we encounter values; yet if there are to be necessity and universality in our values (and, indeed, in our very existence) then this world of consciousness must have its ground in an absolute source of unity and value. The problem thus becomes one of accounting for this source, and Fichte's ontological discourse in the *Anweisung* is his attempt to resolve this problem. It is also a serious transgression of the limitations of transcendental idealism.

Fichte seems to have reified his epistemology, turning merely epistemological distinctions into distinctions regarding reality *as such*. Just as the self must be limited for experience to be possible (a limitation that is genetically deduced from the self's own positing of itself, the radical givenness of its free activity in intellectual intuition, i.e., the notion of *Tathandlung*), so too does Fichte seem to demand that the Absolute must be limited and "posit" its other: "Through his own existence, and by its essential nature, God throws out a part of his existence—that is, such part of it as becomes self-consciousness"[52] (*WBL*, 358). Now, Fichte does qualify himself, noting that consciousness is confined to its finite limits[53] and that thought can never transcend these limitations. This leaves two possibilities, neither of which bodes well for any transcendental idealist reading of the *Anweisung:* (1) if we assume that Fichte has not transcended the limitations of possible human thought (as he states), then we have an *expansion* of the domain of thought such that it is most certainly no longer a *transcendental* philosophy. We then have a Fichte who is closer to the objective idealism of Hegel; or (2) if we assume that Fichte has transcended the limitations of thought, then he has still (obviously) departed from transcendental idealism. In either case, the evidence gives us strong reasons to conclude that Fichte's later *Religionslehre* is incommensurable with the transcendental philosophy of the Jena-period *Wissenschaftslehre.*[54]

Fichte's *Anweisung zum seligen Leben* of 1806 is an important text, both in its own right and in the context of the development of Fichte's thought. I have argued that a mystical reading should be rejected, since it is a reading that seriously distorts both the purpose of the text and the specific claims made therein. We find three motifs in the *Anweisung:* (1) a phenomenology of human spiritual development; (2) a catechetical phenomenology, whereby Fichte "instructs" the reader by leading her—if she animates her discourse with her own spirit—to pose questions to herself (regarding the source of value, spiritual development, etc.) and then to answer those questions via a transformation of her standpoint on sensible reality; and (3) an ontology that grounds finite existence in the necessary manifestation of the Absolute from itself (and thus the intimate connection of the finite and infinite, given this kenotic framework). The first two motifs are both consonant with the earlier *Wissenschaftslehre* (and transcendental idealism *überhaupt*) and stand as important developments of central doctrines of the same. However, the third motif is quite clearly a departure from and a betrayal of the radical finitude that lies at the heart of the early, Jena-period *Wissenschaftslehre.* Whether the ontological doctrines of the *Anweisung* are separable from the phenomenological doctrines is a matter of dispute that is beyond the scope of this chapter.

Notes

1. English-language scholarship devoted to the *Anweisung* consists of four texts: George Seidel, "The Atheism Controversy of 1799 and the Christology of Fichte's *Anweisung zum seligen Leben* of 1806," in *New Perspectives on Fichte,* ed. Tom Rockmore and Daniel Breazeale (Atlantic Highlands: Humanities, 1996), 143–52; Anthony Perovich, "Fichte and the Typology of Mysticism," *in Fichte: Historical Contexts / Contemporary Controversies,* ed. Daniel Breazeale and Tom Rockmore (Atlantic Highlands: Humanities, 1994), 128–41; E. Jeffery Kinlaw, "Fichte's Kenotic Christology," *Idealistic Studies* 22 (1992): 39–51; and C. K. Hunter, "The Problem of Fichte's Phenomenology of Love," *Idealistic Studies* 6 (1976): 178–90.

2. Gueroult appears to subscribe to the mystical interpretation of the *Anweisung.* For instance, in "L'Initiation à la vie bienheureuse (in *Études sur Fichte* [New York: Georg Olms, 1974]; all translations are my own), Gueroult remarks that "there is a reprehensible mysticism, that of the visionary who abandons himself to the blind force of an irrational, arbitrary, and obscure intuition. . . . But there is a highly respectable mysticism, the one of the true religion" (101); and Fichte's *Anweisung* presents such a true religion *qua* mysticism. As Gueroult notes, the *Anweisung* is just this "triomphe de la mystique" (127).

3. Perovich, "Fichte and the Typology of Mysticism," 128–41.

4. Robert Alfred Vaughan, *Hours with the Mystics: A Contribution to the History of Religious Opinion* (London: Gibbons, 1895), 59–60 and 212. Vaughan claims a relation between Fichte and Eckhart regarding the notion of union with the Godhead. For a discussion of the relation of Fichte to German mysticism in general, see Andrew Weeks, *German Mysticism: From Hildegard of Bingen to Ludwig Wittgenstein* (Albany: State University of New York Press, 1993), 218–22 and 227.

5. Hans Waldenfels, *Absolute Nothingness: Foundations for a Buddhist-Christian Dialogue* (New York: Paulist Press, 1976), 37. Waldenfels's interpretation rests in large part on those texts in which Fichte appears to be calling for a complete rejection of one's selfhood.

6. Howard Brinton, *The Mystic Will: Based on a Study of the Philosophy of Jacob Boehme* (New York: Macmillan, 1930), 6, 197n, 215, and 260; see also Andrew Weeks, *Boehme: An Intellectual Biography of the Seventeenth-Century Philosopher and Mystic* (Albany: State University of New York Press, 1991), 207.

7. John Taber, *Transformative Philosophy: A Study of Sankara, Fichte, and Heidegger* (Honolulu: University of Hawaii Press, 1983), 90.

8. Seidel, "Atheism Controversy of 1799," 143–52.

9. Hunter, "The Problem of Fichte's Phenomenology of Love," 178–90. Hunter's paper, one of the few by English-speaking scholars, succeeds in noting the mystical tone that Fichte seems to adopt (and which Hunter is partly correct to attribute to the popular form of the text). However, Hunter distorts the intentions of the text with his various criticisms that Fichte's "phenomenology" of love is insufficient due to its neglect of crucial aspects of the experience of love (e.g., familial relations, sexual relations, etc.). Instead, I will argue later in the present chapter that Fichte offers a "phenomenology of catachetics (or conversion, turn-

ing)," that is, a regimen for animating the reader's spirit and attuning her to the standpoint of idealism.

10. Perovich, "Fichte and the Typology of Mysticism," 128–41.

11. *Anweisung zum seligen Leben oder auch die Religionslehre,* in *GA* 1.9:3–212; in English, *WBL,* 291–496.

12. The very notion of defining something that is ineffable is, at best, highly problematic, and, at worst, absurd. Nevertheless, the need to thematize such experiences has produced a plethora of definitions; for example, the appendix to William Ralph Inge's *Christian Mysticism* (London: Methuen, 1912) lists no less than twenty-six definitions of "mysticism."

13. Nelson Pike, *Mystic Union: An Essay in the Phenomenology of Mysticism* (Ithaca: Cornell University Press, 1992). Pike provides a "phenomenological" analysis of various states of mystical union, focusing exclusively on the tradition of Christian mysticism (and particularly on Saint Teresa of Avila).

14. John N. Findlay, "The Logic of Mysticism," *Religious Studies* 2 (1965): 145–62. Findlay writes that mysticism is as much a universal background to experience as the open sky is to vision" (162).

15. Steven T. Katz, *Mysticism and Philosophical Analysis* (London: Shelly, 1978); and *Mysticism and Religious Traditions* (New York: Oxford University Press, 1983). Katz offers a naturalistic, demystifying account of mysticism. For example, he claims that since all experience is mediated, and since mystical experience purports to offer a non-mediated experience, one can only conclude that the content of mystical experience is purely "contextual" (56–57); that is, social and psychological explanations can account in full for putative "mystical" experiences.

16. William James, *The Varieties of Religious Experience* (New York: Touchstone, 1977), 299–399.

17. Published with the translation of the *Anweisung* as *Characteristics of the Present Age* in *Significant Contributions to the History of Psychology, 1750–1920,* vii–290.

18. We must not discount the possibility that the author may have reasons for explicitly denying that his text is mystical, even as that text expresses unmistakable mystical affinities and sensibilities.

19. Perovich, "Fichte and the Typology of Mysticism," 128. For one who opposes mysticism on philosophical grounds, this is tantamount to "guilt by association." Yet, on philosophical grounds this kind of argument by association is without any merit whatsoever. First, it is merely an argument based on a questionable sampling of various "authorities." Second, the burden of proof is on Perovich to show that the mystical reading is the best inference to an explanation available, yet he *nowhere* in his paper considers other explanations. Third, Perovich simply neglects to perform the most basic exegesis of Fichte's claims, simply assuming that they in some unspecified way correspond to the claims of some or other mystic.

20. See Perovich, "Fichte and the Typology of Mysticism," 130, for his scholarly account of the reception of the *Anweisung* among writers focusing on mysticism and religion. Perovich's sources are Heinrich Scholz, "Preface and Introduction" to *Die Anweisung sum seligen Leben* (Berlin: Deutsche Bibliothek, 1912); R. D. Scmidig, *Gott und Welt in Fichtes Anweisung zum seligen Leben* (Wald: Pontifica Universitas Gregoriana, 1966); Nicolai Hartmann, *Die Philosophie des deutschen Idealis-*

mus (Berlin and New York: De Gruyter, 1974); and Fritz Medicus, "Introduction to Fichte," in *Die Anweisung sum seligen Leben* (Hamburg: Meiner, 1970).

21. Perovich, "Fichte and the Typology of Mysticism," 130.

22. Perovich, "Fichte and the Typology of Mysticism," 130.

23. Perovich, "Fichte and the Typology of Mysticism," 131.

24. Perovich, "Fichte and the Typology of Mysticism," 132.

25. In his discussion, Perovich utilizes the work of William J. Wainright (*Mysticism: A Study of Its Nature, Cognitive Value, and Moral Implications* [Madison: University of Wisconsin Press, 1981]); and R. C. Zaehner (*Mysticism, Sacred and Profane: An Inquiry into Some Varieties of Praeternatural Experience* [New York: Oxford University Press, 1961]).

26. For a pantheistic interpretation, see Antonin Gilbert Sertillanges, *Le christianisme et les philosophies* (Paris: Aubier, 1941). In this text, Sertillanges draws several parallels between Spinoza and Fichte, arguing that the latter's adoption of a form of pantheism results in the traditional mystical conception that "God is All" and that this ultimate unity is accessible via ecstatic revelation (46 and 200–204). Though not mentioned by Perovich, pantheism is not the only possibility, given the monistic reading. Consider the "panentheism" of Karl Christian Friedrich Krause, who was educated at Jena and, while there, came under the influence of Fichte and Schelling. In this view, both nature and human consciousness are parts of the Absolute (God), but the Absolute is not reducible to them.

27. Perovich, "Fichte and the Typology of Mysticism," 132.

28. "Thus, insofar as man is Love—and this he is always in the root of his Life, and can be nothing but this, although it may be that he is but the Love of himself—but especially insofar as he is the Love of God, he remains eternally and forever one, true, and unchangeable as God himself, and *is indeed in reality God himself*" (*WBL*, 469); and "Being and Existence, God and Man, are One; wholly transfused and lost in each other" (*WBL*, 132).

29. "Even in our union with him [the Absolute, God] he does not become our own Being, but he floats before us as something foreign to us" (*WBL*, 365).

30. Perovich, "Fichte and the Typology of Mysticism," 136.

31. Perovich, "Fichte and the Typology of Mysticism," 136.

32. This claim is borrowed from W. H. Walsh, who notes in his *Reason and Experience* (Oxford: Clarendon, 1947) that "if mystical experience is truly cognitive, we should expect those who have it to find ways of referring to different parts or aspects of it which would be intelligible to other mystics at least" (227–28). This approach seems bereft of philosophical merit for (at least) two reasons: (1) it embraces the contradiction of persons experiencing ineffable states somehow communicating those states to one another—that is, if they are truly ineffable, then how could *I* possibly know if my experience is like *yours*? and (2) an inference to a better explanation arguably would refer to various social and cultural contexts that condition the way in which individuals react to paradoxical situations.

33. Perovich, "Fichte and the Typology of Mysticism," 138.

34. "The men of these days are offended at this severity, as if they were thereby grievously ill-treated" (*WBL*, 321). See also Fichte's footnote to his "Aus einem Privatschreiben" (in English in *IWL*, 163), where he writes that "another of [the] for-

mal absurdities of our age is the ridicule and persecution directed against 'one-sole-philosophy' philosophers."

35. "Some people—namely those who have not attained a full feeling of their own freedom and absolute self-sufficiency—discover themselves only in the act of representing things. Their self-consciousness is dispersed and attached to objects and must be gleaned from the manifold of the latter. They glimpse their own image only insofar as it is reflected through things, as in a mirror" (*IWL,* 18).

36. Meister Eckhart, for example, argues that the goal is a life of action that flows forth from contemplation. See Eckhart's sermon on the story of Mary and Martha in his *Deutsche Predigten und Traktate,* ed. Josef Quint (Munich: Hanser, 1963), 280ff.

37. The "age of liberation," directly from external ruling authority and indirectly from reason considered as instinct.

38. Mystics that putatively escape such charges include John Ruysbroeck and Thomas à Kempis, who advocate a life of moral activity. (See F. C. Happold, *Mysticism: A Study and an Anthology* [New York: Penguin, 1963], 280–93 and 299–305, for relevant texts and commentary.)

39. In presenting my interpretation of the *Anweisung,* I will pass over the historical reasons for the lecture series that would become this text. As Xavier Leon (*Fichte et son temps* [Paris: Librairie Armand Colin, 1958]) and Martial Gueroult ("L'Initiation à la vie bienheureuse," 96–144) have noted, the immediate impetus for Fichte's *Anweisung* was the publication in 1804 of Schelling's *Philosophie und Religion.* Fichte opposed what he took to be Schelling's Spinozism (i.e., his conception of the Absolute—God—as a substance); moreover, Fichte felt the need to respond to Schelling's claim that the *Wissenschaftslehre* is one-sided due to its lack of a doctrine of Absolute life and of Blessedness, that is, felicity (Leon, *Fichte et son temps,* 488).

40. I substitute the phrase "moral nature" for Fichte's own language of "spiritual nature," noting that the *Anweisung* is clear in its statement that the spiritual life (the life of the true religion) is incompatible with anything but the life of moral activity. As Fichte notes in the fifth lecture, the fourth and fifth stages of spiritual development, namely, religion and science, "are only percipient and contemplative, not in themselves active and practical" (*WBL,* 378). The true life and the true religion *must* be an active life; indeed, the latter is "essentially active," and if it is not then the putative union with God is merely "deceptive and vain" (*WBL,* 378). Religion "is the innermost spirit that penetrates, inspires, and pervades all our thought and action" (*WBL,* 379).

41. See the "First Introduction" to the 1797 *Wissenschaftslehre* for a discussion of this lively sense that the idealist has of her own agency (*IWL,* 15–19). Indeed, Fichte's insight that "the kind of philosophy one chooses . . . depends on the kind of person one is" (*IWL,* 20) applies also to a person's orientation to (or even recognition of a thing such as) the blessed life.

42. This, of course, conceives of the *Anweisung* as a text and not in its original form, that is, a public communication via live lectures. In the latter case, I would argue that what occurred in the event of those lectures was an encounter between Fichte and the listener in which Fichte conducted something of a performance

piece, one that the listener was advised to follow actively and to animate with her own spirit and thought. In thus following Fichte's discourse actively, the listener would make the same "moves" as Fichte, moves which my interpretation claims to be the move away from dogmatism and toward an idealist position from which philosophy proper could develop.

43. It is important to keep in mind that the title of the lecture series is the "way" toward the blessed life, thus indicating quite clearly Fichte's conception of the work as being a propaedeutic of sorts.

44. Fichte describes the self's captivation by the sensual world in the following terms: "That which is vagrant in the manifold and transitory is dissolved, poured forth, and spread about like water; because of its desire to love this and that and many things besides, it really loves nothing; and just because it would be everywhere at home, it is nowhere at home. This vagrancy [in the manifold] is our peculiar nature, and in it we are born" (*WBL,* 308).

45. Hunter, "Fichte's Phenomenology of Love," 178–90.

46. This is Hunter's criticism: Fichte over-spiritualizes the treatment of love, thus neglecting crucial aspects of the human experience of love. For example, Hunter writes that "the most glaring omission is the lack of treatment of sensual as sexual love" (Hunter, "Fichte's Phenomenology of Love," 184). My interpretation will reveal, it is hoped, the shortcomings of this reading.

47. One could consider these "five" stages as being a further development of an earlier claim that Fichte made regarding human development; namely, his claim in the "First Introduction" to the 1791 *Wissenschaftslehre* that "there are two levels of human development, and so long as everyone has not yet reached the highest level in the course of the progress of our species, there are two main sub-species of human beings" (Fichte, "Introductions to the *Wissenschaftslehre,*" 18).

48. "Show me what thou truly lovest, what thou seekest and strivest for with thy whole heart . . . and thou hast thereby shown me thy Life. What thou lovest, in that thou livest" (*WBL,* 299).

49. This interpretation is heavily indebted to Ellen Bliss Talbot, *The Fundamental Principle of Fichte's Philosophy* (New York: Macmillan, 1906). In her discussion of Fichte's later philosophy (the *Anweisung* in particular), Talbot makes a number of remarks that imply my interpretation (though she does not make it explicit as I do).

50. Daniel Breazeale, "Why Fichte Now?" *Journal of Philosophy* 88 (1991): 524–31.

51. Breazeale, "Why Fichte Now?" 530.

52. Kinlaw addresses this very issue of Fichte's kenotic Christology, showing quite persuasively that Fichte does indeed produce a doctrine in which consciousness/knowing can only be God's existence outside of himself. Such a Christology rests upon an ontology that arguably is incommensurable with transcendental idealism, since there is no evidence within consciousness of this kenosis, nor is it required for the possibility of consciousness. Though Kinlaw does not address this issue, it is, I think, an unmistakable consequence of Fichte's later work (namely, a departure from transcendental philosophy).

53. Fichte notes that "the whole distinction set forth in our former lecture [between Absolute Being and its existence] . . . is thus seen to be only for us, and only

as a result of our limitation; and by no means to have any place, immediately and of itself, in the Divine Existence" (*WBL*, 355). Indeed, this remark that such distinctions are merely "for us" reoccurs frequently throughout the text.

54. This is not to say that there are no connections whatsoever between the early and the later period. Indeed, Radrizzani has noted in his commentary on the *Wissenschaftslehre nova methodo* that this work is a "propaedeutic" of sorts for a transition to Fichte's later "philosophy of the absolute." (See Ives Radrizzani, *Vers la foundation de l'intersubjectivité chez Fichte* [Paris: Librairie Philosophique J. Vrin, 1993].) In addition, see Ellen Bliss Talbot, "The Relation of the Two Periods of Fichte's Philosophy," *Mind* 10 (1910): 336–46.

The Notion of Being in Fichte's Late Philosophy

Johannes Brachtendorf

Transcendental Philosophy and Metaphysics

Transcendental philosophy and metaphysics may be contrasted in various ways. One might say, for example, that transcendental philosophy in the Kantian sense is a philosophy of subjectivity or of the I, whereas metaphysics is concerned with substance or with being. Of course, such a distinction is highly superficial. Fichte himself, *the* philosopher of the I, calls his *Wissenschaftslehre* "metaphysics" in both his early and late writings. In the *Grundlage der gesamten Wissenschaftslehre* (1794), for example, he says the *Wissenschaftslehre* is a metaphysics because it is concerned with "genuine reality" (*ursprüngliche Realität*).[1] In his *Zweite Einleitung in die Wissenschaftslehre,* we read that the *Wissenschaftslehre* is a "metaphysics . . . insofar as it asks about the reason of being for us."[2] In the *Anweisung zum seligen Leben* (1806) Fichte says that, expressed in the "language of the schools," the *Wissenschaftslehre* is the "most profound metaphysics and ontology."[3] And in 1812 he asserts that his *Sittenlehre* should be carried out as a doctrine of being, that is, as a "doctrine of true being, and of proper reality."[4] Thus, it should be called "metaphysics."[5] Fichte never shrinks from aligning his *Wissenschaftslehre* with the metaphysical tradition, which, according to Aristotle, asks about the "causes and principles of being."[6]

To develop a more suitable distinction between transcendental philosophy and metaphysics, one should ask where they each localize the causes and principles of being. It is characteristic of transcendental philosophy to locate the reason of being in a subject, or in the I, which, by means of transcendental acts, constitutes being, now understood as the being of objects. Being is conceived of as a product of a process of constitution, something brought forth through specific acts of the I. So these acts need to be analyzed in order to find the reasons and principles of being. The "true reality," to use a Fichtean word, lies in the I. Traditional metaphysics, however, does not seek the reason of being in the I, but in a being of higher rank, in an Absolute, or in God. According to this tradition, the divine is the "true reality," which means that we cannot understand being without referring to God. Aristotle hints at such a conception when he says that theology is the first philosophy.[7] This way of thinking reached its climax with Plotinus, and philosophers like Augustine and Thomas Aquinas established the same view by distinguishing between "being itself" (*esse ipsum*) and the "thing being" (*ens*).

Which role does subjectivity play in traditional metaphysics? It is often said that this metaphysical tradition overlooks the importance of the I and its functions, and that only modern philosophy starting with Descartes focuses on subjectivity. Recent research on Plotinus[8] and Augustine[9] has proven this idea to be inadequate. Descartes drew heavily on Augustine (although without giving much credit to him),[10] and the problem of self-consciousness that Fichte paid so much attention to is rigorously developed and discussed in both Plotinus and Augustine. This tradition does not overlook subjectivity, but includes it in what could be called a three-step model of reality. First, there is the world of things, above it subjectivity, and God as the supreme principle is placed at the summit. The realm of things can be understood with regard to subjectivity, but the subject on its part needs to be interpreted by recourse to God. If we characterize metaphysics in this way, namely as a three-step theory, including not only the world and the I, but also God as the supreme principle, we would certainly have to call Fichte's late *Wissenschaftslehren,* especially his *Wissenschaftslehre* 1812, metaphysical. In his late lectures, Fichte has certainly kept central ideas of the early *Wissenschaftslehre,* but step-by-step he withdraws his concept of the I as an independent, ultimate principle. According to Fichte's late works, the I must be radically grounded in a divine Absolute. By this point, the I is no more than an "appearance" of the Absolute, with its essence, its existence, and its acts depending on the Absolute as a higher principle. Even Fichte's vocabulary indicates this shift. The word "I" is not missing in the *Wissenschaftslehre* 1812, but it becomes prevalent only at the end of the work. In the beginning, Fichte prefers to use other terms to indicate the dependency of subjectivity. Here he does not speak of God and the I, but of God and God's image, or of "Being" and the "Concept of Being," or, mostly, of the "Absolute" and its "appearance."

The Multiple Meaning of "Being"

When the late Fichte puts forth a metaphysics as a doctrine of true being and of proper reality, his understanding of the terms *metaphysics* and *being* differs from their usage in the *Zweite Einleitung,* where he calls the *Wis-*

senschaftslehre a metaphysics because it asks about the reasons of being for us. The early work aims at a theory of the object as a product constituted by the I. The term *metaphysics* is here used in the rather unspecific sense to mean a "theory of objects." The late *Wissenschaftslehre*, however, is a metaphysics in a very specific sense, namely as a theory of absolute Being as the sole source of the I and its world. In his *Zweite Einleitung*, Fichte says: "The basic claim of the philosopher as such is this: As soon as the I is for itself, another being outside of it necessarily and simultaneously comes into being. The reason for the latter lies in the former; the latter is caused by the former: Self-consciousness and consciousness of something that is not ourselves are necessarily linked."[11] And the *Wissenschaftslehre nova methodo* continues: "This is the true character of proper being, the notion of which was falsely considered primary and immediate."[12] In Fichte's early doctrine, "being" is a definable, and thus derivative, notion that can be reduced to simpler elements and deduced from them. The "true being" of the late works, however, is indeed a primary and original notion; it is non-analyzable, non-derivative, and not deductible from a higher principle such as the first free act of the I, but is itself the highest principle.

Therefore, the words *being*, or *to be*, or *is*, occur in different meanings.[13] In his earlier writings, Fichte limits the meaning of being to the realm of perceptible objects. He also likes to assimilate it to the notion of substance, understanding "substance" as an entity existing in space and time.[14] Being then means "real being" (*wirkliches Sein*). Accordingly, the intelligible realm and especially the pure I are not to be called "being" or "real," but "non-being" or "non-real" in the sense of "over-being" and "over-real." In his *Gerichtliche Verantwortungsschriften*,[15] for example, Fichte says that no sensible predicate like "being" or "substantiality" is applicable to the intelligible world. But Fichte can also take on the reverse perspective, according to which only the principle of the world of objects *is*, whereas the objects themselves *are* not, because they rank lower than the principle. In his *Appellation* Fichte even brings God into play, when he says: "For our philosophy, the intelligible God is Everything in Everything; for it, he alone *is*."[16]

In his propaedeutical works Fichte prefers to employ the common notion of being, according to which the objects of experience *are*. Here his intention is to show the naive, realistically minded reader that this being can be derived, that it has a "genesis," and thus can be nothing true and original.[17] In the *Wissenschaftslehre* itself, however, he takes a stricter viewpoint. Here, being is ascribed only to the realm of principles. Another point on which the late *Wissenschaftslehre* itself differs from the surrounding propaedeutical writings is that the latter focus mainly on liberating the reader from natural realism by showing the I to be the principle of the world of experience. By and large, they do not transcend the I itself, but remain within a two-step framework. Fichte reserves showing that and how the I is grounded in the Absolute for the *Wissenschaftslehre*. The complete three-step model is developed only in the *Wissenschaftslehre*.

The *Wissenschaftslehre* 1812: The Absolute and Its Appearance

At the beginning of the *Wissenschaftslehre* 1812, Fichte solemnly proclaims: "One *is*, and besides the One there *is* absolutely nothing. Hold onto this, and never take any expression of the *Wissenschaftslehre* to contradict this sentence."[18] Further on he says: "One is, nothing is besides it. Everything else is not: this doctrine shall stand immutably and eternally. The notion of the Absolute is held onto."[19] Fichte also calls the One "Being," so that he can say: "Only Being *is*." This characterization of the Absolute leads to the question of what else could be said in the *Wissenschaftslehre*. How can the *Wissenschaftslehre* surpass its very beginning if there *is* absolutely nothing besides the Absolute?

Approaching this problem, Fichte continues: "According to the concept of the One being, there is no being besides it: but the concept is, and it is besides the One. Protestatio facto contraria! When it is said that there is nothing besides it, then there *is* something besides it, namely the act of saying this. . . . Thus, besides Being is its concept."[20] Seemingly, Fichte means that the fact that we can speak about the One, which alone *is*, and know about it, proves that there is another being, namely the concept of Being. But how can the being of the concept of Being be reconciled with the claim that there *is* absolutely nothing besides the one Being? How does the being of the concept go together with the thesis: only the One *is*? Fichte considers two traditional solutions of the problem, but rejects both of them. The first is the understanding of the Absolute as *hen kai pan*, or as oneness which in itself is a multitude without losing its oneness. On the basis of this understanding, the concept of being could be assimilated by the Absolute, so that it would not stand in itself and thus would not be in opposition to the Absolute. Fichte rejects this conception because it gives up the unity of the Absolute. For him, the Absolute is a pure One; it contains absolutely no manifoldness. The second proposal is centered on the idea of participation. According to this view, the concept *is* because it participates in the being of the One. Fichte, however, considers this insufficient, because it implies a change or genesis within the Absolute.[21]

Fichte decides on a third way to solve the contradiction between the singularity of Being and the being of the concept, namely, a distinction of two "forms" of being. But before giving the correct solution, Fichte first expounds an insufficient method of drawing this distinction. The insufficient method is this: it might be said that the One has necessity; it cannot not be. It is independent of its concept and would exist even if its concept were not. It is "absolutely, because it is," and that is why it is called "absolute Being." The concept of being, however, can be thought not to exist. It can be "thought away" (*weggedacht*), as Fichte says.[22] The concept does not exist necessarily, but only factually, which means that we can ask about the reason for its being, that is, about its genesis. According to this view, the Absolute is necessary, while the concept of the Absolute is contingent. To mark this difference, Fichte introduces the notions of "Being" and "being-there." Being indicates necessity, whereas "there" in "being-there" points to facticity, that is, contingency.[23]

Why is this view insufficient? Fichte argues that *Dasein* is contingent only for us, but necessary in itself. Fichte also calls the concept of being the "appearance" of being, or God's appearance. Due to the inseparability of existence and essence in God, God's existence implies his appearance. God does not have the freedom not to appear. For Fichte, God's appearance follows necessarily from his existence. However, Fichte emphasizes that we have no "real notion of the Absolute."[24] This means we are unable to have an immediate insight into the necessity of God's appearance, so the *Wissenschaftslehre* cannot deduce this appearance. We must first realize that the Absolute appears, and this is a matter of life, not of philosophy.[25] Once we have realized this, we can conclude that, since the Absolute does appear, it appears necessarily. At this point, Peter Baumanns objects that Fichte ends up with a double Absolute because he maintains the necessity of both, the Absolute and its appearance.[26] I think Fichte can be saved from this critique. If the Absolute and its appearance do not differ like the necessary from the contingent, this does not mean that there is no difference at all. Rather, they differ like the unconditionally necessary from the conditionally necessary. The concept is necessary under the condition that the Absolute *is*. The Absolute *is* out of itself or through itself, whereas the appearance is derived and thus remains subordinate. To express this in classical terminology, which I find quite convenient here, the Absolute exists *a se* (it has *aseitas*), whereas the appearance exists *ab alio,* namely through the Absolute. These are the two forms of being that Fichte envisaged to clarify the relation between Being and the concept of Being.

The Being and Non-Being of the Appearance

After having learned about the appearance's specific form of being, the reader may be surprised to encounter the following statement: "By its immediate being, by its mere notion, appearance is non-being and thus it does not exclude genesis, but posits genesis."[27] The appearance, whose being should have been secured by the distinction of two forms of being, is now called "non-being." How can the appearance be and not be at the same time? Some Fichte scholars assert that Fichte here entertains a "dialectical" notion of being.[28] To my mind, there is no reason here to bring dialectics into play. I will try to show that Fichte simply employs two different notions of being.

To determine the sense in which the appearance must be said to be, and in which it must be said not to be, Fichte dwells on a consideration concerning the character of an image as such. On the one hand, an image is a reproduction, or a copy, of its original, showing what the original is like and revealing it. On the other hand, an image is not the original itself, but only its image. In one respect the image corresponds with the original, in another respect it differs. How, then, does the appearance as the image of the Absolute match the Absolute, and how does it diverge from the Absolute?

For Fichte, the Absolute is pure unity. Its appearance, however, is what was denied to the Absolute, namely "hen kai pan; one and everything is the same."[29] Further characterizing the appearance, Fichte declares: "The same thing that is one and remains one in eternity also is multiform in infinity, but without losing its unity, and it is one without losing its multiplicity."[30] Here Fichte distinguishes two aspects of the appearance: a unity aspect and a multiplicity aspect. As a unity the appearance matches the Absolute: "We say the image *is* there; we do not say: it comes to be within itself. There is no change in it, no transmutation, no multiplicity, but it is absolutely one, equal with itself, like the Absolute portrayed in it. It is, how it is, complete and equal with itself."[31] Although the image as a whole is *ab alio* and, therefore, has a genesis, it is in itself an immutable unity. To be a unity constitutes its similarity with the Absolute. Due to this similarity, the image *is*. But in its multiplicity, the image is unlike the Absolute, and therefore has no being: "In one respect the image *is,* completely equal with itself: in another respect it is split up, separated, multiple"[32]—and as such, it *is* not.

Apparently, Fichte employs a second notion of being in these analyses, namely, the notion of being as unity and immutability. According to the first notion of being as *aseitas,* the appearance *is* not. Only the One is, and nothing is besides it. According to the second notion of being as unity, however, the appearance *is* insofar as it is uniform, and it *is* not insofar as it is multiform. Or to put it in different terms: the appearance *is* in that it mirrors the Absolute—and it *is* not in that it conceals the Absolute. These two meanings of being are distinguishable and compatible. When Fichte says that the appearance *is,* he does not contradict his notion of the Absolute, but refers to the unity aspect of the appearance. His axiom still holds that only One *is,* namely in the sense of *aseitas.*

Being and Semblance

It has always been part of the program of the *Wissenschaftslehre* not only to free us from the habit of ascribing independent existence (*aseitas*) to derivative entities (see the discussion about the thing in itself), but also to explain on the basis of the true principles how this habit arises. The *Wissenschaftslehre* gives a deduction of semblance, showing both the illusory character and the necessity of semblance. In his *Wissenschaftslehre* 1812 Fichte remains faithful to this program, but in contrast with the earlier *Wissenschaftslehren,* it is no longer the absoluteness of the things that is unveiled as an unavoidable illusion, but the absoluteness of the I itself.

Fichte refers to the mechanism of determination, as known from the *Wissenschaftslehre nova methodo,* to demonstrate the constitution of self-reflection. In 1812 the machinery works like this: the Absolute appears, as life teaches us. The appearance of the Absolute means that it appears *as* the Absolute. Since determinacy comes with negation, the Absolute must bring forth its own opposite, a non-Absolute, to be able to appear *as* the Absolute. This non-Absolute is the Absolute's appearance. The appearance is also that to which the Absolute appears. Thus, the Absolute can appear to the appearance only if at the same time its opposite, namely the appearance, appears to the appearance as well. There is no appearing of the Absolute without an appearing of the appearance to itself, that is, without reflectivity of the appearance. Since the Absolute appears necessarily, the self-reflection of the appearance is necessary too.

Fichte relates the unitary aspect of the appearance to the appearing of the Absolute, whereas the multiplicity aspect is linked to the appearance's self-reflection. Since self-reflection is a process, there is transmutation and genesis within the appearance when it appears to itself. Employing the notion of being as unity and immutability, Fichte concludes that the appearance *is* insofar as it is a manifestation or a self-revelation of the Absolute; and that the appearance *is* not insofar as it is self-reflective. We have to note that the appearance, as being in this sense, is nothing in and through itself, but depends completely on the Absolute, whose image it is. In other words, it is decidedly not *a se.*

As self-reflective, the appearance *is* not, either in the sense of unity, because self-reflection implies multiplicity, or in the sense of *aseitas,* since only the Absolute is *a se.* Nevertheless, the laws of self-reflection inevitably create the illusion in the appearance that it is itself an independent principle. Necessarily, and falsely, the appearance appears to itself as having *aseitas*. How does this semblance of *aseitas* come about? As is well known from the earliest *Wissenschaftslehre,* self-reflection is possible only through self-determination. In 1794 the complete description of the I's self-reflection indicates that the I posits itself as positing itself.[33] In 1812 it is formulated analogously: the appearance appears to itself as appearing to itself.[34] To appear, however, is an activity. Thus, the appearance appears to itself as being active through itself, or as a principle "from itself, out of itself, through itself."[35] Fichte concludes that, since the appearance is constituted by the act of appearing to itself, it conceives of its own existence (its "formal being") as grounded in itself. As soon as the appearance reflects on itself, it understands itself to exist through itself, that is, to be *a se*. But this cannot be true, as the *Wissenschaftslehre* demonstrates. Only One *is* in the sense of *aseitas,* namely the Absolute, so that the appearance cannot truly *be* in this sense. For the appearance, the semblance of *aseitas* necessarily comes with self-reflection, which on its part is a condition for the appearance of the Absolute. Nevertheless, this semblance is illusory. The appearance has no formal being in and through itself. Its being is, as Fichte says, "merely being from and in God." Fichte adds: "Every error without exception consists in mistaking images for being. The *Wissenschaftslehre* has for the first time pronounced how far this error extends through showing that being is only in God."[36]

In Retrospect

It is tempting to cast a retrospective glance from Fichte's late standpoint to the earlier *Wissenschaftslehren,* that is, to compare Fichte's late concept of appearance with his earlier notions of the I and of "absolute knowledge." In a famous passage from the first paragraph of the *Grundlage,* Fichte says: "Self-positing and being are the same, if said about the I. The sentence: I am, because I have posited myself, can also be expressed thus: I am absolutely, because I am."[37] For the early Fichte, the self-positing of the I guarantees its absolute being. Since the I posits itself, it exists out of itself and through itself—or it is *a se.* According to the late Fichte, however, self-positing and being are by no means the same, for the being of self-positing appearance is a mere, if necessary, semblance. The axiom "I am absolutely because I am," seen in the perspective of 1812, represents nothing more than the appearance's erroneous self-interpretation. From the standpoint of the late *Wissenschaftslehre,* this axiom needs to be rephrased: I am not absolutely, but I am grounded in God; and I am not, because I am, but I am, because God appears—if I am at all.

The *Wissenschaftslehre* 1801 represents a position intermediate between the standpoints of 1794 and 1812. What Fichte says in the first paragraph of the *Grundlage,* namely: "I am absolutely, *because* I am; and I am absolutely, *what* I am; both for the I,"[38] seems to be true for the "absolute knowledge" of the *Wissenschaftslehre* 1801 too: "Knowledge is absolutely *what* it is, and *because* it is."[39] However, Fichte's further analyses in 1801 show that only the existence of knowledge, its "being, because it is," is rooted in its own free act. "Absolute knowledge" is "an absolute self-generation, from nothing."[40] But the quality of this knowledge, that is, *what* it is, is no longer thought to stem from knowledge itself, but from an "absolute Being." When knowledge comes to recognize that it is not the origin of its own quality, it is led to the Absolute as "mere pure being."[41] In 1801, "absolute knowledge" still is absolutely, because it is, but it is no longer absolutely *what* it is. The reason for its "what" now lies in the Absolute.

Fichte's seemingly paradoxical statements of 1801, such as that absolute knowledge "floats between its being and its non-being,"[42] or that it is "being non-being,"[43] can be interpreted when related to the notion of being as *aseitas* as developed in 1812. In this perspective, absolute knowledge *is* not, because its quality does not stem from itself, but it *is,* because it itself is the source of its existence and formal being. Whereas the *Wissenschaftslehre* 1801 ascribes formal being to "absolute knowledge," the *Wissenschaftslehre* 1812 removes all its self-sufficiency completely. As an image of God, the appearance receives its quality, that is, that what it is and what it shows, from God. Furthermore, its existence, that is, the fact that it is, does not result any more from a free act of I-hood, but from the necessity with which the Absolute appears. To return to my distinction from the beginning of this chapter, transcendental philosophy is now completely transformed into metaphysics.

Notes

1. *FW* 1:286; *GA* 1.2:416. In the notes for this chapter, references are made to *Fichtes Werke* (*FW*), the edition of Fichte's works by I. H. Fichte. The corresponding passages in the Academy edition are added (where possible).

2. *FW* 1:456; *GA* 1.2:212.

3. ". . . in der Schulsprache die tiefste Metaphysik und Ontologie" (FW 5:416).

4. About a "Sittenlehre" conceived in the light of the "Wissenschaftslehre" Fichte writes: "Durch diese Ansicht verwandelt sich nun dasjenige, was man bisher Sittenlehre genannt hat, in eine Seinslehre: (in Lehre von dem wahren Sein, der eigentlichen Realität)" (*FW* 11:34).

5. *FW* 11:34.

6. Aristotle, *Metaphysics* 6.1.1025b3.

7. See Aristotle, *Metaphysics* 6.1.1026a10–32.

8. See J. Halfwassen, *Geist und Selbstbewusstsein: Studien zu Plotin und Numenios* (Mainz, 1994).

9. See J. Brachtendorf, *Die Struktur des menschlichen Geistes nach Augustinus: Selbstreflexion und Erkenntnis Gottes in De Trinitate* (Hamburg: Felix Meiner, 2000).

10. See Descartes' letter to Colvius of November 14th, 1640, in *Oeuvres de Descartes,* ed. Charles Adam and Paul Tannery (Paris, 1964–76), 3:247.

11. "Die Grundbehauptung des Philosophen, als eines solchen, ist diese: So wie das Ich nur für sich selbst sey, entstehe ihm zugleich nothwendig ein Seyn ausser ihm; der Grund des letzteren liege im ersteren, das letztere sey durch das erstere bedingt: Selbstbewusstseyn und Bewusstseyn eines Etwas, das nicht wir selbst—seyn solle, sey nothwendig verbunden" (*FW* 1:457–58; *GA* 1.4:212).

12. "Dieß ist der wahre Charakter des eigentlichen Seins, deßen Begriff man mit Unrecht für einen ersten unmittelbaren gehalten hatte" (*WLNM* [1982], 41).

13. See *Thatsachen des Bewusstseins,* in *FW* 9:422.

14. See *Appellation an das Publicum gegen die Anklage des Atheismus,* in *FW* 5:216; *GA* 1.5:434–35.

15. *FW* 5:261; *GA* 1.6:46.

16. ". . . der übersinnliche Gott ist ihr [unserer Philosophie] Alles in Allem; er ist ihr derjenige, welcher allein *ist*" (*Appellation,* in *FW* 5:223–24; *GA* 1.5:440).

17. See *Einleitungsvorlesungen in die Wissenschaftslehre* (1813), in *FW* 9:16–17, 43–50.

18. "Eins *ist,* und außer diesem Einen *ist* schlechthin Nichts. Dies festgehalten, und nie irgend einen Ausdruck der WL so genommen, als ob diesem Satze widersprochen werden sollte" (*FW* 10:331).

19. "Eins ist, außer diesem Nichts. Alles Andere *ist* nicht: dieser Satz stehe unveränderlich und ewig fest. Der Begriff des Absoluten wird *gehalten*" (*FW* 10:331).

20. "Außer ihm ist seinem Begriffe nach kein Sein: aber der Begriff ist, und *ist* außer ihm. Protestatio facto contraria! Indem *gesagt* wird, es sei Nichts außer ihm, *ist* Etwas, eben dieses Sagen, außer ihm" (*FW* 10:327).

21. See *FW* 10:330–31.

22. See *FW* 10:329.

23. "Diesen Unterschied [zwischen notwendig und zufällig] haben wir bezeichnet durch *Sein* und *Dasein:* so drückt es, falls ich nicht irre, die *Sprache* aus: es ist eben *da*" (*FW* 10:333). Fichte's concept of *Dasein* has little to do with Heidegger. While Fichte holds that *Dasein* is grounded in the Absolute, Heidegger emphasizes the non-derivative facticity of *Dasein.*

24. See *FW* 10:344.

25. "Die Realität kann aber eintreten nur in dem wirklichen Erscheinen, nicht in der WL. Zwar haben wir so eben gesagt, als WL redend, was die *Realität* sei, im bloßen Begriffe. Dies kann nun freilich die WL, und thut es. Aber die Realität selbst kann sie nicht, und soll sie nicht nachweisen. . . . In Absicht der Realität verweist sie an das *Leben,* wie sie denn überhaupt daran verweist" (*FW* 10:340).

26. See P. Baumanns, *Kritische Gesamtdarstellung seiner Philosophie* (Freiburg, 1990), 349.

27. "Dagegen die Erscheinung: die durch ihr unmittelbares Sein, durch ihren bloßen Begriff, das Nichtsein ist, und so die Genesis gar nicht ausschließt, sondern setzt" (*FW* 10:333).

28. See M. Brueggen, *Fichtes Wissenschaftslehre: Das System in den seit 1801/02 entstandenen Fassungen* (Hamburg, 1979), 116, 136.

29. "Hen kai pan; Eins und Alles ist dasselbe. Alles in dem Einen, alles Eins. Allerdings, nemlich in der Einen Erscheinung" (*FW* 10:336–37).

30. "Dasselbe, was Eins ist, und ewig fort Eins bleibt, ist, ohne seine Einheit zu verlieren, auch ein vielfaches, und ins Unendliche Mannigfaltiges, und ohne seine Mannigfaltigkeit zu verlieren, Eins" (*FW* 10:336).

31. "Dieses Bild *ist* da, sagen wir: keinesweges etwa: es *wird* innerhalb seiner selbst. In ihm ist darum eben kein Wandel, Veränderung, Mannigfaltigkeit, sondern es ist absolut Eins, und sich selbst gleich, eben so wie das in ihm abgebildete Absolute. Es ist, wie es ist, ganz und sich selbst gleich" (*FW* 10:334).

32. "In Einer Rücksicht das Bild *Eins,* durchaus sich selbst gleich: in einer andern gespalten, gesondert, ein *Mannigfaltiges*" (*FW* 10:337).

33. See *FW* 1:276; *GA* 1.2:409.

34. ". . . daß sie [die Erscheinung] erscheint sich, *als* sich erscheinend" (*FW* 10:367).

35. "Die Erscheinung soll allerdings und muß erscheinen als absolutes Princip von sich, aus sich, durch sich, also als Wesen und Realität" (*FW* 10:372).

36. "Aller Irrthum ohne Ausnahme besteht darin, daß man Bilder für das Sein hält. Wie weit dieser Irrthum sich erstrecke, den ganzen Umfang desselben hat wohl zuerst die WL ausgesprochen, indem sie zeigt, daß das Sein nur in Gott sei, nicht außer ihm" (*FW* 10:365).

37. "Sich selbst setzen und Seyn sind, vom Ich gebraucht, völlig gleich. Der Satz: Ich bin, weil ich mich selbst gesetzt habe, kann demnach auch so ausgedrückt werden: Ich bin schlechthin, weil ich bin" (*FW* 1:98; *GA* 1.2:260).

38. ". . . ich bin schlechthin, weil ich bin; und bin schlechthin, was ich bin; beides für das Ich" (*FW* 1:98; *GA* 1.2:260).

39. "Das Wissen ist absolut, *was* es ist, und *weil* es ist" (section 10, *FW* 2:20; *GA* 2.6:151).

40. "Das absolute Wissen ist für sich schlechthin, *weil* es ist, heisst daher: die intellectuelle Anschauung ist für sich ein absolutes Selbsterzeugen, durchaus aus Nichts" (section 19, *FW* 2:38; *GA* 2.6:169).

41. "blosses reines Seyn" (section 26, *FW* 2:60; *GA* 2.6:193).

42. "Es [das absolute Wissen] schwebt zwischen seinem Seyn und seinem Nichtseyn" (section 23, *FW* 2:51; *GA* 2.6:182–83).

43. "das seyende Nichtseyn" (section 24, *FW* 2:53; *GA* 2 6:184).

Fall and Freedom: A Comparison of Fichte's and Saint Paul's Understandings of Original Sin

Holger Zaborowski

> Is it too much to say that the novelist . . . is one of the few remaining witnesses to the doctrine of original sin, the imminence of catastrophe in paradise?

Modern Philosophy and the Secularization of the Doctrine of Original Sin

Original Sin and Its Transformation in Modernity

Varying a famous quote of Fichte, Peter Koslowski has argued that one could categorize a particular philosopher's philosophy by analyzing his understanding of the doctrine of original sin. Koslowski argues as follows:

> Der Typus der Theorie der Gesamtwirklichkeit, die ein Denker vertritt—sei sie die theologisch-philosophische, die gnostische und die mythologische Theorie der Gesamtwirklichkeit-, und der Typus der Theorie der Wandlung der Welt folgt aus der Art und Weise, wie der Sündenfall gedacht wird. Man könnte so weit gehen zu sagen, daß mit der Art der Sündenfalltheorie, die man hat, entschieden ist, welche Art von Philosoph man ist.[1]

Modern philosophy can, to a certain extent, be read as a detailed footnote to this very doctrine. These footnotes, however, do not simply comment on the doctrine; rather, they modify and alter its meaning in a way which frequently crosses the boundaries of what one might call an orthodox approach to this doctrine.[2] Indeed, this doctrine and its understanding have significantly changed in modernity while yet playing a substantial role, particularly for Kantian philosophy, for German idealism, for Søren Kierkegaard, and for Martin Heidegger's existential analysis too.[3] There is an underpinning of gnosticism in modern thought: philosophy was to replace theology, and the exercise of rationality was to substitute for the practice of religion. Many philosophers claimed, as Fichte indeed did, to be a "priest of science" (*ein Priester der Wissenschaft*).[4]

Johann Gottlieb Fichte is often said to be the philosopher of freedom par excellence, both as far as his private life is concerned and in his philosophy.[5] There is an obvious link between the notion of freedom and the doctrine of original sin. The doctrine aims at explaining why humans are free to do both good *and* evil. It is a way of justifying freedom against the background of the experience of manifold constraints. It is thus a way of justifying God and his creation as well and strives, loosely speaking, to provide an answer to the following issues:

1. How can the relation between the infinite and finite be conceived?
2. Is there such a phenomenon as freedom? What is the relation between freedom and necessity?
3. How does evil come into existence?
4. How can history be understood?

Orthodox Christian theology tried to answer these questions in the following ways:

1. This relation is characterized by the utter dependency of the creation on the creator.
2. There is freedom, as humans are created in God's image.
3. Evil is due to human freedom; that is, it is due to a fall which happened either ontologically or "historically" prior to human history.
4. History is a process from fall to redemption. The infinitely loving God is the cause of redemption by means of the gracious, that is, not-necessary, incarnation.

The Aim of This Essay

In the essay which follows, I shall focus on three of Fichte's more popular writings: *Die Bestimmung des Menschen* (published in 1800), the lecture series *Die Grundzüge des gegenwärtigen Zeitalters*[6] (delivered in 1804–5 and published in 1806), and the lecture series *Anweisung zum seligen Leben oder auch Religionslehre*[7] (delivered and published in 1806). I shall look at how the middle Fichte understands and reinterprets the doctrine of original sin. I want to argue, against the background of what has been proposed by

Peter Koslowski, that Fichte continuously engages in a dialogue with the doctrine of original sin. Unfortunately, I cannot discuss the 1813 *Staatslehre* and *Sittenlehre* in any detail due to limits of space in this chapter. A more precise analysis of these writings could shed light on Fichte's philosophical, religious, and political development.

What I do not intend to do, however, is to argue that Fichte is engaged in a conversation with a particular understanding of this doctrine. For this can hardly be convincingly argued. What can be argued convincingly, though, is that this doctrine somehow constitutes a background for Fichte's understanding of history, sinfulness, blessedness, sanctification, justification, and redemption. Still, the account below of Saint Paul's understanding of original sin and justification shall demonstrate how closely Fichte comments upon this doctrine. I shall also propose to understand the doctrine in a rather broad sense, for it can be understood as a theory of the whole of reality, of creation, fall, and redemption. The doctrine thus includes an account of the origin of reality, of the process of its history, and of the character of mankind as the actor of the historical process, that is, a nuclear anthropology.

Fichte refers to this doctrine and its setting within the Christian teaching both implicitly and explicitly, however infrequently these references can be found. It seems to me, however, that if there is one Christian doctrine he refers to the most (apart from the Christological doctrine), it is the doctrine of original sin. This is all the more interesting a feature of his philosophy, as Fichte frequently refused the notion of creation (for there is no origin, as he argues in the *Grundzüge,* but simply one timeless and necessary Being,[8] and this is why neither the philosopher nor the historian can comment on the origin of world, nor on that of mankind) and as his thought arguably moved toward a philosophy which deals with religious and Christian issues on the one hand and historical and political issues on the other. The crucial role of moral concept, largely indebted to his *relecture* of Kant's practical philosophy in his early thought, was increasingly taken over by concepts with a religious origin, such as the "mystical" union with God.

Yet the account below will be a narrative of the idealist transformation and annihilation of the doctrine of original sin in its original sense rather than of an orthodox interpretation. It will thus be shown how modern philosophy draws decisively on its Christian heritage while yet transfiguring it substantially. Fichte's adoption of this doctrine is obviously influenced by Rousseau's and Kant's thought. Yet I shall refrain from tracing back Fichte's thought to other modern philosophers. The first part of this essay shall draw attention to the Christian understanding of original sin. In what follows I shall rather exclusively focus on Paul's understanding of sin and justification in Romans 5–7, for "in the New Testament no one takes sin as seriously as does Paul, and nowhere does he treat it as fully as in Romans, especially chapters 5–7."[9] The emphasis will be laid upon features which best provide a sharp contrast to Fichte's understanding of sin and justification. This will facilitate an understanding of the philosophical transformation of Christian doctrines in Fichte's philosophy. In the *Grundzüge,* though, Fichte is very critical of Paul. Fichte draws a sharp distinction between Saint Paul and John, who, as he argues, knows none but the true God and focuses his teaching on mankind's inward sense of truth.[10] John's teaching is, according to Fichte, as old as the world and is the first original religion.[11] Fichte even lauds John in that he rejected unconditionally and without mildness Judaism as a result of the subsequent deterioration of this original religion.[12] Paul, however, is to be criticized, since he attempted to unify the Christian and Jewish systems and interpreted Christianity as a religion which is the result of a historical development.[13] Paul overemphasizes, as Fichte states, the historicity of Jesus and his death and presupposes an arbitrarily acting God.[14] Fichte goes on to modify his rejection of Paul's theology and argues that Paul's teaching is right as long as he does not strive to reconcile Judaism and Christianity, that is, his own Jewish past and his having become a Christian.[15] Otherwise, it would be difficult to understand why Fichte highly appreciates the Reformation and the pietist movement, the main ideas of which are apparently deeply indebted to Paul.[16] In the 1813 *Staatslehre,* Fichte's positive appraisal of Saint Paul has become even stronger.

Why does Fichte draw extensively on the doctrine of original sin, which is a Pauline *theologoumenon* rather than a Johannine one and could seem to be at odds with Fichte's reading of John and his stress on the inward experience of the divine? It is, I suppose, due to Fichte's interest in history and in means by which he could explain the historical process. Fichte needed a state of original innocence and, moreover, a fall which made up the very beginning of history. If history is understood (1) as a movement toward the full realization of freedom and (2) as a circular process, the notion of original innocence and a fall from this original state of affairs, as it were, cannot be omitted. This demonstrates as well why modern philosophy did not simply abolish the doctrine of original sin: the transformation of this doctrine is deeply tied up with the modern narrative of how history proceeds. If the modern account of a straightforward movement of history toward, say, freedom is a secularization of Christian eschatology, the presupposition of Christian eschatology, that is, the anthropology of a fallen mankind, cannot simply be given up. Already at this stage of this essay one can suppose that modernity substantially transformed Christian soteriology too.

Saint Paul's Understanding of Fall and Justification in Romans 5–7: The Universality of Sin in Adam and the Universality of Salvation in Christ

In her collection of essays on Paul, Morna D. Hooker draws attention to the problematic issue of how to interpret Paul properly. She writes: "Whenever I imagine I have grasped the true significance of his arguments, I find myself stumbling over a passage which apparently undermines my interpretation." Additionally, "it is well to remember that Paul's own thinking also changed and developed over the course of the years."[17] The problem does not become at all easier if one raises the question of whether and in what ways Paul's teaching is compatible with, say, the Gospels, as their interpretation is itself very controversial and diverse. Furthermore, many difficulties arise because Paul's theological oeuvre consists of letters, the true character of which is not at all wholly laid bare as to whether they are meant to be theological treatises of general importance or, alternatively, whether they are rather determined by a particular question, or by the problematic situation of their addressees. This is an important issue to emphasize, particularly as regards Romans.[18]

Since Paul aims at understanding Christ and the universality of salvation and grace in him by means of looking at Christ's "counterpart" Adam (Romans 5:18–19), the *universality* of sin in Adam plays a crucial role too in the account of justification in Romans. For the "account of man's wickedness," as Hooker concludes with regard to Romans, "has been deliberately stated in terms of the biblical narrative of Adam's fall."[19] Adam was, as Paul states, the "type of the one who was to come" (5:14).[20]

Sin has been a key notion for Paul, enabling him to understand the fallenness of mankind, the origin of death, and thus the process of history too, and also to develop a counter-account of redemption. "For the wages of sin *is* death; but the gift of God *is* eternal life through Christ our Lord" (6:12). Death and lack of freedom in Adam are opposed to life and freedom *in* Christ. The Christ event overcomes what one might call the Adam event which leads to the current sinful state of mankind. Humans used to be enslaved by sin, but are freed by Christ. Consequently, law, which came into existence "to increase the trespass" (5:20), is opposed to grace. According to Kittel, the "state of sin already present . . . is actualized through the command of the Law in transgression."[21] In 7:4, Paul argues that Christians die to the law through the *body* of Christ, that is, law has been overcome through that which is closely tied up with sin among humans.[22]

It is, however, difficult to understand what Paul means by life *in Christ.* Leon Morris underlines that the idea of an interchange with Christ, that is, being in Christ, is crucially important for Paul's Christology. A precise interpretation, though, is hard to achieve, "but at least we can say that it emphasizes the closeness of the tie between the saved and the Saviour and that it also indicates something of the unity that binds all Christ's own."[23] Moreover, it says much more about the saved, since to be in Christ presupposes the very negation of one's former sinful self. To overcome the consequences of Adam's original sin, that is, to surpass both sin and death, entails to die to sin. This seems paradoxical. It is, however, a rather straightforward application of Paul's Christocentric view. To be baptized, that is, to die to sin, means to follow Christ into his own death and then to be united with him and thus to participate in his resurrection.

The atonement by Christ is, according to Paul, opposed to how sin came into the world. Because of one single man, sin and death came into the world. All mankind participates in sin and death. Not even Moses and those "whose sins were not like the transgression of Adam, who was a type of the one who was to come" (5:14), could escape from the universal dominion of sin. Without proposing the idea that sin is inevitably inherited from Adam (this notion would indeed abolish human freedom and lead to fatalism), Paul asserts that there is "an indissoluble connection between the act of Adam, the fate of death and the general state of sin."[24] In Romans 1:21, he explains what sin really is: "For although they knew God they did not honor him as God or give thanks to him, but they became futile in their thinking and their senseless minds were darkened." Thus, the current state of sin is deeply tied up with Adam's disobedience to God's command.

To fully understand Paul's appraisal of redemption, one needs to take into account what seems to be a *paradoxon*. The freedom of those who participate in the redemption embodies and, furthermore, entails, a new enslavement. This enslavement is due to the life *in* Christ. Consequently, Paul calls himself a "servant of Jesus Christ" (1:1). Paul's letter to the Romans starts off with this self-characterization, whereas none of the other Pauline and pseudo-Pauline letters employ this notion explicitly, except Philippians (1:1) and Titus (1:1). Paul, of course, refers implicitly to this notion in that he regularly calls himself an "apostle of Christ." The letter opening in Romans is rather illuminating, for it sheds light upon the crucial role of the dialectic of slavery in Romans. Attention has been drawn to the fact in particular that the letter opening of Romans elaborates hugely the ordinary ancient letter opening ("a to b. Greetings."). John Ziesler has emphasized that this elaboration is due to Paul's intention to embody substantial matters of Christian teaching already in the opening of his letters. According to Ziesler, there are three main themes dwelled upon in the opening of Pauline letters: first, a theological rather than a biographical self-interpretation; second, an interpretation of Christ as regards God's plan for humanity; and third, a stress on the universality of the Christian mission.[25] The apparent stress on being a servant of Christ plays through all these themes, particularly since it ought to be read against the background of the Pauline teaching that all mankind is to become a servant of Christ rather than of sin. Paul's self-identification as a servant of Christ apparently refers back to the (self-)understanding of Abraham, Moses, and some prophets as servants of God.[26] It does not, however, distinguish Paul from the Christian community, as "having been set free from sin, have become slaves of righteousness" (6:18). To assert that he is a servant of Christ implies also a reference to his Jewish ancestors. "The Jewish worshipper quite naturally thought of himself as God's slave."[27]

In Romans 6, Paul contrasts the life in Christ to the sinful one in Adam in what is a deeply dialectical thought. To overcome the sinful life in Adam, that is, our old human being, in Adam means intrinsically to die to the old life. The term "our old self" ('ὁ παλα ι ὸς ἡμῶν ἄνθρωπος'; 6:6) is also based on the Adam-Christ typology. Christ is, as Ernst Käsemann has commented upon this passage, "according to Eph 2:15, 4:24 . . . the 'new man' and the exhortation in Col 3:9f. carries the antithesis of the old and new man into anthropology."[28]

The idea that Christians have to die to what brought about death, that is, sin, is crucially important for Paul's understanding of salvation. This negation of negation constitutes a condition of salvation which cannot be omitted. For Paul, the sacrament of baptism causes the death of the sinful self. This is a *theologoumenon,* the roots of which, it has been argued, may possibly be found in ancient mystery cults.[29]

We died to sin (6:2), we were baptized into Christ's death (6:3), and we were buried into death by our baptism (6:4). As we are united with Christ in his death, we will also be united with him in his resurrection (6:5). Death, in general, and Christ's death in particular are the keys to fully understand the redemption, for there is a link between sin and death: Adam's sin brought death into the world (5:12), but only Christ's death can reconcile God with mankind: "Then as one man's trespass led to condemnation for all men, so one man's act of righteousness leads to acquittal and life for all men" (5:18). Christ's death has made an end to our being slaves to sin. Paul, however, is not simply dealing with the contemporaneity to Christ of the Christians who have already gone through death by being baptized. His account of salvation is characterized by an eschatological dimension as well, as indicated by the juxtaposition of the aorist δικαιωθέντες and of the future σωθησόμεθα in Romans 5:9, or the differentiation between sanctification and its end, that is, eternal life, in Romans 6:22.

The new life in Christ demands the negation of one's former self, that is, of one's "body of death" (7:24), one's members (7:23), or one's flesh (7:14, 18). Then the new spiritual self can enjoy the law of God in one's inmost self (7:22). The law of sin has been overcome by the law of God (7:25). The spiritual reality of the unity with Christ in grace, which is still to be accomplished, replaces the sinful reality of the life beyond Eden, which intrinsically implies death and the law of sin. Faith is substantially important for the overcoming of sin, "for whatever does not proceed from faith is sin" (14:23).

Mankind is justified by faith (5:1), but this does not mean that justification presupposes a somehow autonomous act of faith. For it cannot be understood independently of Christ's death, which Paul interprets as both a *cosmic*—Adam brought sin into the world (κοσμός) and therefore Christ's death freed the world from sin and death—and a *historical* event. The *historicity* of Christ's death constitutes one of the major differences between Paul's sacramental theology and the notion of death as conceived by ancient mystery cults. It brings about the reconciliation between God and mankind and it anticipates today what is yet a gift of the future. History has wholly been changed, as the cross has brought about a wholly new dimension for both the present and the future life. It is now possible to turn to Fichte's philosophy in order to see how the Pauline understanding of reality has been transformed in modernity.

The Vocation of Man, the Lost Innocence of His Soul (*Geist*), and the Justification by Faith

Doubt and the Necessity of Nature

In 1800 Fichte published *Die Bestimmung des Menschen* (*The Vocation of Man*),[30] a treatise which "is not intended for professional philosophers, for they will find nothing in it that has not been already set forth in other writings of the same author."[31] It is, however, "intended to attract and animate the reader, and to elevate him from the world of sense into a region beyond it."[32] Fichte's starting point is a question as traditionally philosophical and religious as "What am I myself, and what is my vocation?"[33] Particularly in its emphasis on the *Übersinnliche*, or what is *beyond* our everyday experience, and on the crucial role which is played by faith in its third part, this writing anticipates what Fichte was still to develop. It is, so to speak, an *Introduction into the Blessed Life avant la lettre*. The focus, though, is slightly different from his later work, particularly with regard to the central role of practical reason and the *Sittengesetz* (moral law). In his later writings, Fichte focuses on the unity with the Divine rather than on the *Sittengesetz*. Blessedness is, as he argues in the *Die Anweisung zum seligen Leben* (*Guide to the Blessed Life*), the unification with God as the One and absolute.[34]

The first part of *Die Bestimmung des Menschen,* called "Zweifel" ("Doubt"), is on certainty rather than on doubt. It aims at demonstrating what, from a certain point of view, I am. Fichte concludes that

> I know what I am, and wherein the nature of my species consists. I am a manifestation, determined by the whole system of the universe, of a power of Nature which is determined by itself alone. To know my particular personal being by knowing its deepest sources is impossible, for I cannot penetrate into the innermost recesses of Nature. . . . I do not truly act at all: Nature acts in me. To make myself anything other than that which Nature has intended is something I cannot even propose to myself. I am not the author of my own being; Nature has made me what I am and everything that I am going to be.[35]

The proposed solution to the question of what I am and what my vocation is proves rather sobering and disillusioning. In fact, I am not myself, for I am merely a contingent expression within the in-itself wholly necessary system of Nature. Having said this, Fichte expresses almost dramatically his grief about this account of what the all-embracing necessity of Nature appears like: "I was destined to this misery, and it is in vain that I mourn the lost innocence of soul which can never return." Fichte interprets his getting to know what man really is as a loss of innocence and as a destiny which, presumably, could not have been avoided once the aforementioned issue of what I am had been raised. Fichte, though, in the most emphatical way, does not accept the "anguish-evoking"[36] idea of humans being merely parts of an overall natural necessity. He then goes on to elaborate a counter-account which he calls *Wissen* (knowledge), since it focuses on what is undoubtedly known to us. He calls for his inner self and his readers to "have the courage to become truly wise."[37]

Knowledge and the Exclusivism of Freedom

This second part in fact justifies consciousness and freedom (as opposed to Nature). Reason (*Verstand*) is fully satisfied, but at a very high cost too. For the result of this narrative is the following: "The reality in which you formerly believed—a material world existing independently of you, of which you feared to become the slave—has vanished; for this whole material world arises only through knowledge; and it is itself our knowledge.

But knowledge is not reality—just because it is knowledge."[38] There is no such thing as insurmountable natural necessity anymore, since "our consciousness of external things is absolutely nothing more than the product of our own presentative faculty, and . . . with respect to such things, we know only what is produced through our consciousness itself, through a determinate consciousness subject to definite laws."[39]

A dilemma that is both ontological and epistemological is to be faced. Either, on the one hand, one acknowledges nature and its necessity and thus, inevitably loses the notion of consciousness as characterized by freedom, or, on the other hand, one succeeds in defending freedom and consciousness and thus sees nature herself wholly vanishing.

Faith and the *Sittengesetz*

Fichte, though, proposes a solution to this dilemma in the third part of *Die Bestimmung des Menschen*. This chapter is called "Faith" and develops a way to defend both human freedom and the reality of the outer world. Fichte's answer to the question of how to reconcile freedom and system (and thus of how to solve the most urgent problem of post-Kantian German philosophy) is based on a narrative of the notion of the *Sittengesetz*. Both freedom and nature are reconcilable in that humanity inevitably implies the demand to act according to the *Sittengesetz*. Humans are therefore members of two orders: "I stand in the center of two entirely opposite worlds: a visible world, in which action is the only moving power; and an invisible and absolutely incomprehensible world, in which will is the ruling principle."[40]

The two worlds—"the one purely spiritual, in which I rule by my will alone; the other sensuous, in which I operate by my deed"[41]—are ideally deeply interwoven with one another. The idea of the purely spiritual world and its immediate presence is apparently a philosophical transformation of what is theologically called *realized eschatology*. Theologically, however, there is an insurmountable tension between realized and future eschatology. This difference does not wholly vanish in Fichte's thought, for his philosophy of history, as already present in *Die Bestimmung des Menschen,* takes over the role of futuristic eschatology, though in a detranscendentalizing and secularizing way. History is determined by the "mighty World-Spirit" (*mächtige Weltgeist*) and by freedom, "which you (i.e., the mighty World-Spirit) are now constrained to adapt to your plans with labor and contrivance."[42] Fichte's rather sketchy account of the process of history and particularly of the current state of affairs indicates that he is in a continuous dialogue with the Christian doctrine of original sin. The manner in which he describes his own epoch is apparently reminiscent of the biblical account of the existence *beyond* Eden: "Our species still laboriously extorts the means of its subsistence and preservation from an opposing Nature. The larger portion of mankind is still condemned through life to severe toil in order to supply nourishment for itself and for the smaller portion which thinks for it; immortal spirits are compelled to fix their whole thoughts and endeavours on the earth that brings forth their food."[43]

Conclusion: A Gnostic Narrative of Redemption

In *Die Bestimmung des Menschen,* Fichte proposes an almost entirely secularized narrative of how one could possibly get redeemed; it is an account that is substantially different from the theological position developed by Saint Paul. One gets justified by faith alone, as Fichte states in this treatise. "Faith," however, does have an arguably secularized meaning. It is constituted by what can be *shown* philosophically and can then be clearly seen,[44] rather than by what can be ultimately proven, but it is based on *philosophy*. It thus depends on illumination, on getting a new organ, which opens up a new world.[45] "The mist of delusion," as Fichte emphatically asserts, "clears away from before my sight."[46] Fichte's account of faith does lack the Christocentric and historical dimension of Saint Paul's understanding of justification by faith (5:1–2). In Fichte, religious revelation is replaced by the awareness of one's own freedom and its practical claim. The *Sittengesetz* replaces what is traditionally understood as providence. Faith means to experience the practical dimension of one's freedom. It entails that we become aware of our two-worldliness and of the universal *ought to* of the *Sittengesetz*. It is made up by the experience that "I *am* immortal, imperishable, eternal, as soon as I form the resolution to obey the laws of reason; I do not need to become so."[47] Therefore, Fichte argues, "I become the sole source of my own being and its phenomena, and, henceforth, unconditioned by anything without me, I have life in myself."[48] Fichte's emphasis lies on the issue of how to get redeemed from sin. Faith is the obvious answer. This faith, though, has become a matter of philosophy, of education and initialization. It has become dependent on the courage to think about one's own vocation. "Blessed be the hour in which I first resolved to inquire into myself and my vocation."[49]

Fichte's Understanding of Sin in the *Grundzüge des gegenwärtigen Zeitalters*

History and Transcendental Philosophy

In 1794 Fichte claimed to provide the *Wissenschaftslehre* as a "pragmatic history of the human being,"[50] for it is precisely the tensional relation between the I and the not-I from which time can be deduced. However, for Fichte, it takes some further years to more exhaustively consider history and its development. Particularly in his popular lectures for a wider audience, he draws attention decisively to the process of history against the background of his transcendental philosophy, as outlined in the different lecture series on the *Wissenschaftslehre*. History is the necessary process of fall, justification, and redemption of mankind; it is thus the self-becoming of the divine life, the development of the higher life (*das höhere Leben*).[51] Fichte's idea of history is thus intriguingly close to Hegel's understanding of history, particularly from *Glauben und Wissen* (*Faith and Knowledge*) and from the *Phänomenologie des Geistes* onward. It is important to note that Fichte does not engage in empirical history: he remains a transcendental philosopher even in his philosophy of history. What he is more or less exclusively interested in is a priori history, as can be deduced from the principles of the *Wissenschaftslehre*. He leaves empirical history to whomever knows world and mankind, to the *Welt- und Menschenkenner*,[52] as he slightly ironically states. His popular lectures do not abandon the insights of his *Wissenschaftslehre*; rather, they presuppose what Fichte systematically deduces in the different lecture series entitled *Wissenschaftslehre* without, of course, deducing it again.

The *Grundzüge*: History as Process from Innocence via Sinfulness to Justification

In the first lecture of the *Grundzüge des gegenwärtigen Zeitalters* (*The Characteristics of the Present Age*), Fichte defines the purpose of the life of mankind. This purpose is to arrange everything in this life, first, with freedom, and second, according to reason (*Vernunft*).[53] Fichte lays stress on the freedom of mankind rather than on individualistic freedom. This understanding of the purpose of humanity involves an initial and rather sketchy categorization of history. There seem to be two main periods, one of which is before the realization of what the definition demands from mankind, and the other of which is after this reasonable arrangement of life with freedom. History appears thus to be a continuous process toward a more fully realized expression of reason and freedom. There is an underlying plan of history, which unquestionably must be met. This plan is that mankind becomes in this life, with freedom, a pure impression of the absolute.[54] This, in fact, will be the realization of the all-embracing unity of the absolute. For there is, as Fichte claims to authentically interpret Christianity (particularly John's Gospel),[55] no being and no life apart from the immediate divine life. This is in manifold ways disguised, but is also disclosed by humans who are devoted to God in their life and deeds.[56]

In the following, Fichte develops a more elaborate narrative of mankind's endeavor to fully realize freedom and reason. He draws on the theological notions of sin and justification to comprehensively describe the descending and the ascending lines of this necessary evolution. There are five different periods of the deterioration and of the following maturation of mankind. There is, first, the period of the unconditioned dominion of reason by instinct, which is the period of mankind's innocence. In that Fichte speaks of the effectiveness of reason by natural instinct (as opposed to that by freedom), it is indicated very clearly that Fichte's understanding of nature has considerably been modified toward a rather Schellingean notion, for in Fichte's earlier work, nature was strictly opposed to reason. There is, however, also a purely natural drive which is opposed to the reasonable one.

There is, second, the epoch of positive systems of teaching and life. Instinct has become an externally compelling authority. This is the period of beginning and increasing sin. There is, third, the period of liberalization from the coercing authority, from the instinct of reason and from reason itself. This period Fichte calls that of utter indifference toward any truth whatsoever and of an absolute lack of constraint. It is the period of accomplished sinfulness. The fourth period is that of the science of reason (*Vernunftwissenschaft*),[57] when truth is acknowledged as the highest and is loved most highly. This is the time of the beginning and increasing justification. The fifth period, finally, is that of the accomplished justification and sanctification (*der Stand der vollendeten Rechtfertigung und Heiligung*).[58] Fichte interprets this whole process as a circular movement; it is nothing but the return to the origin. However, it is an intrinsically necessary and therefore good way,[59] as he states, for mankind is living life and not simply dead, an unmovable or solidified being. Without this history of mankind, life would not have been realized at all.

In the *Anweisung zum seligen Leben,* Fichte modifies the idea of five distinctly different historical periods. In fact, there are still five different ways to approach the world (*die Welt zu nehmen*), but they are not characteristic of any historical period any more, for all of them can be found simultaneously. The first way is merely to trust the sensual experiences, and the second standpoint is characterized by the aim to understand the world as a law of order (*als Gesetz der Ordnung*). Freedom and humanity are to be thought of as opposed to the law of nature. The most eminent philosopher of this standpoint, as Fichte argues, is Kant. The third standpoint is that of true and high morality. Truly real are the holy, the good, and the beautiful. Examples for this point of view are provided by Plato and Jacobi. The religious standpoint is the fourth way. From this point of view, the good, holy, and beautiful appear to be the revelation of God. This is the disclosure of the inner essence of the divine. It becomes clear that only God exists and that we are God's immediate life and dwell in the divine. This notion of God, however, is still rather shadowy. The last approach to the world is the scientific one (*die aus dem Standpunkt der Wissenschaft*); it is that worldview which is based on the one, absolute, and in-itself accomplished science. Only science transforms religion, as Fichte has it, into vision (*Schauen*):

> Zweitens weiß, und erkenne ich, mit derselben Evidenz, folgendes: daß man nur durch das eigentliche, reine und wahre Denken, und schlechthin durch kein anderes Organ, die Gottheit und das aus ihr fließende selige Leben, ergreifen, und an sich bringen könne; daß daher die angeführte Behauptung der Unmöglichkeit, die tiefere Wahrheit populär vorzutragen, auch gleichbedeutend ist, mit der folgenden: nur durch systematisches Studium der Philosophie könne man sich zur Religion und zu ihren Segnungen erheben, und jeder, der nicht Philosoph sei, müsse ewig ausgeschlossen bleiben von Gott, und seinem Reiche.[60]

The Philosophical Consummation of Theological Language

In the *Grundzüge,* Fichte continues to draw on the theological doctrine of original sin. He essentially transforms the view of humanity and of human history that is provided by this doctrine from the position of his philosophical view of these issues. Mankind awoke to life in paradise where it could do well without knowledge, trouble, or art (*Kunst*).[61] Once mankind dared to live its own life, an angel expelled it from the place of its innocence and peace. This angel, however, wears a fiery sword of the obligation to do well (*Rechtsein*).[62] The expulsion from paradise makes up the starting point of history as sketched in the five-stage periodization of mankind's evolution.[63] The second lecture will explain where Fichte thinks we are today, that is, in Fichte's time. This time is, as Fichte says very polemically to his contemporaries, particularly with regard to contemporary intellectual life, the third period, that of accomplished sin.

How Fichte transforms the doctrine of original sin can also be shown by what I would call his transcendental Mariology as set out in the *An-*

weisung zum seligen Leben. Mary, who is said to be free of original sin, particularly by the Catholic tradition, is, according to Fichte's implicit, yet very obvious reference, an example of someone who lives the blessed life to which the *Wissenschaftslehre,* as Fichte argues, leads.

> Aber die Urquelle der Schönheit ist allein Gott, und sie tritt heraus in dem Gemüte der von ihm Begeisterten. Denken Sie sich z. B. eine heilige Frau, welche, emporgehoben in die Wolken, eingeholt von den himmlischen Heerscharen, die entzückt in ihre Anschaue versinken, umgeben von allem Glanz des Himmels, dessen höchste Zierde und Wonne sie selbst wird—welche—allein unter allen—nichts zu bemerken vermag von dem, was um sie vorgeht, völlig aufgegangen, und verflossen in die Eine Empfindung: Ich bin des Herren Magd, mir geschehe immerfort, wie er will.[64]

Conclusion

Let us summarize Fichte's understanding of sin against the background of what has been said about his understanding of history.

First, Fichte's panentheistic notion of the absolute de-realizes sin. If anything that is the case is an expression of the absolute, then it follows that there can be no real sin. In the *Staatslehre*[65] (1813), for instance, Fichte notes that to believe that one could really disturb the divine world plan is sinful arrogance on the part of mankind.[66] Sin is, as Fichte has it, nothing (*eine Nichtigkeit*).[67] This is equivalent to what he wrote in the *Anweisung*. In the last few paragraphs of the sixth lecture, Fichte brings out his interpretation of sin. According to John, Christ does not atone for the sins of the world to an angry God; he rather carries away all sins. Paul, though, stresses that "while we were enemies we were reconciled to God by the death of his Son" (Romans 5:10). Humans, as John has it according to Fichte's interpretation, do merely exist in God; otherwise, they are dead and do not exist at all. Fichte then wonders how a nonexisting being could possibly disturb God's plan. He then inquires about how an existing being (i.e., someone who lives in Christ and in God) could commit any kind of sin, since God cannot sin against himself.[68] If the only human existence is that of self-negation and becoming the mirror of the absolute, there is no way to speak of sin. Sin is simply nothing, and the whole historical process, however necessary this might be, is nothing too. In the seventh lecture, Fichte speaks of the "truly sinful arrogance" (*wahrhaft sündliche Hochmut*) of the people who are still at the first level, but, interestingly, since they do not exist at all (*denn sie sind gar nicht da, und es gibt gar keine solche Sie*), they cannot sin.[69] In them, however, there is the blind necessity of nature, and, as Fichte says, this tree cannot carry other fruits (sic!). Here, the allusion to the biblical account of original sin in Genesis is obvious. There is nothing but one reality, that of fully realized freedom which is virtually the same as that of the eternal absolute. This notion *seems* to be comparable to the link between death and sin in Saint Paul. Paul says that "as sin reigned in death, grace also might reign through righteousness to eternal life through Jesus Christ our Lord" (5:21). Paul, however, takes the reality of sin much more seriously (e.g., 1:18ff.). For Paul, sin is not simply nothing (since sinners do not simply not exist) but implies, and leads to, the nothingness of death. His understanding of sin is also tied up with his emphasis upon God being creator, for people sinned "because they exchanged the truth about God for a lie and worshipped and served the creature rather than the Creator" (1:25). Paul's teaching is part of a prayer, hence he finishes off by saying, "the Creator, who is blessed for ever! Amen" (1:25). Fichte's doctrine of sin, though, belongs to the philosophical endeavor of laying bare which unity of one single principle underlies the plurality of our experience.[70]

There is, secondly, neither a *historical* nor a *metaphysical* need for an external redeemer, such as Christ, for the process of the self-becoming of the divine is both utterly necessary (i.e., philosophically foreseeable) and intrinsically good. Eternal life in Christ is, as Paul contrarily states, a "free gift" (5:15–16; 6:23) dependent on grace and God's love: "God shows his love for us in that while we were yet sinners Christ died for us" (5:8). An act of love and grace cannot be deduced transcendentally. Transcendental philosophy cannot but become aware of its intrinsic limits (as Schelling would argue in his later philosophy) when facing realized freedom, revelation, and empirical history.

One might, thirdly, think it appropriate to accuse Fichte of gnosticism. This accusation, though, needs to be put forward more precisely. Fichte does indeed think of a progressive *self-redemption* of mankind; not, however, by means of every single individual's full self-realization and self-divinization, but by means of a progressive *self-negation* of mankind in the course of the evolution of the "mighty World-Spirit,"[71] as he puts it in the *Die Bestimmung des Menschen*. For mankind is subject to the necessary and intrinsically good evolution of the World-Spirit.

Fichte also relies extensively on religious and particularly on mystical language. Ernst Benz has drawn attention to the mystical language which is characteristic of a great deal of German idealist writings:

> Finally, the terminology of religious idealistic philosophy itself is drawn consciously from the language of the mystics, in which they interpreted their mystical experience of divinization. It is not by chance that Fichte not only developed his ideas in systematic treatises, but also in his *Anweisung zum seligen Leben* (Introduction to the Blessed Life; or Spiritual Guide to the

> Blessed Life). The title is reminiscent of the literary tradition of mysticism, which produced a great number of "spiritual guides" read especially in German pietistic circles.[72]

Yet it is philosophy, and not religion as traditionally understood, which is to provide salvation. Christianity has so far, as Fichte argues, not yet been generally and publicly disclosed in its true character.[73] It is, furthermore, Fichte's *Wissenschaftslehre,* rather than the historical Christ event (Romans 6:18–19), which is the turning point of history, for only by means of the *Wissenschaftslehre* can mankind get justified. Fichte is therefore not simply a "priest of science,"[74] since he, to a certain extent, aims at replacing Christ himself.

Fichte himself, finally, claims to authentically interpret Christianity, particularly the Logos speculation of John. Furthermore, in the *Anweisung* he makes clear that Christianity must prove its accordance with reason if it intends to claim validity.[75] Even despite his emphasis on unity with Christ, Fichte's account of sin and redemption differs hugely from Saint Paul's deeply historical view. Fichte's merely transcendental understanding of history seems to imply that he does not take history, and therefore sin and evil, as seriously as Paul does. Paul's dialectic of sin, death, and new life in Christ (6:3ff.) is replaced by Fichte's dialectic of nothingness, self-negation, and freedom. Since Fichte does not develop an account of creation (for he refuses, quite in contrast to Paul, the idea of creation and upholds that there is only one eternal being), the whole historical process remains utterly mysterious. Fichte cannot answer questions as to why there is history at all. Nonetheless, as he affirms, history is utterly necessary. Quite in contrast to Paul, Fichte opposes sin to freedom. It needs to be asked, though, what makes up the sinfulness of sin, if not freedom. In Paul, freedom is deeply ambivalent. Paul speaks, of course, of the "slaves of sin" (e.g., 6:17), but this does not deny the freedom of the sinners, be it Adam (e.g., 5:12; 6:18–19) or the whole of mankind (1:18ff.). Consequently, sin is opposed to the life of faith and grace, that is, to the freedom of Christ. This freedom, as has been shown above, consists of the obedience to the law of Christ, that is, grace (6:14ff.).

The *Wissenschaftslehre* as a Transformation of the Doctrine of Original Sin

I have suggested reading Fichte's popular writings as a continuous struggle with the doctrine of original sin. Particularly his understanding of the process of history and of the progressive self-realization of the *Sittengesetz,* as far as his earlier writings are concerned, or, as far as the later ones are concerned, of love and of the absolute Being indicate that he constantly refers to the doctrine of original sin. He also provides a narrative of how humanity can obtain redemption. Redemption and blessedness are to be achieved through philosophy.

If it is granted that Fichte's popular writings are authentic reformulations of the *Wissenschaftslehre,* it must be asked if and how the *Wissenschaftslehre* is a transformation of the doctrine of original sin too. This is all the more interesting as *Die Bestimmung des Menschen,* for instance, is not simply a reformulation of the previous *Wissenschaftslehre* but rather a developed (if not substantially revised) version of it. This is, therefore, also a very difficult question because there is arguably no such thing as *the Wissenschaftslehre,* for Fichte constantly revised what he called *Wissenschaftslehre* (he chose this term because he wanted to translate the Greek-derived word *philosophy* into German; his claim was that the *Wissenschaftslehre* was the new *prima philosophia*). Fichte's *Wissenschaftslehre,* though, strives to provide an answer to issues which the doctrine of original sin aimed at answering too, such as what the relations are between the absolute and the relative, between *Urbild* and *Abbild,* between time and eternity, between the finite and the infinite, and between freedom and necessity. What is history? How do freedom and nature relate to one another? What does blessedness, or redemption consist of? How is the distinction between *Sein* and *Dasein* to be overcome? This also leads to the question of whether or not Fichte's reference to Christian teaching, to Saint John, and to the doctrine of original sin is simply rhetorical. Did Fichte just want to avoid being accused of atheism, nihilism, or deism again? There is, of course, the need to take Fichte's self-estimation very seriously. And if this reference is indeed not simply rhetorical, how is his *Wissenschaftslehre* to be understood? It certainly does not provide an orthodox interpretation of Christianity (even if *orthodox* is understood very broadly), but it could provide a transformation, a secularization, or what I suggest calling a "metaphorization," of a feature of Fichte's teaching, which has its own legitimacy independent of any previous Christian teaching.

These are important questions for further research and discussion. Insofar as Fichte's philosophy of religion is deeply ambivalent and also changes over the course of his philosophical development, there will certainly be no simple answer to these questions.

Notes

The epigraph is from Walker Percy, "A Novel About the End of the World," in *The Message in the Bottle* (New York, 1989), 106. For Percy's review, see also Jeremiah

Alberg, *Die verlorene Einheit: Die Suche nach einer philosophischen Alternative zu der Erbsündenlehre von Rousseau bis Schelling* (Frankfurt: Peter Lang, 1996), 21.

1. Peter Koslowski, "Sündenfälle: Theorien der Wandelbarkeit der Welt," in *Die Wirklichkeit des Bösen: Systematisch-theologische und philosophische Annäherungen,* ed. Peter Koslowski and Friedrich Hermanni (Munich: Wilhelm Fink, 1998), 99–131, 128.

2. For the modern understanding of the doctrine of original sin, see, for example, Alberg, *Die verlorene Einheit;* Christoph Schulte, *Radikal böse: Die Karriere des Bösen von Kant bis Nietzsche* (Munich: Wilhelm Fink, 1991); Christoph Simm, *Kants Ablehnung jeglicher Erbsündenlehre* (Münster: Lit, 1991); Julius Gross, *Entwicklungsgeschichte des Erbsündendogmas seit der Reformation,* vol. 4 of *Geschichte des Erbsündendogmas* (Munich: Reinhardt, 1972); Elfriede Lämmerzahl, "Der Sündenfall in der Philosophie des deutschen Idealismus," in *Neuere Deutsche Forschungen* (Berlin: Junker und Dünnhaupt, 1934); Heinrich Wimmershoff, *Der Sündenfall in der Philosophie Schellings, Baaders und F. Schlegels* (Freiburg: Sollingen, 1934). See also R. W. Schanne, *Sündenfall und Erbsünde in der spekulativen Theologie: Die Weiterbildung der protestantischen Erbsündenlehre unter dem Einfluß der idealistischen Lehre vom Bösen* (Frankfurt: Peter Lang, 1976).

3. For Heidegger's philosophy of fallenness as a secularization of the doctrine of original sin, see Robert Spaemann, "Über einige Schwierigkeiten mit der Erbsünde," in *Zur kirchlichen Erbsündenlehre: Stellungnahmen zu einer brennenden Frage,* ed. Christoph Schönborn, Albert Görres, and Robert Spaemann (Freiburg: Johannes Verlag Einsiedeln, 1994), 37–66, 57–58.

4. *Über das Wesen des Gelehrten, und seine Erscheinungen im Gebiete der Freiheit* (1805), in *SW* 6:437.

5. See, for example, Walter Schulz, "Johann Gottlieb Fichte: Vernunft und Freiheit," in *Johann Gottlieb Fichte, Sören Kierkegaard* (Pfullingen: Günther Neske, 1977), 5–31, 7ff.

6. *GGZ.*

7. *ASL.*

8. *GGZ,* 137.

9. Leon Morris, *The Epistle to the Romans* (Leicester: Inter-Varsity, 1992, repr.), 190; see also Gerhard Kittel, ed., "Hamartánÿ," in *Theological Dictionary of the New Testament,* trans. and ed. Geoffrey W. Bromiley, 1:267–316, (Grand Rapids, Mich.: Eerdmans, 1964), 309.

10. *GGZ,* 102.

11. *GGZ,* 102.

12. *GGZ,* 102. It can be said that Fichte's view on Judaism led to an instrumentalizing interpretation of his philosophy by German Nazism, though one must also note that the key notions of Fichte's thought are utterly irreconcilable with any kind of totalitarian ideology.

13. *GGZ,* 103.

14. *GGZ,* 107–8.

15. *GGZ,* 107–8.

16. *GGZ,* 246.

17. Morna D. Hooker, *From Adam to Christ: Essays on Paul* (Cambridge: Cambridge University Press), 1.

18. For the interpretation of the purpose of Romans, see James D. G. Dunn, *Romans 1–8,* Word Biblical Commentary, vol. 38a (Dallas Word Books, 1988), liv–lviii; see also Karl P. Donfried, 'False Presuppositions in the Study of Romans," in *The Romans Debate,* ed. Karl P. Donfried, rev. and exp. ed. (Edinburgh: T&T Clark, 1991), 102–25; Robert J. Karris, "The Occasion of Romans: A Response to Professor Donfried," in *The Romans Debate,* 125–27; and Peter Stuhlmacher, "The Purpose of Romans," in *The Romans Debate,* 231–42.

19. Morna D. Hooker, "Adam in Romans 1," in *From Adam to Christ,* 78.

20. For the Greek New Testament text and the English translation, see *Nestle-Aland, Greek-English New Testament* (Stuttgart: Deutsche Bibelgesellschaft, 1992).

21. Kittel, "Hamartány̆," 310.

22. See ibid. for how the link between the carnal being of humans and sin ought to be understood in a proper way.

23. Morris, *Epistle to the Romans,* 257; see also Morna D. Hooker, "Interchange in Christ," in *From Adam to Christ,* 13–69.

24. Kittel, "Hamartány̆," 310.

25. John Ziesler, *Paul's Letter to the Romans* (London: SCM, 1993), 55.

26. Morris, *Epistle to the Romans,* 37.

27. For numerous Old Testament references, see Dunn *Romans 1–8,* 7.

28. Ernst Käsemann, *Commentary on Romans* (London: SCM, 1980), 169.

29. Käsemann, *Commentary on Romans,* 160–61.

30. *VOM.*

31. *VOM,* 3.

32. *VOM,* 3.

33. *VOM,* 5.

34. *ASL,* 72.

35. *VOM,* 25.

36. *VOM,* 35.

37. *VOM,* 35.

38. *VOM,* 82.

39. *VOM,* 74.

40. *VOM,* 118.

41. *VOM,* 124.

42. *VOM,* 117.

43. *VOM,* 102.

44. *VOM,* 128.

45. *VOM,* 116.

46. *VOM,* 116.

47. *VOM,* 125.

48. *VOM,* 125.

49. *VOM,* 144.

50. Johann Gottlieb Fichte, *Science of Knowledge (Wissenschaftslehre), with the First and Second Introductions,* ed. and trans. Peter Heath and John Lachs (New York: Appleton-Century-Croft, 1970), 198–99.

51. *GGZ,* 44.

52. *GGZ,* 22.

53. *GGZ,* 11.

54. *GGZ,* 20.
55. *ASL,* 334.
56. *ASL,* 87.
57. *GGZ,* 15.
58. *GGZ,* 15.
59. *GGZ,* 17.
60. *ASL,* 28.
61. *GGZ,* 15.
62. *GGZ,* 15.
63. *GGZ,* 15–16.
64. *ASL,* 139–40.
65. Dirk Schmids, "Das Christentum als Verwirklichung des Religionsbegriffs in Fichtes Spätphilosophie 1813," in *Sein—Reflexion—Freiheit: Aspekte der Philosophie Johann Gottlieb Fichtes,* ed. Christoph Asmuth, Bochumer Studien zur Philosophie, vol. 25 (Amsterdam and Philadelphia: B. R. Gründer, 1997).
66. *Staatslehre oder über das Verhältnis der Urstaates zum Vernunftreiche,* in *FW* 4:562.
67. *Staatslehre,* in *FW* 4:562.
68. *ASL,* 101.
69. *ASL,* 108.
70. *GGZ,* 8.
71. *VOM,* 117.
72. Ernst Benz, *The Mystical Sources of German Romantic Philosophy,* trans. Blair R. Reynold and Eunice M. Paul (Allison Park: Pickwick, 1983), 25.
73. *GGZ,* 194.
74. *Über das Wesen des Gelehrten,* in *SW* 6:437.
75. *ASL,* 88.

Fichte and the *Ursprache*

Andrew Fiala

During the winter of 1807–8, Fichte delivered a series of lectures, *Addresses to the German Nation*, that were intended to inspire the German people to struggle against the tyranny of French occupation. In these lectures Fichte, the transcendental philosopher par excellence, addresses a political audience in a rhetorical voice. He intends to inspire his audience as much as he intends to educate them. Indeed, in these addresses Fichte deliberately muddies the distinction between inspiration and education: in order to create the conditions for the possibility of a new German spirit, Fichte must inspire the people to create a new form of education. Given the political context in which Fichte delivered his *Addresses*, it is easy to understand why he might occasionally overstate his case about the virtue of the German spirit. It cannot be denied, however, that Fichte's *Addresses* contain a nationalistic tone that appears to be at odds with the transcendental concerns of his systematic philosophy.

Much of the argument in the *Addresses* is centered on the relation between the nation, politics, language, and culture. His conclusion in the *Addresses* is to call for the rebirth of the German nation from out of its bondage to the French invaders of 1806. Fichte claims: "Only a complete regeneration [*Umschaffung*], only the beginning of an entirely new spirit [*eines ganz neuen Geistes*] can help us."[1] Fichte concludes by criticizing his fellow Germans for not being level-headed enough to see that French domination did not result in liberation. Fichte goes so far as to claim that enthusiasm for the French ought to sound ludicrous when uttered in the German language because the German language itself is "formed to express the truth": "No! Good, earnest, steady German men and countrymen, far from our spirit [*Geist*] be such a lack of understanding, and far be such defilement from our language, which is formed to express the truth [*zum Ausdrucke des Wahren Gebildeten Sprache*]!"[2] This nationalistic rhetoric finds its basis in Fichte's understanding of language and its connection to politics.

The implicit theory of language we find in the *Addresses* is thus different from Fichte's earlier theory of language as developed in his 1794 essay

"On the Linguistic Capacity and the Origin of Language." There are three main differences:

1. In 1807 Fichte extends his consideration of language in an explicitly political direction, explicitly linking language to the concept of the nation.

2. In the *Addresses,* Fichte revises his earlier theory of the *Ursprache* (i.e., primal language) by linking the *Ursprache* more explicitly to the concept of spiritual freedom.

3. Finally, in the *Addresses,* Fichte ties his whole argument about the political nature of language around his view that language is, in a sense, the transcendental ground for the possibility of both nationality and individuality.

In 1794, as Fichte wrote his essay on language, he was caught up in an attempt to discover the transcendental ground of language. In 1807, as Fichte addressed his German audience under the French occupation, he was concerned with finding a way to renew the German spirit and inspire the creation of the German nation. While these two projects are quite different in intent, the second is only possible on the basis of the first. The German spirit is conceived by Fichte in terms of language; it is not primarily a racial or geographical concept.[3] The spirit of a people is the connection between its language and the original source of language which, Fichte maintains, is the human need to communicate. Fichte goes so far as to explicitly define "spiritual culture" (*geistige Bildung*) as "thinking in an *Ursprache*" because such a primal language remains linked to the living root of human life.[4] This living root is human intersubjectivity and freedom. In an *Ursprache,* Fichte continues, spiritual culture "is itself the life of one who thinks in this way."[5]

Although Fichte's comments on language in the *Addresses* represent the changed focus of his thought toward very practical political matters, he does not reject the conclusions of his earlier transcendental account of language. In 1794 Fichte understood the transcendental basis of language in terms of the intersubjective nature of human reason. This pointed him toward a social interpretation of language that he left undeveloped in the 1794 essay. In 1807 Fichte extended this reflection on language and reached the radical conclusion that language is the basis of both nationality and individuality. It would not have been possible to reach this conclusion if he had not already rejected an asocial theory of language in 1794. In the early essay, Fichte rejected both the view that language was given to man by God and the view that language evolved from primitive animal instinct. Instead, he understands language as a necessary consequence of the social nature of the human spirit. Thus Fichte's social interpretation of language in the *Addresses* stems from the view which he developed in 1794 that the transcendental ground of language is the intersubjectivity of human freedom.

While Fichte's specific nationalistic conclusions about the virtue of the German *Ursprache* must be taken with a grain of salt, his general consideration of language in the *Addresses* deserves to be taken seriously for the following reasons.

1. He links his transcendental account of the origin of language to empirical/historical manifestations of language. This may give us some insight into Fichte's transcendental idealism, especially the connection between theory and practice in his thought. In the *Addresses,* Fichte seems to hint that the history of language can influence the history of philosophy and vice versa.

2. Fichte also admits that philosophy must be articulated in real historical languages and that different languages are more or less philosophical. Fichte's philosophy of language in the *Addresses* thus attempts to explain why people fail to comprehend the truth of transcendental philosophy. Thinking that occurs in dead languages, which do not speak an *Ursprache,* is unable to reach the depth of transcendental philosophy.

3. Finally and more generally, Fichte's philosophy of language redefines the relation between thought, language, individuality, and culture. Fichte rejects the view that individuals are atomic selves who come up with ideas prior to language and who then search for words with which to express their thoughts. Rather, Fichte has a social interpretation of thought, language, individuality, and culture. Fichte claims that spirit speaks through individuals and that individuality must thus be understood in relation to a given historical culture, language, and philosophical tradition.

From 1794 to 1807

Jere Surber's excellent translation and analysis of Fichte's 1794 essay, "On the Linguistic Capacity and the Origin of Language," raises a number of questions for those of us interested in Fichte's political writings and Fichte's place within the history of German politics and philosophy. This is especially true since Surber links Fichte's essay on language to a tradition of reflection on the political nature of language that culminates in Habermas. Surber claims that Fichte's analysis of language was based upon a sensitivity to the "transcendental-political context" of language.[6]

Indeed, Surber claims that according to Fichte, "the development of language, far from appearing as a potential obstacle to political freedom, must be seen as its absolute precondition."[7] Surber concludes by claiming that with regard to Fichte's 1794 essay on language, "what is most important to notice is his explicit recognition that linguistic considerations always have political implications and that political questions cannot be adequately treated without an acknowledgment of the centrality of language to the discussion."[8]

Surber bases these claims on Fichte's repeated recognition of the transcendental basis of language in the communicative nature of free human beings: language originates in the human desire to communicate with and be recognized by other human beings.[9] In other words, the transcendental basis of language can be found in the intersubjective nature of human freedom. Fichte claims that human freedom is tied to a drive to communicate with and be recognized by another human being. As Fichte says in the 1794 essay, "as soon as he has actually encountered a being of his own kind in a reciprocal relation, it is precisely this drive that would have to produce in him the wish to indicate his thoughts to the other with whom he has become connected, and, on the other hand, to be able to obtain from the other a clear communication of the other's thoughts."[10] Fichte argues for the intersubjective basis of language throughout his essay. Moreover, he makes it clear that intersubjectivity, the transcendental condition for the possibility of language, has different levels of empirical expression. In the early essay, Fichte distinguishes two different levels, the family and the tribe. Fichte understands the empirical development of language as a development from family to tribe: signs develop and are used within a family; these signs are then exported to the larger community of the tribe. The social and political development of empirical languages can be traced back to an original *Ursprache* which is the first way in which human beings express thoughts to one another. In this early essay, Fichte understands the *Ursprache* as giving voice to the basic level of intersubjective communication grounded in the human drive to communicate. Fichte claims that the aim of language is "signification [*Bezeichnung*] . . . for the sake of mutual reciprocity of our thought."[11] He further clarifies this by stating that "through association with human beings, there awakens in us the idea of indicating our thoughts to one another through arbitrary signs—in a word, the idea of language."[12] This basic desire to communicate is the ground of the *Ursprache,* the immediate expression of inner thought which is developed further in both familial and tribal interaction.

In this early essay, however, Fichte leaves unanalyzed the explicitly political development of language, that is, the development of diverse national languages. He does not extend his account of the development of language beyond a primitive tribal level and does not consider the connection between language and the modern nation-state. While he does point beyond the *Ursprache* to a more advanced, more "spiritual," cultured, or civilized language,[13] he leaves this undeveloped. Almost at the end of the 1794 essay, Fichte claims that a more culturally advanced language would eventually "supplant" (*verdrängten*) the *Ursprache:* "For as the nation [*die Nation*] advanced further in its culture, it would necessarily have to find new forms adequate to its concepts and soon forget about the older ones while using the new ones."[14] Here Fichte uses, for the first time in this essay as far as I can tell, the word "nation" (*die Nation*) and indicates, if only in outline, the direction that his thinking on language would take in his politically inflammatory *Addresses to the German Nation.*

This direction can be roughly indicated as follows. In the *Addresses,* Fichte extends the political context of language to an explicit consideration of the link between the nation, its language, and the spiritual development of its culture. Fichte says in the *Addresses* that it is crucial for a nation to remain in touch with its proper linguistic heritage. A nation's spiritual life flourishes when the people speak a "living language" (*lebendige Sprache*): "Among the people with a living language, spiritual culture [*Geistigesbildung*] influences life; whereas among a people of the opposite kind, mental culture and life go their separate ways."[15] Fichte here attempts a taxonomy of peoples based upon the *lebendigkeit* of their various languages.

As we shall see in the next section, the criterion of Fichte's taxonomy represents a crucial shift away from his analysis in the 1794 essay. Before we turn to this crucial difference, let us note that, in the *Addresses,* Fichte was still concerned with something that could be called the transcendental condition for the possibility of language and that this transcendental condition is still the intersubjective nature of human reason. In the *Addresses* Fichte stressed the fact that human progress is transcendentally grounded on the creative activity of human being: "The real destiny of the human race on earth . . . is in freedom to make itself what it really is originally."[16] Fichte here emphasized the creative power of human freedom. In the *Addresses,* however, Fichte extended the notion of intersubjectivity in a radically political direction. What is important in the *Addresses* is that Fichte recognizes that the creative power of human freedom is always tied to some empirical basis in space and time, most importantly the nation. Fichte continues: "This making of itself deliberately, and according to rule, must have a beginning somewhere and at some moment in space and time. . . . In regard to the space, we believe that it is first of all the Germans who are called upon to begin the new era."[17] Fichte's goal in the *Addresses* is to link the project of freedom to the German nation and especially to the German language. Fichte thus continues to maintain that the intersubjective nature of human freedom is the transcendental ground of empirical languages, but in the *Addresses* he recognizes that these empirical languages vary according to national differences. He concludes that the German language is the language that is closest to the completion of the project of human freedom because it alone remains clearly linked to the transcendental ground of language. German is the proper language in which to comprehend the essence of human freedom because German remains tied to the "force of nature" (*Naturkraft*) from which language first issued forth.[18] In other words, in evaluating national differences among languages, Fichte's criterion remains linked to the nature of human freedom and its need to communicate with other human beings—this is the "force of nature" of which Fichte speaks. He concludes that German is the language in which the connection between language and human freedom remains clear.

German Destiny and the *Ursprache*

Given that Fichte remained committed to Kant's universal morality, one wonders why Fichte felt it was necessary to specifically address the *German* nation. After all, Fichte was aware that the history of culture is a European, if not a global, affair: his first "Address" locates the *Addresses* within the context of his speculations about European or world history as found in *The Characteristics of the Present Age*. However, for Fichte the decisive moment which confronted world history in 1807 was uniquely German: it was the Germans who were to usher in a new epoch in history by creating a new, more spiritual world. In the *Addresses* Fichte both attempts to prove that the proper manifestation of the new spiritual world is the German nation and attempts to show the, as yet, nonexistent German nation how it might come to create this new world. The means of creating the new world are political, philosophical, and poetic. The new era will be a German era, Fichte argues, because only in the German language and culture are politics, philosophy, and poetry united.

While there are certainly chauvinistic and contingent historical reasons why Fichte's *Addresses* are addressed specifically to the Germans, he attempts to provide a philosophical justification for the fact that "it is first of all the Germans who should be recognized as those who begin the new era—as forerunners [*vorangehend*] and exemplars [*vorbildend*] for the rest [*für die übrigen*] [of the human race]."[19] In this formulation of the German task, it is clear that Germany is not to be a conquering nation but an exemplar for the rest of the human race that will then lead humanity forward into the new epoch of history. Fichte's German nationalism is thus more than naively chauvinistic; it is based on a philosophical claim about progress in history. Fichte claims that to Germany alone belongs the spiritual destiny of bringing forth a new epoch in world history because Germany is the highest exemplar of the European spirit.

Fichte's philosophical justification of his claims about the unique historical mission of Germany is based on what he claims is the uniquely philosophical nature of the German language and way of thinking. Germans speak a living primal language, an *Ursprache,* in which alone truth can be authentically thought. The *Ursprache* connects living German speakers with their original destiny and provides the means for completing this destiny, the means for making life into that which it ought to be. Most significantly, this *Ursprache* is a living connection between theory and practice, between life and thought:

> In this way, I say, spiritual culture [*geistige Bildung*]—and here is meant especially thinking in a primal language [*Ursprache*]—does not exert an influence on life; it is itself the life of him who thinks in this fashion. Nevertheless it necessarily strives, from the life that thinks in this way, to influence other life outside it, and so to influence the life of all about it and to form this life in accordance with itself. For, just because that kind of thinking is life, it is felt by its possessor with inward pleasure in its vitalizing [*belebenden*], transfiguring [*verklärenden*], and liberating [*befreienden*] power.[20]

Fichte claims that theory and practice are united in the spirit of the *Ursprache.* Thinking in the *Ursprache* leads to the real invigoration, transfiguration, and liberation of political life. This connection between theory and practice only occurs within the *Ursprache,* the primal language which Fichte elsewhere characterizes as a "living language" (*lebendige Sprache*) and a "mother-tongue" (*Muttersprache*).

Fichte had developed the notion of the *Ursprache* in the 1794 text on language. The differences between this early account of the *Ursprache* and Fichte's account in the *Addresses* are significant. In the early text, Fichte described the *Ursprache* as a primitive language that was a direct imitation of nature: "Just as nature signified something to men through sight and hearing, exactly thus did they have to signify it to one another in freedom. One might call a language constructed on this basic principle the *Ursprache* or Hieroglyphic language."[21] In the early essay, Fichte did not claim any special ontological or spiritual status for the *Ursprache.* While all languages remain connected to their origin in some way, this connection to the origin of language is gradually effaced by the progress of culture.

Fichte claimed in 1794 that as culture progresses, the *Ursprache* "will gradually perish and be replaced by another which carries in itself not even the slightest trace of the former."[22] This progress occurred as the original words of the *Ursprache* "were replaced by signs which better corresponded to the civilized spirit of the people."[23] In this early text, then, Fichte sees the overcoming of the *Ursprache* as a sign of spiritual progress.

This is not so in the *Addresses,* where progress is understood as reviving the spiritual power of the *Ursprache.* In the *Addresses,* Fichte claims that German culture is progressive because the actually existing German *Ursprache* affords Germans the most comprehensive appropriation of the original "force of nature" that is at work in language. This claim is in direct contradiction to his earlier claim that the *Ursprache* is overcome by civilization. Fichte even goes so far in his early text on language as to claim that, with regard to grammatical rules about the placement of adjectives, French "has a decided advantage over the German."[24] In the *Addresses,* Fichte does not have a single kind word to say about the French language. Indeed, he indicates that the demise of European culture can be blamed in part on the "mongrelization" of culture that has occurred in Romance languages like French that have appropriated Latin and thus remain tied to a dead language.[25]

Fichte's reevaluation of the value and power of the *Ursprache* is based on three factors. First, Fichte seems to have reestimated the political, philosophical, and poetic power of language. This makes sense, since the goal of the *Addresses* is to use the poetic power of language to inspire the German spirit and bring forth the German nation. In 1794 Fichte was concerned with language and its ability to represent objects. In 1807 Fichte was interested in the creative power of language to generate new developments in history. In both 1794 and 1807, Fichte maintained that the transcendental condition for language, the "force of nature" that gave rise to language, was human freedom. In 1807 Fichte emphasizes that this force is a creative and not merely a representational activity. In the *Addresses* Fichte states that in a living language, the highest thoughts remain tied to sensuous life. Only in an *Ursprache* is living philosophical thought possible because in such a living language, "the symbol is directly living and sensuous; it re-presents [*wieder darstellend*] all real life and so takes hold of and exerts an influence on life."[26] Creative advancements in thought must be tied to real life and this is only possible when such thought is articulated in an *Ursprache.*

Second, in 1807, after the failure of German politics and the French invasion, Fichte is forced to recognize that the uniqueness of German culture is not political but cultural. The German culture has always existed beyond the confines of a political state in the shared spiritual milieu of those who speak the German language. This leads Fichte to conclude that the spirit of the German nation is found in the unifying power of the German language. He claims that what is unique about German as opposed to French or English is its link to its own etymological past. Fichte emphasizes that German possesses both Latinate and Germanic words that are synonymous. However, he claims that the Germanic terms are more powerful stimuli to thought and action because they do not require translation into sense images.[27] Fichte claims that there is a "national power of imagination" (*Nationaleinbildungskraft*) and that words in the *Ursprache* (as opposed to foreign words introduced into this language) stimulate this imagination directly.[28]

Third, in 1807, Fichte understands progress in terms of a living connection to the origin of human culture. This only happens in a living language in which philosophical, artistic, and even political investigations are linked to the transcendental ground of language in "spiritual nature itself" (*geistigen Natur selbst*).[29] This connection is, Fichte claims, only found in the German spirit and Germany thus ought to be the forerunner of progress in history.[30] French civilization seems to have failed to live up to its promise by exchanging the ideals of revolution for the lust of empire. Fichte links the failure of French culture to the remnants of imperial Roman culture in the French language. The German language remained unpolluted by Roman culture. Instead, it remains linked, as an *Ursprache,* to the basis of language in the intersubjectivity of human freedom.

Language, Politics, and Poetry: The Golden Age

Fichte's comments about the importance of the *Ursprache* are significant for both his political and philosophical agendas. He claims that philosophy and all of spiritual culture grow out of real, historical, political life and that only a certain type of political life will lead to the full fruition of philosophy. In particular, for Fichte, making the German people into a real political nation in which thinking in the *Ursprache* can proceed without external constraint will open the possibility for the completion of a living mediation between politics and philosophy. For the living truth expressed in the *Ursprache* to become self-conscious and complete, this truth must be made real by way of real political transformations in the lives of those who speak the *Ursprache.* In short, the philosophical truths which can only be thought in the *Ursprache* will be completed and comprehended when the Germans are politically and spiritually free. This will, in turn, be an example for the rest of mankind, who will then follow Germany into the new epoch in which mankind will freely "fashion itself by means of itself" (*die Menschheit sich selber durch sich selbst erschaffen*).[31] One can see here the linkage to Fichte's more theoretical work in which freedom is understood as the ego positing itself. Fichte understands the new German epoch as a philosophical epoch because such freedom can only be enacted "through knowledge" (*durch die Erkenntnis*).[32] Such philosophical self-determination can only occur within an *Ursprache* because only within such an *Ursprache* is thinking organically connected to its origin in freedom.

When the living truth that is implicit in the *Ursprache* is finally allowed to express itself, when thought determines itself in accord with its origin, it will do so, Fichte claims, by means of the transformative power of poetry. Fichte agrees with his contemporaries Schiller, Schelling, and Hölderlin when he claims that "the thinker [*der Denker*] . . . is a poet [*Dichter*]."[33] A truly original thinker re-presents in images, as the poet does, the truth of sensual life and in this re-presentation actually overcomes the old world and creates a new one. Within an *Ursprache* in which thought and life are organically connected, poetic thought thus has direct political consequences: "To such a language, therefore, poetry is the most excellent means of flooding the life of all with the spiritual culture that has been attained."[34] We can see, then, that Fichte justifies his own flurries of poetic rhetoric by stating that poetry is at least as useful as philosophy for transforming people's lives. Fichte thus moves beyond Kantian rationalism in claiming that political transformation will occur, not by reasoned argument as Kant might claim, but by the power of persuasive speech and the poetic art of imagination.

Fichte concludes his remarks on language with a brief account of "the golden age." This golden age would be reached when life, language, and thought interpenetrate each other mutually.[35] Fichte notes, however, that with such a completion comes a subsequent decline. He acknowledges that it is possible for poetry, politics, philosophy, and life to be completed at a given stage of historical development. However, such completion inevitably results in death; after a people celebrates its golden age, "the source of poetry runs dry."[36] This source is the force of nature that leads us to strive to produce new poetry, philosophy, and politics, that is, it is human freedom. In the *Addresses*, Fichte concludes that at the present stage of historical development, the German spirit alone remains close to this source and thus has a unique task in the future of the development of the human race. Indeed, Fichte states that the criterion for being called "German" is whether or not "you believe in something absolutely primary and original in man himself, in freedom, in endless improvement, in the eternal progress of our race [*unsers Geschlechts*]."[37] German politics, philosophy, and poetry thus point beyond the golden age promised by spiritually dead languages toward the eternal progress that is the work of freedom.

Conclusion: Fichte's Philosophy of Language

What then is Fichte's philosophy of language as articulated in the *Addresses*? As we have seen, this question is not tangential to his project in the *Addresses*. Indeed, Fichte explicitly states that "a consideration of the nature of language in general [*das Wesen der Sprache über haupt*]" is necessary as part of his larger project of inspiring the German people.[38] Fichte's philosophy of language can be summed up in the following epigram: "Men are formed by language far more than language is formed by men" (*Mehr die Menschen von der Sprache gebildet werden, denn die Sprache von den Menschen*).[39] There are two ways in which Fichte develops this view, a strong way and a weak one. In both of these he is arguing for a reversal of the commonsense view of the relation between language and individuality, language and the community, and indeed language and thought. The commonsense view holds that individuals, communities, and thoughts exist prior to language and that we learn particular languages in order to express our inner thoughts to other members of our community. Such, for example, is Augustine's view (famously used as a foil by Wittgenstein at the very beginning of the *Philosophical Investigations*) that both will and thought are prior to language and that we learn language in order to be able to express our thoughts and our wills.[40]

In the *Addresses,* Fichte rejects this theory of language. In the strong version of his theory, he claims that language is the basis of individuality, community, and thought. He states that with regard to individual language speakers, "They do not form language, it is the language that forms them" (*So bilden nicht sie die Sprache, sondern die Sprache bildet sie*).[41] Individuals, even in their most deeply held thoughts, are all formed by language. Fichte further elaborates this claim in a more political direction: "The people does not express its knowledge, but its knowledge expresses itself out of the mouth of the people" (*Nicht eigentlich dieses Volk spricht seine Erkenntniss aus, sondern seine Erkenntniss selbst spricht sich aus aus demselben*).[42] This claim is, in turn, explained by the following: "It is not really man that speaks, but human nature that speaks in him and announces itself to others of his kind" (*Nicht eigentlich redet der Mensch, sondern in ihm redet die menschliche Natur, und verkündiget sich anderen seines Gleichen*).[43] According to this strong claim, individuals are merely conduits for the life of spirit that is found in the totality of language and community.

The weaker form of Fichte's claim can be found in the following:

> What an immeasurable influence on the whole human development of a people [*eines Volkes*] the character of its language may have—its language, which accompanies the individual into the most secret depths of his mind in

> thought and will and either hinders him or gives him wings, which unites within its domain the whole mass of men who speak it into one single point and common understanding [*gemeinsamen Verstanden*], which is the true point of meeting and mingling for the world of the senses and the world of spirit [*der Sinnenwelt und der der Geister*], and fuses the ends of both in each other in such a fashion that it is impossible to tell to which of the two it belongs itself.[44]

Here Fichte moderates his view slightly and recognizes that there is a mutual interplay between the individual and the spirit of his or her community. Nonetheless, language is crucial for it acts as the medium in which individual and community are interrelated. Indeed, Fichte concludes above that there is no way to dissolve the mediating function of language and that we cannot tell whether the individual or the community is prior to their juncture in language. Thus, even this weaker claim, which allows some room for the individual beyond language, still results in a subordination of the individual to language. In both versions of this theory, then, it is clear that Fichte rejects the view that individuals and their thoughts are somehow prior to language.

Fichte provides us with two arguments for the priority of language: a transcendental argument and a practical-moral argument. The transcendental argument is similar to the argument he made in the 1794 essay on language. In that essay, Fichte claimed that language originated in the human drive to be recognized by another human being: the transcendental condition for the possibility of language is the intersubjective nature of human freedom. In the *Addresses,* Fichte claims that language originates in a force of nature which is unitary and necessary: "It ever remains nature's one, same, living power of speech, which in the beginning necessarily arose in the way it did" (*Bleibt es immer dieselbe Eine, ursprünglich also ausbrechenmüssende lebendige Sprachkraft der Natur*).[45] He even goes so far as to claim that there is a "fundamental law" according to which "every idea becomes in the human organs of speech one particular sound and no other."[46] Fichte does not explain this fundamental law in any detail but it might, perhaps, be explained as a law of onomatopoeia wherein human speech originates out of an imitation of sounds in nature.[47] Behind this must be, however, the transcendental condition of human intersubjectivity which makes the imitation of nature in speech necessary to begin with. In the *Addresses,* this transcendental condition seems to be what he calls the "force of nature," which he refers to as "language in its original emergence from life" (*der ursprüngliche Ausgang der Sprache*).[48] Language emerges from the intersubjective basis of human freedom. It is thus prior to individuality because individuality can only form on the basis of communication between selves which is itself only made possible by language.

The practical-moral argument is linked to Fichte's call for a new form of education. Fichte's *Addresses* are dedicated to inspiring the German nation. This will occur, he claims, when Germany creates a new form of education for its youth. According to Fichte, there could be no such thing as moral education if the individual were a selfish atom which comes into existence somehow prior to his or her community. If it were true that children were naturally selfish and viewed themselves as atomic selves, it would be impossible to educate them:

> Nothing can be created from nothing, and the development of a fundamental instinct, no matter to what extent, can never make it the opposite of itself. How then could education ever implant morality in the child, if morality did not exist in him originally [*ursprünglich*] and before all education? It does, therefore, actually exist in all human children that are born into the world; the task is simply to find out the purest and most primitive form in which it appears.[49]

Fichte claims that he knows that children have this fundamental moral disposition both as the result of empirical observation and as the result of his own speculative philosophical thought. Speculative philosophy in the *Wissenschaftslehre* reaches the conclusion that the self and the not-self mutually determine one another and that the self strives to recognize and to be recognized by the not-self. In the *Addresses* Fichte explains this as "the most primitive form of morality," which he calls "the instinct for respect."[50] He further elaborates this: "The bond, therefore, which makes men of one mind, and the development of which is a chief part of education for manhood, is not sensuous love, but the instinct for mutual respect."[51] This instinct for mutual respect is linked to the intersubjective nature of human freedom and thus to Fichte's discussion of language. Language is the medium which allows individuals to respect one another. According to Fichte, then, we do not acquire language because we are pre-formed homunculi looking for the means of expressing our selfish desires. Rather, language occurs because we are moral and social beings whose basic instincts require that we create a medium in which we can respect one another.

The details of Fichte's view on language thus changed significantly between 1794 and 1807 while its underlying kernel did not. Fichte revises his estimation of the *Ursprache* and argues that the best language is the language that stays closest to its roots in the intersubjective nature of human being. Nonetheless, Fichte retains his view that language originates in intersubjectivity. In the later text he argues more vigorously for the view that language is prior to the development of finite individuality and that society is thus, in some sense, prior to the individual. Finally, in the later text, he explicitly claims that the German language is the modern language that has stayed closest to its roots in the human *Ursprache* and in which the intersubjective truth of human nature can best be developed. While this is obviously a nationalistic exaggeration on his part, it is clear that this exaggeration is dependent, in part, on the historical context in which he offered his *Addresses*. Indeed, this exaggeration might be expected because the *Addresses* and the oppressed German people to whom they were addressed formed part of the ongoing political struggle for recognition and mutual respect which Fichte found at the basis of language itself.

Notes

1. *AGN,* 243; *FW* 7:476.
2. *AGN,* 247; *FW* 7:480.
3. Fichte says, for example: "Let the original people [*Stammvolke*] who speak this language incorporate as many individuals of other races [*Stammes*] and other languages; if they are not permitted to bring the sphere of their observation up to the point from which, from now on, the language is to develop, then they remain dumb in the community and without influence on the language, until the time comes when they themselves have entered into the sphere of observation of the original people" (*AGN,* 62; *FW* 7:319–20, translation modified).
4. *AGN,* 78; *FW* 7:333.
5. *AGN,* 78; *FW* 7:333.
6. Jere Paul Surber, *Language and German Idealism* (Atlantic Highlands: Humanities, 1996), 41.
7. Surber, *Language and German Idealism,* 62.
8. Surber, *Language and German Idealism,* 64.
9. For example, Fichte writes: "As these [supersensible] ideas now become clearer and clearer to a human being, the drive to acquaint others with what he had discovered would begins to stir in him, for never is the drive to communicate livelier than in the case of new and sublime thoughts" (Johann Gottlieb Fichte, "On the Linguistic Capacity and the Origin of Language," in Surber, *Language and German Idealism,* 132).
10. Fichte, "Linguistic Capacity and the Origin of Language," 123.
11. Fichte, "Linguistic Capacity and the Origin of Language," 124.
12. Fichte, "Linguistic Capacity and the Origin of Language," 124.
13. Fichte, "Linguistic Capacity and the Origin of Language," 144.
14. Fichte, "Linguistic Capacity and the Origin of Language," 144; *GA* 1.3:127.
15. *AGN,* 73; *FW* 7:329.
16. *AGN,* 46; *FW* 7:306.
17. *AGN,* 46–47; *FW* 7:306.
18. "The difference [between Germans and other Teutonic people] arose at the moment of the separation from the common stock and consists in this, that the German speaks a language which has been alive ever since it first issued from the force of nature [*dass der Deutsche eine bis zu ihrem ersten Ausstromen aus der Naturkraft lebendiges Sprache redet*]" (*AGN,* 68; *FW* 7:325).

19. *AGN,* 47; *FW* 7:306.
20. *AGN,* 78; *FW* 7:333.
21. Fichte, "Linguistic Capacity and the Origin of Language," 125.
22. Fichte, "Linguistic Capacity and the Origin of Language," 144.
23. Fichte, "Linguistic Capacity and the Origin of Language," 144.
24. Fichte, "Linguistic Capacity and the Origin of Language," 138.
25. *AGN,* 84–87.
26. *AGN,* 76; *FW* 7:332.
27. *AGN,* 67.
28. *AGN,* 65; *FW* 7:322.
29. *AGN,* 86; *FW* 7:339.
30. *AGN,* 86; *FW* 7:339.
31. *AGN,* 46; *FW* 7:306.
32. *AGN,* 46; *FW* 7:306.
33. *AGN,* 78; *FW* 7:333 (my translation).
34. *AGN,* 78; *FW* 7:334.
35. *AGN,* 80.
36. *AGN,* 80; *FW* 7:335.
37. *AGN,* 125; *FW* 7:374.
38. *AGN,* 55; *FW* 7:314.
39. *AGN,* 55; *FW* 7:314.
40. "But I, by longing and cries and broken accents and various motions of my limbs to express my thoughts, that so I might have my will and yet unable to express all I willed, or to whom I willed, did myself, by the understanding which Thou, my God, gavest me, practice the sounds in my memory. When they named any thing, and as they spoke turned towards it, I saw and remembered that they called what they would point out by the name they uttered. And that they meant this thing and no other was plain from the motion of their body, the natural language, as it were, of all nations" (Augustine, *Confessions,* trans. Edward B. Pusey [New York: Collier Books, 1961], bk. 1, p. 16).
41. *AGN,* 62; *FW* 7:320.
42. *AGN,* 56; *FW* 7:315.
43. *AGN,* 56; *FW* 7:314–15.
44. *AGN,* 69; *FW* 7:326.
45. *AGN,* 57; *FW* 7:315.
46. *AGN,* 56; *FW* 7:314.
47. This seems to be a new twist in the *Addresses.* The 1794 essay on language emphasized written language at the expense of spoken language, and indeed interpreted the *Ursprache* in terms of written hieroglyphics. In the *Addresses,* Fichte seems more interested in the spoken word. The political and hermeneutical context of the *Addresses* might explain this difference: in the *Addresses,* Fichte is himself speaking German and is acutely aware of the power of his own voice to inspire the German people.
48. *AGN,* 63; *FW* 7:321.
49. *AGN,* 172; *FW* 7:414.
50. *AGN,* 172; *FW* 7:414.
51. *AGN,* 174; *FW* 7:416.

"The Logic of Historical Truth": History and Individuality in Fichte's Later Philosophy of History

Angelica Nuzzo

Emil Lask and the History of German Idealism

In his 1902 dissertation *Fichtes Idealismus und die Geschichte,* Emil Lask, one of the most brilliant of Heinrich Rickert's students, assumes the problem of irrationality as the guiding principle for his analysis of the development of German idealism in general and of Fichte's philosophy in particular. In so doing, Lask moves along the lines established by the still young tradition of Heidelberg neo-Kantianism. One need only recall Wilhelm Windelband's attention to the problem of contingency in the history of philosophy[1] or Alfred Bäumler's study of the problem of irrationality in Kant's *Critique of Judgment*[2] in order to place Lask's research in its historical context. Moreover, Lask's interpretation of the internal development of Fichte's philosophy takes up the typical neo-Kantian issues dictated by a philosophy and logic of values. In this connection, irrationality is necessarily linked to what Lask calls, following contemporary terminology, *Wertindividualität,* that is, the issue of the source and legitimacy of the specific value proper to the structures of individuality.

In his historically oriented reconstruction, Lask pursues two objectives. First, he aims at showing how classic German philosophy departs from Kant's transcendental turn by starting precisely from the point at which Kant, while leaving irrationality—namely, the entire empirical realm—out of the strict logic of understanding and reason, still remains trapped in the unavoidable need for it. The solution of the dualism that separates concept and sensible intuition is eventually reached by Hegel's metaphysical monism—or, in Lask's terminology, by Hegel's "emanational logic." However, according to Lask's neo-Kantian reading of the history of German idealism, the treatment that individuality receives in Hegel's logic is ultimately not so different from the way Kant's "analytic logic" initially dealt with it. In both cases, even if for very different reasons, the individual in its monadic existence has no intrinsic value. Analytic logic denies the individual any value since it places it outside the realm of all possible knowledge, at the bottom line of a hierarchy in which the thing in itself occupies the opposite—yet specular—side. In Kant's epistemology, the individual can be known only in its being as a logical instance of the *abstract* universal; it can never be known in its *empirical* individuality, since this cannot be deduced from the concept of the genus. In this way, empirical individuality remains for Kant an irrational remainder; namely, something that can by no means be comprehended,[3] or something that must be left as transcendentally "contingent" (*zufällig*).[4] Consequently, the only notion of individuality allowed by Kant's analytic logic is the abstract individuality of formal logic. Yet *transcendental* logic, being a logic of real cognition and not simply a logic of abstract thinking, needs to assume the irrationality of empirical individuality as a given or *factum* that fulfills the same systematic function as the thing in itself. However, at the margins of Kant's philosophy—that is, in a realm that lies beyond the jurisdiction of logic *tout court*—Lask discovers two legitimate occurrences of true individuality that will be of crucial importance in post-Kantian philosophy. On the one hand, if individuality remains an inscrutable mystery for human knowledge (which is always and necessarily *discursive* knowledge), it can be claimed as object of a hypothetically assumed *intuitive*, divine understanding. On the other hand, Kant's third *Critique* discloses the realm of aesthetics as the sphere in which empirical individuality can be ascribed an independent value In neither case, however, is Kant able to propose a specific logic to govern the different occurrences of empirical contingency.

The "emanational" logic proposed by Hegel only apparently saves the value of the individual by sublating the abstract universal in the notion of a "concrete universal." As monistic totality, the concrete universal is individual and is the only true individual. Lask sees correctly that Hegel's philosophy is the attempt to claim the force of Kant's divine intuitive understanding for human cognition—for knowledge as such. Along with the upper limit of the thing in itself, Hegel eliminates the lower limit of the empirical irrationality as well. The emanational model transforms the logical relation between universal or genus and individual into the metaphysical relation between the totality and its parts. Thereby the manifold of the individuals emanates from the unique totality, which constitutes itself by making its parts possible. The particular is "particularization" (*Besonderung*) of the whole; the individual is its "individualization." In Lask's interpretation, this move implies a destruction of the ontological and epistemological independence of the individual, for it posits an all-embracing, unique totality by which the empirical individual is eventually swallowed up as a mere part. The individual has now indeed a value, yet is not valuable "in-and-for-itself." The individual owes its ontological and epistemological validity to the totality of which it appears as a merely subordinated part or function.

This view of the general development of German idealism leads to the second task of Lask's book, which can be summed up in the following question: what is the position occupied by Fichte's philosophy in the historical constellation dominated by the two alternative models of Kant's analytic logic and Hegel's metaphysical emanationism? Against this background, the problem of irrationality guides Lask in the discussion of Fichte's philosophical development along four different stages. In the first phase—that of the *Grundlage der gesamten Wissenschaftslehre* of 1794—Fichte clearly reacts to the insufficiencies of Kant's transcendental philosophy with a metaphysics very close to Hegel's emanationism; the crucial turn of the *Zweite Einleitung* of 1797, however, brings Fichte back to Kant's analytic logic; what follows is a transition period (1798–1801) in which Kant's pre-critical positions are recuperated[5] and developed into a type of "positivism"[6] that opposes speculation to life[7] and establishes the high value of feeling or *Gefühl*[8]—the faculty that both in its moral and aesthetic use is able to capture the value of the particular; finally, starting from 1801, Fichte reaches his unique position of compromise between the analytic and emanational models. This compromise is the foundation of Fichte's conception of history.

At the final stage of this development—and at this final stage alone (a stage that, in Lask's account, is subjected to yet further transformations)—Fichte is able to present for the first time a complex and coherent philosophy of history. Thus, the topic announced by Lask's title—*Fichte's Idealism and History*—occupies only the third part of his book. Lask's primary concern is to provide the theoretical framework for a discussion of the "logical structure of history,"[9] and only subsequently to offer the analysis of the structure of history itself.[10] At this point, however, Lask leaves a whole set of crucial questions totally unexplored. What is the necessary assumption that places the problem of irrationality at the very heart of a *philosophy of history*? Why is it precisely in *history* that *logic* finds its necessary counterpart (and this is true at least since Leibniz's distinction between *verité de raison* and *verité de fait*)? Why is a reconciliation between logic and history such an important and yet almost unsolvable issue for the philosophers of German idealism? Since Lask never addresses these questions despite their going directly to the heart of his general thesis, the topic of a philosophy of history—in Fichte but also in Kant and Hegel—does not receive the attention that one would expect given the theoretical premises of his book. Moreover, neither Lask's discussion of Kant's analytic logic nor his examination of Hegel's emanationism touches on the problem of history, on its relation to logic, or on the role played by individuality in historical processes. Is there a philosophical reason why a theory of history becomes possible for Fichte only in the later development of his thought?

My aim in this chapter is to carry Lask's analysis a step further, and to inquire into the general systematic conditions for a theory of history in Fichte's later philosophy. For this purpose, I will concentrate on Fichte's "metaphysics" of history, or on the metaphysical claims that reveal Fichte's awareness of the necessary link between logic and history. I will confine my discussion to the *Grundzüge des gegenwärtigen Zeitalters* (1806; *The Characteristics of the Present Age*), which, in Lask's periodization, represents the first text of Fichte's new philosophy of history. Despite—and indeed beyond—its specifically neo-Kantian problematic and terminology, Lask's study remains important to me because precisely the point left unexplored and unthematized by Lask is the point that creates the possibility of addressing in Fichte's philosophy the same crucial issue that we find so clearly and explicitly developed later on by Hegel—an issue that, at first glance and to a great number of interpreters, seems to be totally absent in Fichte.

That Hegel's system produces a tension between the alleged all-encompassing "closure" of speculative logic on the one hand and the openness of historical reality on the other is a well-known and difficult issue, which has been interpreted variously by Hegel scholars. The relation between logic and history is due to the speculative and dialectic nature of logic itself, and expresses its function both as method of philosophical knowledge of reality and as method of immanent constitution of the reality of knowledge itself. Fichte's philosophy, on the contrary, is not guided by the rigorous logical claim that dominates Hegel's theory. Yet his philosophy of history reveals a curious need for a logical structure that reaches far more deeply than the schematic distinction of epochs, peoples, and mediating principles for the transition between different epochs and civilizations. According to Fichte, a logical claim distinguishes the approach to history proper to the philosopher from that of the historian, and distinguishes *Wahrheit* from *Wahrscheinlichkeit* to be discovered in history. Hence my claim is that in Fichte's philosophy we have the best case for an analysis of the peculiar relation between logic and history in the theory of history.

In this essay, I will discuss Fichte's philosophy of history by focusing on the following question: in what sense is a philosophy of history grounded by a *logic of history*, and what is the general structure of this logic? In developing this issue my analysis will move, more or less explicitly, between Lask's suggestions and Hegel's solutions. Fichte recognizes, beyond Kant, the need for a specific logic or philosophical justification of empirical individuality; and yet, unlike Hegel, he does not generate empirical individuality directly from logic. The result is Fichte's constitution of the sphere of "history proper" (*eigentliche Geschichte*).

In bringing Fichte close to Hegel on the common issue of the logic of history—a point that must be considered crucial, being always regarded as the origin of Hegel's alleged "panlogism"—I present an interpretative thesis that not only reaches opposite conclusions in relation to Lask's book but also runs directly against the positions of distinguished Fichteans such as Georges Gurvitch[11] and Reinhard Lauth.[12] In all these interpreters the desire to perceive Fichte's *Wissenschaftslehre* as separated by the deepest distance from Hegel's all-encompassing logic arises more from an insufficient knowledge of the nature and function of Hegel's logic (always more feared than understood) than from the conviction of the absence, in Fichte's own philosophy, of the same problematic that dictates Hegel's solutions. Not having anything to fear from Fichte's closeness to Hegel on this point, I will set out to explain the reasons for what I claim to be a common problematic.

The Systematic Place of the Concept of History: Physics and History; History and the Philosophy of History

At the end of his programmatic work of 1794, *Über den Begriff der Wissenschaftslehre,* Fichte presents a list of philosophical sciences or theories that are grounded in the practical part of the *Wissenschaftslehre* to constitute the system of philosophy. Fichte includes all those philosophical disciplines that Kant developed both in the third *Critique* and in his moral writings: aesthetics (a theory of the "pleasant, the beautiful, the sublime"), a theory of nature ("the free obedience of nature to its own laws"), a psychology ("the so-called common sense or the natural sense of truth"), and finally a theory of "natural law and morality."[13] No mention of history is made in this plan. A "philosophy of history" is absent from the horizon of Fichte's early philosophy. As the title for a part of the philosophical science, the expression appears only late in Fichte's development, and its significance will oscillate for a long time. In the *Reden an die deutsche Nation* (1808) it still has only a negative meaning.[14] Indeed, since 1794 in the aftermath of the Enlightenment, Fichte has been reflecting on the issue of a progress of mankind; at that time, however, his claims on this topic could not yet constitute a "philosophy of history" proper. In the

Naturrecht (1796), Fichte presents a scheme of the development of mankind based on the principle of the use of reason.[15] However, the idea of assuming theoretical reason as the guiding principle for the progress of mankind was ruled out already by Kant—one of the reasons for this being the impossibility of including anthropology in a philosophy of history based on the principles of theoretical reason. This argument should have been even more convincing for Fichte. But if theoretical reason could not provide the principle of historical progress, the criterion of morality had to be excluded as well as being a merely internal principle not subject to any development. This explains Kant's choice of the idea of right as the rational thread of human history. Fichte's difficulties with a philosophy of history should be brought back to his criticism of Kant's moral formalism and to the project of developing a "material" theory of morals.

Even before addressing the specific material question of the guiding principle of history, Fichte tries to define the ontological and epistemological sphere that should be assigned to history and historical knowledge in a system of philosophy. This is the crucial question from which Fichte's reflections on the problem of history first develop. It follows that Fichte's solution to Kant's problem of empirical irrationality is not meant, in the first place, to find the new logic that allows him to think the empirical beyond the limits of transcendental knowledge, but rather to assign to the whole realm of the empirical its own sphere of competence and legitimacy in philosophical discourse. In the ninth lecture of the *Grundzüge des gegenwärtigen Zeitalters,* Fichte sees history as "part of science in general, namely the second part of the *empirical* [*die zweite Teil der Empirie*] next to physics."[16] The "empirical" is here a transcendental concept describing the relation between a twofold modality of being and cognition. The empirical as such is immediately a part of science—and not, as for Kant, only in its being taken up and mediated by the categories of the understanding and its schematism. The empirical is at the same time the object of *Wissen* and the modality of that *Wissen.* It is one and the same object that in its static, objective unity is called *nature,* addressed in its regularities by a knowledge called *physics;* and in its dynamic, teleological development is called *history* and is itself knowledge unfolding in time, filling up the sequence of time. From the outset, history is for Fichte both empirical knowledge and the empirical reality which constitutes the object of that knowledge. It is precisely this transformation of the empirical essence of history into a form of knowledge that sets the first condition of possibility for Fichte's "philosophy of history."

If nature is the first manifestation of the eternal unity of divine being, knowledge that "develops *in it* [*an ihm*] according to the flow of a temporal series"[17] is not the knowledge of physics itself but the knowledge that belongs to the "*second* part of the empirical next to physics," namely history. However, if this simple and formal characterization (i.e., the idea of a dynamization of nature along the lines of the temporal series in the form of *Wissen*) grounds the systematic order established between physics and history (this last being the *second* part of the empirical), the concept of history is not sufficiently established by it yet. To this purpose, Fichte must add a material characterization: "The empirical which in its regularity is directed to fill up this temporal series is called *history*."[18] Thereby Fichte brings the distinction between *formal* and *material* aspect right to the center of the concept of the empirical as constituting the specific realm of history. From this first distinction follows the recognition of two essential parts of "history proper" (*eigentliche Geschichte*), which eventually merge into one another, namely (1) an a priori and (2) an a posteriori part.

(1) The a priori part constitutes the idea of a "Weltplan," that is, the structure that orders the development of mankind through the five epochs of its history. This *a priori* provides the idea of a necessary *succession* in history according to which one can determine without any previous historical and factual knowledge, "*that* the five epochs must follow one another"[19] in the past as well as in the future. In this perspective, however, cognition proper of history is not itself historical; it presents a whole as "in a single overview" (*in einem einzigen Überblicke*)[20]—the totality of history beyond history (and before history). Cognition is here referred to the "whole of time," and presupposes a "unitary concept of this time" that is necessarily formal and does not include the determinations of the "process that fills up that time."[21] The a priori determination of history reaches therefore only as far as the notion of a "history *in general*" (*Geschichte überhaupt*);[22] it does not grasp the "proper" nature of history yet. In other words, the a priori part of history provides for Fichte only a philosophical consideration of history, not a true, full-fledged "philosophy of history."

(2) The sphere of a philosophy of history proper is first reached by the a posteriori part of history, that is, by its "pure empirical" nature. The real development of history is not only a generic succession but a process in which the formal succession is materially determined by the causality of "alien forces" and diversion factors, by the *Trägheit* in which freedom constantly finds its hindrance. These forces bring a disturbance in the *Weltplan* that can neither be calculated nor deduced a priori from it;[23] and yet it is precisely this irrational element that constitutes the historical development in its *particular* direction and material significance. Compared to Kant, Fichte reverses the relation between the a priori and the a posteriori element of history. To put Fichte's claim in a paradoxical way, we can say that *in history the a priori does not precede the a posteriori but follows from it.*

Fichte does not simply maintain that the empirical and irrational element cannot be deduced from the a priori concept; he further claims that history in its proper sense (as *eigentliche Geschichte*) does not consist in the a priori *Weltplan* but rather in the purely empirical development in which the idea of a *Weltplan* first receives its meaning. It is the logic of the irrational, not the logic of the abstract and universal a priori notion—the logic of *Unbegriffenes*, not the logic of *Begriff* or *Begreifen*—that is responsible for establishing the peculiar logic of a philosophy of history. This idea implies a strong polemic claim against the assumption that the necessary and sufficient condition for a philosophy of history is to establish the formal principle or the criterion for the historical progress of mankind. The notion of a *Weltplan* is not sufficient, according to Fichte, to determine any of the empirical—and yet structural and essential—characters of history. It determines neither the nature of historical teleology nor the limits of the realm of history; neither the character of the agents of the historical development nor the direction of their freedom.

Since the logic of history is *determined* by its a posteriori and not by the a priori part (more precisely, it is determined by the a posteriori on the basis of which the a priori is eventually recuperated), knowledge of history is, in turn, *historical* knowledge. It cannot take place in the closure of the synthetic overview of a whole but necessarily unfolds as an infinite progress. "All pure a priori science can be completed, and its research brought to conclusion. . . . *Only the empirical is infinite* [*unendlich ist nur die Empirie*]: both the empirical which is static, i.e., nature, in physics, and the empirical which is in flow, i.e., the appearances of mankind in time, in history."[24] Fichte's crucial point consists in the further claim that in history the infinite progress of the empirical is regulated by a "*logic of historical truth*" (*Logik der historischen Wahrheit*).[25] This logic provides a *determinate* notion of the realm of history—of what belongs to it of the specific problems it addresses (excluding, for example, "metaphysical" and mythological questions regarding the origins of mankind), and of the method that reason should employ in it. Only a logic of historical truth can ground a philosophy of history, bringing the accidental wandering of knowledge to the secure path of its advancement.

To sum up these first results: in the *Grundzüge des gegenwärtigen Zeitalters* Fichte assigns to history the systematic place of the second part of the empirical next to physics. The *reality* of history is one with the *knowledge* of history, and this, in turn, reveals itself to be *historical* knowledge. Fichte distinguishes a formal and a material aspect of history; a "history in general" from what he calls "history proper." Only the latter is the topic of a philosophy of history—or more precisely, as we will see,[26] a philosophy of history deals with the transition between "history in general" and "history proper." Its construction runs through a "logic of historical truth" that *is not* the same as an a priori construction of history. This logic displays both an a priori and an a posteriori element; in addition, however, it provides the method that allows one to think of their relation, that is, the method for thinking the "unthinkable," the *Unbegreifliches,* and the irrational; for thinking that which constitutes the absolutely empirical beyond all possible conceptualization, and yet for thinking it as part of an a priori concept.

Once the empirical has been inserted in the realm of philosophical knowledge under the title of history, the task becomes to present and justify the specific method for its comprehension. As Kant correctly saw, for the comprehension of the irrational no rule of formal logic can be applied; while transcendental logic is unable to preserve the irrational status of the empirical. However, the irrational remains an essential part of philosophical knowledge. In order to account for the necessity of the irrational, and in agreement with Hegel on this point, Fichte singles out the realm of history. Yet, while Hegel obtains the realm of history from the idea of a logic that is neither formal nor transcendental but dialectical and speculative, Fichte generates the concepts of a "logic of historical truth" from the need of thinking the empirical realm of history and from its metaphysical foundation.

Fichte's "Metaphysical Proposition": The Essence and Realm of History

Fichte's systematic division of the empirical part of philosophy is grounded on a "metaphysical proposition" from which such division immediately follows. A closer examination of the realm of history and its logic is possible only on the basis of this metaphysical assumption. Thereby, Fichte establishes the two central theses of his philosophy of history. First, history is the point of transition between absolute necessity and sheer contingency. This transition grounds the *possibility of freedom.* Second, the central problem of a philosophy of history is the explanation of the multiplicity that constitutes both its process through time and its differentiation in space. This is the issue of the *realization of freedom.*

God's Existence and History: Contingency and the Conditions of "History in General"

Fichte's "metaphysical proposition" states: "What is only effectually there, is there with absolute necessity, and therefore is with absolute necessity there as it is; it could neither not be there, nor be different than it is."[27] This proposition entails the paradox from which the thought of history arises. The law of necessity is the law of the divine being as *ens necessarium.* Accordingly, the divine being exists with absolute necessity both in the sense that it is absolutely necessary that the divine being exists (it cannot not be) and that it could not be different than it is. The absolute self-sufficiency and necessity of this being makes all change, beginning, and end impossible. Brought back to this proposition, the metaphysical problem of history is nothing less than the problem of creation, the problem of thinking the unthinkable, namely, how the necessity and uniqueness of God's being allows for contingency, change, and multiplicity. History is not thought of according to a dualist Platonic model as the other realm opposed to the eternity and necessity of the divine being; history is rather the very relation (the possibility of a relation) that links the eternity of the one to the temporality of the many. Fichte's solution of this paradox is the argument that bringing history back to the necessity of the *ens necessarium* seems to make history as such impossible. This argument appeals to the fundamental notion of *Wissen.* Moreover, in showing how historical change is compatible with God's necessary existence, Fichte comes very close to the fundamental thesis of Kant's pre-critical work *Der einzig mögliche Beweisgrund zu einer Demonstration des Dasein Gottes* (*The One Possible Basis for a Demonstration of the Existence of God*).

God is neither the cause nor the ground (*Ursache, Grund*) of something that is assumed to follow from him; God is neither the cause nor the ground of cognition, but is rather cognition itself. *Wissen* is the *immediate Dasein* of God, whereas the *world* is his *mediated* form of existence—his "factual existence" (*faktisches Dasein*). On the basis of its intentional structure, cognition is a principle of differentiation and exteriorization. It is a "complete image [*Abbild*] of the divine force." Yet it only reflects one aspect of God's being which becomes its object, and thereby "appears" to cognition as "something determined" and therefore contingent, as something that "could also be different than what it is."[28] History is introduced by Fichte at this crucial transition from necessity to contingency, since it is precisely this transition that creates the possibility of *freedom* and its development in time. We have already seen the systematic meaning of the twofold appearance of the object of cognition in which the divine being is manifested both as nature and as history. Since world and knowledge are nothing but two different manifestations of the divine existence, none of them can prevail upon the other or exhaust the other; that knowledge is the mediation of the world does not mean that the world is a manifestation of knowledge. Knowledge of history is a peculiar kind of knowledge. It owes its specific character to the fact that history is first introduced at the point in which knowledge meets the unknowable and even generates the very necessity of the unknowable. The same contingency that makes cognition possible as *determinate* cognition (or as cognition of a determinate object) establishes the limits of what cannot be penetrated by conceptual knowledge. Fichte reverses Kant's position with the argument that presents the irrational as a norm for the necessary "development" of knowledge in time. Thereby, knowledge of history accomplishes the metamorphosis of eternity into time.[29]

Starting from the necessity of the divine being, Fichte's metaphysical argument gains the notion of history through three different stages. The *first stage* seems to posit the radical negation of all change (*Veränderung*) in God's necessary being. However, a passage from the later work *Die Thatsachen des Bewußseins* (1810) helps us understand how Fichte sees the possibility of generating change from the absolute being in the fact that the absolute being itself is, in a certain sense, already affected by change. The One (*das Eine*) that produces a multiplicity of appearances (*Erscheinungen*) is an "unchangeable being" since "it does not pass over into any of these changes" or appearances. According to the principle of contradiction, "transformations [*Veränderungen*] exclude one another in time," that is, they are possible only successively in a time sequence. The unchangeable One, on the contrary, "is thoroughly out of time"—yet not because it does not change. It is rather out of time because "*even if it transforms or changes itself in time,* all these transformations do not affect it in its most proper being."[30] Fichte's One is herein thought of according to a model that combines the notion of an infinite "force" or a pervasive "life"—hence notions explicitly opposed to the idea of a substrate—with Kant's pre-critical notion of existence. The life of the unchangeable being is "a simple force, *pure force without any substrate;* it does not appear at all in its immediacy, and for that reason it *is also not intuited. . . . What is thought in it, is not an appearance but rather that which grounds the possibility of all appearances*"[31] and therefore lies beyond them in the dimension of the "Unvordenkliches"—to use a terminology that is not Fichte's but adequately portrays the relation between God's existence and historical existence. Fichte's suggestion is that the origin of history is metaphysical, not historical. History is grounded on a prehistorical dimension as the manifold of factual existence is grounded on the possibility of all existence that precedes existence itself. The historical existence of mankind (the pure empirical realm of history) rests upon a condition that "lies beyond all factual existence [*faktisches Dasein*] and all empirical elements" and makes it possible for the first time. The ground of history is not in turn history. It is rather, as it were, a metaphysical proposition, a "Philosophem." The conditions of empirical existence established by that proposition are presupposed by the "possibility of all history."[32]

The *second stage* of the argument that presents the "essence of history"[33] concerns the production of a first *determination* through the intentional and relational structure of cognition. Fichte has been pursuing the same line of thought since his early period: the transition from the universality of the "überhaupt" to its determination (*Bestimmung, Beschränkung*) is achieved by the introduction of the empirical. Herein, "all deduction comes to an end." Determination is thereby "that which is *absolutely contingent* and provides the pure empirical element of our knowledge."[34] In Fichte's philosophy of history, contingency grounds both the possibility of freedom and the method of our knowledge of history.

The *third stage* finally shows how determination develops into a *process* (*Entwicklung*) in which time is first introduced. The eternity of the One is transformed by cognition into the two realms of nature and history.[35]

Fichte attributes to his philosophy of history three tasks corresponding to the three different stages of his metaphysical argument. The *first task* is *metaphysical.* Its major claim is that *the possibility of history is the necessity of God.* Philosophy must establish the "conditions of empirical existence." This leads to an inquiry into the "*mere possibility of a history in general*" (*die bloße Möglichkeit einer Geschichte überhaupt*)[36] and brings the philosopher back to the absolute *necessity* of the ground of all existence. Thereby, philosophy outlines the specific "territory" (*Grund und Boden*) of historical research. Fichte claims that history cannot even begin before this task has been fulfilled. Indeed, this claim has to be taken literally.

The *second task* addressed by Fichte's philosophy of history is the transition from the "mere *possibility* of history *in general*" to its *actual* and *particular* development. This task can be summed up in the claim that *the actuality of history is human freedom.* The method of a philosophy of history should have both an a priori and an a posteriori component. A philosophy of history is neither pure metaphysics nor mere historiography. The contingency proper to the empirical reality of history makes (human) freedom possible. Freedom becomes for Fichte the *immanent* principle of historical development. Freedom is both the necessary and the sufficient principle of historical explanation. Historical epochs are directly produced by the agency of human freedom. In this way, Fichte's argument rules out both the intervention of an "unknown," "external force"[37] or an immanent *impersonal* principle that works like Hegel's *List der Vernunft*,[38] and something like a mechanistical and evolutionary view of historical processes, namely, the absurd claim that history leads "from the orang-outang to a Leibniz or a Kant."[39] In the *Reden an die deutsche Nation* (1808) Fichte suggests that "the peculiar age of mankind as well as all human relations are made and produced by human beings themselves and by no means by a force lying outside of them." This claim immediately implies an appeal to human responsibility and agency in history: "Do not let the thought of relying upon the activity of others or upon something else that lies outside of you make you lazy; do not count on the inscrutable wisdom of the age according to which every age produces itself without any human intervention, on the sole ground of an unknown force."[40] Human beings produce their own human history; they should not wait for history to produce itself. Moreover, freedom has to struggle against the *Trägheit* that leads men to passively abandon themselves to events and creates a "habit" (*Gewohnheit*) that eventually makes even slavery bearable. "Those who live without any attention for themselves and let circumstances shape them in whichever way these may wish to shape them, they soon get used to every possible order of things."[41]

Finally, there is the *third task*, the comprehension of historical processes proper to a philosophy of history reveals itself as the comprehension of what in principle cannot be comprehended. Methodologically, *knowledge of history is the impossibility of conceptual knowledge.* The sphere of philosophy of history is the realm of the *Unbegreifliches*. Philosophy as metaphysics sees herein its end. In this sphere neither genetic nor causal explanations are allowed.[42] The comprehension of history starts rather from the dimension of the *present*—from the "life of the present" or the *gegenwärtiges Zeitalter*[43]—and constructs from here the sequence of empirical facts. That this sequence constitutes a historical development is known by the "logic of historical truth," not by the formal logic of deduction. In other words, historical processes in their factual existence can never be deduced from the a priori notion of a *Weltplan;* they can only be obtained by recognizing that they constitute what *in that same a priori concept* necessarily remains *überhaupt Unbegriffenes*[44]—non-conceptualized because in principle non-conceptual. Yet the essential "incomprehensible"—that is, irrational and individual—nature of historical processes constitutes the historical character of the knowledge proper to a philosophy of history. It is the norm that establishes the open horizon for the philosophical science of history: "Only the empirical realm is infinite."[45]

Fichte builds his idea of a philosophy of history upon a paradoxical argument. He pushes to the extreme the claim of the bare empirical nature of history as the realm of the irrational, not-conceptual, not rationalizable, and thoroughly contingent reality. Yet he maintains that philosophical knowledge of history is possible—although neither as deductive nor conceptual nor genetic knowledge. Against the fictitious notion of historical *Wahrscheinlichkeit* Fichte holds on to the notion of "historical truth" and to its "logic." Moreover, despite its radically empirical character, history can be constructed a priori. The metaphysical claim that grounds the possibility of history in general establishes that the bare "factual existence" of historical processes is grounded upon the *unvordenkliches* existence of the absolute totality of the divine existence.

The One and the Many: Contingency and the Development of "History Proper"

Because of its metaphysical foundation, Fichte's philosophy of history meets the crucial problem of the transition from the absolute *totality* of history beyond time to the empirical *multiplicity* of individuals in time and space. If philosophy requires both an "overview of the *whole* of history" (*eine Uebersicht über das Ganze der Geschichte*) and the attention to "the *universal* [*das Allgemeine*] that remains always identical to itself,"[46] the task of the philosopher of history is to explain how multiplicity, particularity, and diversity come about and become the guiding principles of history. In Lask's terminology, the problem of historical explanation in philosophy is the problem of the "value" of historical individuality. Fichte asks, very concretely, "How are the different human races possible—races so different in color and physical constitution . . . ; how does inequality among men arise—the inequality that we find everywhere since history has begun?" These are not de facto questions of concern only for the historiographer. They are *de iuris* questions that cannot be answered "just in general," since they require the position of a "determinate modality"[47] of being and knowledge. The same issue is raised in discussing the way in which the unitary whole of life differentiates itself not only in time but also in space, and thereby becomes *individual* life—the life of different persons and different peoples on earth. "The one life [*das Eine Leben*] is completely in myself, but is at the same time in my neighbor, and is at the same time for example in America, maybe also on Sirius. How can it be in so many places at the same time?"[48] To be sure, this is not just a puzzle for individual consciousness. This is a crucial question for Fichte's theory of history because of the role played by space and time as formal *intuitions* in the constitution of historical development.

As we have seen, Fichte rejects the view that the absolute manifests itself in history "emanationally"—as Lask would have said—so as to be totally present in its manifestations and to be nothing beyond them. In Fichte's account the movement of history is the immanent development of human freedom not the immanent manifestation of God's presence in the world. The "logic of historical truth" is only the *logic of human freedom.* This is also the only way to save from contradiction the claim that the eternal absolute is subject to time:[49] if the absolute does not "appear" in its modifications, time does not affect its essence. But if the infinite, divine force is not a substrate that "immediately appears, [then] it cannot be intuited," it cannot be revealed by any form of possible intuition, that is, it is neither in space nor in time. The necessary existence of the absolute is not the existence of a fact given in intuition but rather the existence of what "lies to the basis of all possible appearance" and intuition. This situation places the origin of history in the "incomprehensible" realm of the "supersensible." "What cannot be in any way the object of an intuition is called not-sensible, supersensible, spiritual [*geistig*]." The origin of history lies in the paradox of what is "spiritual"[50] and, as such, always individual. The gap that divides the supersensible from the sensible is maintained by Fichte as necessary for the development of history. This gap guarantees that historical processes are not a sort of gradual evolution. Moreover, this gap posits the moral end of history as well as the task of human agency in it. The aim of free action is not eternity as such but only the earthly preparation to it. We have to work "in order to grasp eternity already in this life, fulfilling the ends that are commanded to us."[51] What this work makes *visible* is the immanent end of history, not what lies beyond it as the ground of its general possibility. History is a thoroughly immanent process toward "visibility" (*Sichtbarkeit*) that reveals its unaccomplished end, not its imponderable ground. Only the former, not the latter, can be "made the object of an intuition" through the work of freedom.[52]

This metaphysical construction frames Fichte's need to introduce in the epochs of history the idea of the "peoples," carriers of the different principles of civilization and agents of historical development.[53] With a significant inversion, Fichte's philosophy of history aims at constructing, in the first place, the "eigentliches Menschengeschlecht der Geschichte"[54]—not the "Geschichte des Menschengeschlechts." The metaphysical standpoint of this construction is the standpoint of history taken as an a priori complete totality that as such precedes both historical development and historical agents. Accordingly, this construction aims at finding out the human agent that brings history out of the ahistorical totality into the manifold manifestation in time and space. At this point Fichte introduces the notion of *Volk,* which is first presented in the still ahistorical figure of the *Normalvolk* or the *Erdgeborene.*[55]

Individuality and Idea in History

According to Lask's typology of the forms of irrationality, "individuality" is the main figure of irrationality. We have seen how Fichte's "logic of historical truth" attributes to the individual the function of realizing the transition from "history in general" to that determinate development in time and space which is "history proper." Our analysis has already disclosed how historical agency manifests itself through the principle of freedom in the individual figure of a "people." Fichte suggests that history is not the continuous process through which civilization spreads among different peoples. History is rather the discrete movement of a confrontation of peoples—each *Volk* being the carrier of a different principle of civilization.[56] We need now turn to Fichte's treatment of the role of individuality in history, and see what the relation is between this figure and the general logic of history.

The logical claim that guides the development of history (as history *of* individuals and *through* individuals) is brought forth by the "idea." The "idea" recapitulates Fichte's metaphysical proposition and establishes the peculiar dialectic between individuals and historical totality. In the *Grundzüge* Fichte declares:

> Under the term "individuality" we understand *only the personal and sensible existence of the individual* [*die persönlich sinnliche Existenz des Individuums*] as the common meaning of the word itself suggests. Yet by no means do we intend to deny—indeed we explicitly underline and emphasize—that the one eternal Idea, in every particular individual which it permeates with life, shows itself in an entirely new figure that has never been there before. This happens independently of sensible nature, through the idea itself and its proper legislation—namely not through *sensible individuality* [*sinnliche Individualität*] but rather in a way that destroys this sensible individuality: the idea determines itself purely out of itself to *ideal individuality* [*ideale Individualit ät*] or, as it is called more correctly, to *originality* [*Originalität*].[57]

Fichte distinguishes between two different notions of individuality. The first is the notion of the purely empirical and "*sensible* individuality" of an existing person. In this case, the *principium individuationis* is *Sinnlichkeit* as such. Both ontologically and epistemologically the empirical individual owes its existence to factual circumstances The empirical individual is therefore radically contingent. This is the perspective of Leibniz's monadology, which views individuals as atomistic entities and denies the possibility of an immanent link among them. But it is also the perspective of that "egoism" that Fichte identifies, since the very beginning, with Spinozism. The second notion is that of "*ideal* individuality." "Ideal individuality" is by no means understood by Fichte as opposed to the first notion, for it is as contingent as empirical individuality. This second notion of individuality integrates and complements the first, or to put it in another way: by claiming that individuality is a thoroughly empirical and contingent form of existence (strictly speaking individuality is not even a concept), Fichte does not deny that individuality has an "ideal" dimension. The task of a philosophy (or logic) of history is precisely to reveal the ideal significance of empirical individuality; to show how the *principium individuationis* lies, this time, not in sensibility but in the Idea. The ideal significance is added on to the empirical one, and even if the ideal dimension eventually "cancels/destroys" (*vernichtet*) the empirical one, it cannot cancel the essential contingency of the individual.

In the ideal perspective, the individual is brought back to the eternal and unique Idea. The idea—as the logical form of eternal "life"—shows itself in the particular figure or shape (in the *Gestalt*) of a multiplicity of individuals. It is the internal *logic* of the eternal idea that produces the individual agents and the particular determinations of history. The relevance of this metaphysical claim for Fichte's theory lies in the historical significance attributed to the contingent manifestations of the idea. The process of "individualization" is the production of absolutely new figures that have neither been there before nor "have been experienced before,"[58] that is, it is a process that unfolds in time and presupposes a continuity of consciousness in time. Moreover, with an almost dialectical argument, Fichte contends that the "law"[59] according to which the "new" is produced in history is the absence of any law—that is, it is radical contingency. This *Gesetzlosigkeit,*[60] however, is nothing but the peculiar "legislation" (*Gesetzgebung*)[61] of the idea. *It is precisely for this reason, that is, for the fact that the absence of any law proper to the individual becomes the law of the idea, that we find the logic of individuality displayed in history.* This dialectical turn, on the other hand, generates the possibility of "absolute freedom." Thus, to the question: "According to which rule or according to what law . . . is the infinite force determined [to bring the new into reality]?" we have to answer: "According to no law. *The new arises out of the universal with absolute freedom,* as an absolute creation brought into the sphere of reality."[62]

We need now to discuss two further issues concerning the relation between individuality and the totality of the idea on the one hand, and the ethical significance of this relation in the development of history on the other. With regard to the first issue, in his 1805 lectures *Über das Wesen des Gelehrten und seine Erscheinungen im Gebiete der Freiheit,* Fichte presents the relation between idea and individuality, stressing the function that the totality has as the foundation for the individual's own value. Fichte claims that each single individual empirically maintains itself through its own self-sufficiency and independency. Consciousness of this self-sufficiency is "self-love."[63] The ideal dimension of individuality, however, brings it back to the "eternal and divine idea" that "comes to existence in single human individuals." The same relation of love is established for this *Dasein* in the human shape assumed by the divine idea. The peculiar character of the *Gelehrter* is described by Fichte in terms of this relation: the *Gelehrter* is the man who revives in himself the same *Liebe zur Idee*[64] through which the eternal idea constituted itself as individual. The idea is thereby transfigured into the totality of mankind. At this point, Fichte significantly explains the loving relation between totality and individuals in two rhetorically different ways: "*If we take on the customary language of an illusory appearance* [*Schein*], we say that this particular man loves the idea and lives in the idea; *but if we want to be faithful to truth,* we have to say that it is the idea that lives in the place of that man, and in his person it is the idea that loves itself; this person is only the sensible appearance of the existence of the idea."[65] In *Die Thatsachen des Bewußtseins* Fichte further develops this argument, suggesting that the individual is not "a particular mode of being proper of life but is rather a mere *form* of it, and more precisely a *form of its absolute freedom.*" The individual form represents the necessary counterpart to the absolute freedom of the idea in its being a *zufällige Form*—the form of sheer contingency. The historical process is nothing but the development of this relation between absolute freedom and radical contingency made possible by the *unmittelbares Band*[66] that brings the individual back to the universal idea.

With regard to the second issue, Fichte, as we have already seen, opposes the impersonal view of historical development and proposes a model in which individuals are the active and immanent forces responsible for the outcome of historical events. He claims that "the peculiar age of mankind is produced by the work of human beings themselves"; it should not wait for the intervention of alien forces, nor should it be abandoned to the passivity of human habits and their consequences.[67] Moreover, Fichte clearly states that *agency* is possible only in the form of individuality: "Kein Handeln außer in der individuellen Form." Indeed, only in its individual form can life become a "*practical* principle."[68] The idea or universal life functions as the mere "faculty" (*Vermögen*) or capacity for the production of historical reality; whereas it is only the individual that is able to give determinate actualization to that faculty. The individual transforms the abstract force of life into a "real" force.

Fichte opens the *Grundzüge* with a series of claims that recapitulate both views on the relation between idea and individuality. On the one hand, he maintains that the topic of history—the subject of the "progress of life on earth"—is the human species (*Gattung*), not the individual.[69] On the other hand, however, Fichte recognizes that all historical events (including the succession of the five epochs) take place only because "the starting point is the individual."[70] The historical agent is still the individual. In a formulation similar to Hegel's famous claim in the *Philosophy of*

Right, Fichte suggests that "individuals are products of their own time; in them their age is expressed in the most clear way." Individuality becomes thereby "universal individuality,"[71] that is, properly *historical* individuality.

Lask maintains[72] that the two arguments just discussed—namely, the claim that posits the individual as a function of the universal idea, and the notion of individual agency as opposed to the abstract possibility of the idea—represent the two radically alternative ways under which Fichte conceives individuality. Lask's point is that these two views cannot be reconciled either theoretically or logically. My suggestion, on the contrary, is that these two explanations can be reconciled coherently (and must eventually be reconciled) if they are thought together in the dimension of *history.* Indeed, Fichte's aim in constructing these arguments is to think the sphere of history not according to *Wahrscheinlichkeit* as a historian, but according to the "logic of historical truth" as a philosopher. Accordingly, he does not oppose the metaphysical subordination of the individual under the idea to the claim of the independent agency of the individual in history. His argument is far more complex and stringent than the construction of this opposition. If individual agency were not grounded in a universal structure (in the form of "history in general" and in the logic that establishes its very possibility), history itself would be impossible. Individual agency could only be thought in the way proposed by the "egoist" or by a Leibnizian philosopher. In this model, individuals would be nothing more than the atomistic "numerical repetition of the one and only life," with the consequence that neither "originality" nor contingency nor the production of the "new" could be accounted for. Individuals would live and act representing radically "separated worlds," with no possibility of establishing among them something like the spiritual dimension of historical development. In any case, if individual agency is the one and only principle of action, *historical* agency needs the foundation of the individual in the continuity of the more comprehensive structure provided by the idea. Fichte has been proposing the inclusion of individuality in the structure of an ideal or intelligible order since 1798. The fact that the individual agent that produces "history in the proper sense," that is, the empirical sequence of events, acts within the comprehensive structure of a universal totality guarantees the immanent character of historical praxis. Moreover, the relation between the individual and the totality of history has an ethical, and not only a metaphysical, significance. Fichte's argument is that the final goal of history is within reach of each single individual agent of history precisely *because* it lies in the "universal force" that constitutes a *zusammenhängendes Ganze*—a thoroughly interconnected whole. Fichte's principle is that "what is possible in general (i.e., what lies in the universal force) is also absolutely possible for each individual."[73]

Finally, Fichte's dialectical determination of the relation between individual and idea constitutes the double character of the movement of history: the *continuity* of the process of the whole is experienced by each individual consciousness as radical *discontinuity*. In the perspective of the totality of history, progress is the continuity of the "possible line of freedom and action carried on ad infinitum."[74] In the perspective of the individual, on the contrary, the issue of the *Fortsetzung* of the process becomes a moral command. To bring history forth, to guarantee the continuation of the process through generations is the ethical task of the individual in history—is a task that, according to Fichte, could not even be proposed to Leibniz's monadic subject.

Notes

1. W. Windelband, *Die Lehren vom Zufall* (Berlin, 1870).
2. A. Bäumler, *Das Irrationalitätsproblem in der Ästhetik und Logik des 18. Jahrhunderts bis zur Kritik der Urteilskraft* (Halle, 1923).
3. See E. Lask, *Fichtes Idealismus und die Geschichte* (Tübingen: Mohr, 1902), 145; see also T. Rockmore, "Fichte, Lask, and Lukács's Hegelian Marxism," *Journal of the History of Philosophy* 30 (1992): 557–77, 571.
4. Lask, *Fichtes Idealismus und die Geschichte,* 38–39.
5. Lask, *Fichtes Idealismus und die Geschichte,* 145ff.
6. Lask, *Fichtes Idealismus und die Geschichte,* 148.
7. Lask, *Fichtes Idealismus und die Geschichte,* 161ff.
8. Lask, *Fichtes Idealismus und die Geschichte,* 157ff.
9. See the "Preface" to Lask, *Fichtes Idealismus und die Geschichte,* 3ff.
10. Furthermore, because of his neo-Kantian orientation, what is most relevant for Lask—in explicit contrast with all classical German philosophers—is not the logic of history but rather the logic of historical knowledge (the logic of the *Geisteswissenschaften*).
11. G. Gurvitch, *Fichtes System der konkreten Ethik* (Tübingen: Mohr, 1924).
12. R. Lauth, "Die Handlung in der Geschichte nach der Wissenschaftslehre," in *Transzendentale Entwicklungslinien von Descartes bis zu Marx und Dostojewski* (Hamburg: Meiner, 1989), 397–410.
13. *GA* 1.2:151; in English, *EPW,* 135.
14. See C. Cesa, *Introduzione a Fichte* (Bari: Laterza, 1994), 174–75.
15. *GA* 1.3:336–37.
16. *SW* 7:129 (the translation is always mine).
17. *SW* 7:131.
18. *SW* 7:131.
19. *SW* 7:139 (my emphasis).
20. *SW* 7:139.
21. *SW* 7:6.
22. *SW* 7:135. See also *SW* 2:648 for the distinction between a development of

the force of life "in general" and according to a "determinate development." However, this distinction can be considered typical of Fichte's philosophy from its early period.

23. *SW* 7:139.

24. *SW* 7:107 (my emphasis).

25. *SW* 7:107–8.

26. See below in the section titled "The One and the Many: Contingency and the Development of "History Proper."

27. *SW* 7:129

28. *SW* 7:130.

29. *SW* 7:130–31.

30. *SW* 2:642 (my emphasis).

31. *SW* 2:642 (my emphasis).

32. *SW* 7:132.

33. *SW* 7:129.

34. *SW* 1:489 (*Zweite Einleitung in der Wissenschaftslehre;* my emphasis).

35. *SW* 7:131.

36. *SW* 7:131–32 (my emphasis).

37. *SW* 7:487.

38. See *SW* 7:487.

39. See *SW* 7:134.

40. *SW* 7:487.

41. *SW* 7:445.

42. See *SW* 7:136.

43. See, for example, *SW* 7:137.

44. See *SW* 7:139.

45. *SW* 7:107.

46. *SW* 7:135.

47. *SW* 7:135–36.

48. *SW* 2:643.

49. Different is, of course, Hegel's response to the same dilemma. The crucial difference lies obviously in the dialectical nature of his logic.

50. *SW* 2:642.

51. *GA* 1.8:440.

52. *SW* 2:661–62.

53. Following the general aim of this chapter, what I want to point out are the reasons that bring Fichte to certain philosophical claims, not the specific content of those claims. For this reason, I am not going to discuss Fichte's division of history in any detail.

54. *SW* 7:138.

55. *SW* 7:134.

56. This is a well-known model already introduced by Herder.

57. *SW* 7:69 (my emphasis).

58. *SW* 2:648.

59. *SW* 2:648.

60. See also *SW* 9:515, which presents the pure empirical materiality of the world as something "durchaus gesetzlos."

61. *SW* 7:69.

62. *SW* 2:648 (my emphasis).

63. *SW* 6:356.

64. *SW* 6:356, also 377, 383.

65. *SW* 4:356 (my emphasis).

66. *SW* 2:640 (my emphasis); see also *SW* 2:647.

67. See *SW* 7:487, commented on above.

68. *SW* 2:641.

69. *SW* 7:7.

70. *SW* 7:11.

71. *SW* 7:13.

72. See Lask, *Fichtes Idealismus und die Geschichte,* 210ff.

73. *SW* 2:649.

74. *SW* 2:646.

Fichte on Knowledge, Practice, and History

Tom Rockmore

After he left Jena, Fichte deepened and developed his interest in history as part of his distinctive approach to knowledge. It has too often been said that Fichte wanted to perfect Kantianism without understanding the way in which he surpassed Kant in helping to inaugurate a new conceptual stage.

To grasp Fichte's contribution, one must see that his position takes shape not before but after the great French Revolution.[1] This political event divides the philosophical debate into two parts. At the dawn of the modern period, philosophy invents a concept of the subject in order to understand objectivity on the basis of subjectivity. But this subject remains abstract, and the sort of knowledge that emerges is without a historical dimension. In pointing to the transitory, hence historical character of political institutions, the French Revolution engenders what can be called the rise of historical consciousness as well as a transformation of the conception of the subject.

After the French Revolution, and through the formulation of a concept of history, philosophy struggles to find the theoretical means to rethink the epistemological subject as a historical being and knowledge as rooted in history. Fichte contributes to this movement in reformulating the ahistorical Kantian position on the basis of the primacy of practical reason.[2] Though he is interested in history, his a priori approach finally prevents him from going beyond an analysis of practice to make the transition to a historical conception of philosophy and knowledge.

Two Epistemological Turning Points in Modern Philosophy

Fichte contributes to this historical turning through his progressive, but never finished "tightening" of the link between knowledge and history. Since this link concerns the problem of knowledge in general, or epistemology, we can begin with several epistemological remarks before we come to history. This problem is obviously not limited to the modern period, nor is it even specifically modern. It was neither created by Descartes nor does it end, as some believe, in Kant. In a way, philosophy has always been concerned with epistemology.

The entire Western philosophical tradition is composed of a series of analyses of knowledge that are opposed in an ongoing struggle across the centuries and whose end is still not in sight. We recall the analyses of knowledge by Plato and Aristotle as well as earlier by Socrates and the pre-Socratics. Hegel is not wrong to see the problem as going back at least to Parmenides. It obviously continues after Kant, and beyond German idealism, for instance in such varied philosophical tendencies as phenomenology, Anglo-American analytic philosophy, American pragmatism, Marxism, and so on, which are all present tendencies that turn on the problem of knowledge.[3]

In the modern period, the two best-known epistemological turning points are linked to the names of Descartes and Kant. As their positions are well known, we can go quickly here. Claims for knowledge are invariably claims for objective knowledge. Following in the footsteps of Montaigne, Augustine, and others, Descartes introduces a "subjective element" into the concern for objective knowledge. If not before, at least since Descartes it becomes clear that access to objective cognition necessarily passes through subjectivity. This is the first main turning point in modern epistemology.

The second turning point, which is just as well known, consists in carrying further the dependency of objectivity on subjectivity in understanding the cognition object through the subject, which is held to "construct" it, so to speak, as a necessary but not a sufficient condition of knowledge. This idea is clearly anticipated by Vico, an early anti-Cartesian, in his slogan *verum et factum convertuntur.*[4] According to the Neapolitan thinker, God alone can know nature because he is its source. Man can know only history, since he creates it. This idea returns in a different, ahistorical form in the well-known "Copernican revolution." Kant, who believes that he can identify the general conditions of knowledge, underlines the need to bring about a correspondence of the object to the subject that literally constructs (*herstellen:* "to produce") what it knows.[5]

These two very different epistemological turning points share an emphasis on subjectivity as the means of access to objectivity. Through this bias, the subject becomes the key to the problem of knowledge. However, at this level the subject is neither more nor less than an abstract principle, which is invoked on merely epistemological grounds. Neither Descartes nor Kant, though Descartes more than Kant, understands the subject of knowledge as a finite human being. However, both point in this direction. For as soon as one introduces the subject as a necessary epistemological element, one points, so to speak, at least in implicit fashion toward human being. Heidegger is hence correct to see, if not in Descartes, then at least starting with him, the conditions of an inevitable anthropological transformation that continues throughout the later discussion.[6]

The Historical Turning in Modern Philosophy

Fichte participates fully in the subjective and Copernican turning points as well as in a third, anthropologico-practical turning point. In the same way as Descartes and Kant, he bases his theory in a conception of the subject. Like Kant, he understands the subject as the source of its cognitive object. But Fichte distances himself in transforming the subject and the entire debate. For Descartes and Kant, the subject is no more than an epistemological principle understood on the basis of a normative view of knowledge. In inverting this approach in order to grasp the subject as finite human being, Fichte basically transforms the discussion of knowledge.

Up until Fichte, the debate on knowledge concerned the theoretical analysis of the possibility of knowledge in general, which in turn gave rise in Montaigne, Descartes, and others to a concept of the subject.[7] After Fichte, this debate turns on specifying the nature and limits of human knowledge. In substituting a concept of human being for the epistemological concept, he helps to transform the traditionally abstract account of knowledge into an increasingly concrete debate that in post-Kantian idealism increasingly becomes a social and historical theory.

There is a difference between an anthropological and then a historical conception of human being. The former precedes the latter. This anthropological and then later increasingly historical turning, which begins late in the eighteenth century, constitutes the main epistemological change after the Cartesian introduction of the subjective principle. Fichte reinforces this tendency, which he does not begin and which he does not think through to the end.

The theme of history, which is already raised by Vico and others, is everywhere in German philosophy beginning with Herder. Besides Fichte and Herder, other German philosophers concerned with history include Kant, Friedrich Schlegel, Humboldt, Schelling, Hegel, and Marx.[8] In German idealism, the two extremes are represented by Kant, who thinks history in separating it rigorously from knowledge, and Hegel, who, in trying "to think life,"[9] or again "the life of spirit that is inseparable from history,"[10] reduces it to historical knowledge.

The link between knowledge and history in the critical philosophy points to the difficulty of bringing both together in a conception of historical knowledge. Kant begins the discussion of history in German idealism. In his minor writings, reacting against Herder, his former student, he creates the outlines of a theory of history. As a transcendental thinker, he is less interested in historical facts than in their general possibility. Following the same approach he utilizes everywhere in his mature position, he raises the transcendental question of the a priori possibility of history.[11]

Kant in his own way follows historical events. But even in his posthumous writings, he constantly maintains an impermeable separation between history and philosophy,[12] between facts and knowledge. For this reason he is unable, and in fact does not even make the effort, to integrate knowledge into history. Though he formulates a concept of history, Kant continues to favor the well-known conception of philosophy as a reliable source of supra-temporal knowledge, hence as supra-historical, an approach that Hegel denies in his definition of philosophy as the thoughtful grasp of its own historical moment. In effect, if each of us belongs to his own time, and if the philosopher belongs to his historical moment, then philosophy is not beyond but rather is fully integrated into history.

Fichte, Kant, and History

The critical philosophy dominates its period, and perhaps even the discussion that follows it. Like Schelling and Hegel, Fichte considers himself to be and is in a sense a Kantian. But despite what Fichte says concerning the supposed faithful continuity between his position and Kant's, it would be a mistake to take his claim literally, and hence it is incorrect to "reduce" his position to Kant's. For to do this is to make it more difficult, perhaps even impossible to grasp the specific novelty of his own position.

In order to grasp Fichte's contribution to the historical turn, it will be useful to evoke the relation of his position to Kant's in a little more detail. Fichte shared the widespread contemporary enthusiasm for the critical philosophy. The idea that philosophy can realize itself is a central theme in the reception of the critical philosophy. After the appearance of the *Critique of Pure Reason,* numerous thinkers, beginning with Reinhold, tried to carry the Copernican revolution further than Kant with the idea of ending philosophy, with the aim of putting an end to philosophy. We know that, after Hegel, numerous thinkers believed that philosophy had reached its end.

Fichte carries the identification of his position and Kant's very far. One can speculate that there are two main reasons for this public identification with the author of the critical philosophy. First, Fichte doubtlessly sincerely believes in the importance of Kant's philosophical contribution. Second, especially in his early period, when he was still unknown, Fichte was obviously concerned to call attention to his own views. He goes so far as to affirm that his position is nothing other than Kantianism correctly understood,[13] and he insists as well that he has discovered a new foundation on which to construct a systematic philosophy. He even suggests that his position is the one that Kant ought to have advanced if he had clearly understood the critical philosophy.[14]

The suggestion that there is in fact no difference, or no significant difference, between Kant and Hegel leads to a "deformed" vision of the Fichtean position. This vision was transmitted to the later debate by Hegel, but Fichte must also assume at least in part responsibility. It is mistaken to read Fichte, as Hegel reads the latter, in reducing Fichteanism to a simple variation, no matter how brilliant, of Kantianism. Following Fichte's own suggestions, Hegel is the first to propose such an analysis, which he already advances in his first philosophical text[15] and in all his later writings. But an important philosophical position, such as Fichte's, which belongs to the very restricted circle of the most important philosophical theories, can never simply be reduced to its predecessors.

The Hegelian thesis, which has long influenced the comprehension of German idealism, is simply false.[16] Since it is a question of the relation between knowledge and history, several remarks about the difference of perspective between Fichte and Kant are in order. To begin with, Kant, who is not indifferent to history, distinguishes rigorously between knowledge and history. From the perspective of the critical philosophy, there can be knowledge of history, but knowledge is not itself historical. Knowledge and history are basically different.

There is an obvious tension between the Kantian concern to separate knowledge and history, and the role of the critical philosophy in defending this distinction. Kant's way of thematizing history in the critical philosophy contributes to later efforts to sublate the well-known concept of historical knowledge. But Kant does not draw this inference. On the contrary, he affirms his own version of the familiar canonical thesis of the abstract nature of knowledge. In a word, he steadfastly insists on the abstract character of knowledge. According to this thesis, knowledge appears in time but does not depend on it. Fichte, on the contrary, starts down the path leading to a historical conception of knowledge. In other words, though he is a self-described Kantian, and though Kant remains attached to so-called pure reason, Fichte immediately substitutes what we can call impure reason for pure reason. This is the path on which we still find ourselves, and whose importance has still not been grasped.

It will be useful to recall several ways in which, through his ameliorations of the critical philosophy, and despite what he may say or think, Fichte breaks with Kant. Like Descartes before him, Kant famously asserts that claims for knowledge are apodictic. He says that to change anything, anything at all in his position, is to run the risk of a general collapse of human knowledge.[17] Following Kant, Fichte also insists on the impossibility of refuting his position. Yet, on the contrary, in the short metaphilosophical text accompanying the *Foundation of the Entire Wissenschaftslehre* (*Grundlage der gesamten Wissenschaftslehre*), he affirms that philosophical science is circular, hence hypothetical.[18]

Another difference concerns the concept of the subject. The author of the critical philosophy understands the epistemological subject, which he calls the transcendental unity of apperception, as no more than what has been called an epistemological placeholder, as distinguished from finite human being. Fichte, on the contrary, quickly rethinks the subject as human being. Kant strives to grasp forms of knowledge through forms of activity attributed to the subject to grasp their possibility, without, however, being able to think the unity of the subject. Fichte, on the contrary, "inverts" this approach in thinking the forms of activity on the baiss of the subject understood literally as activity. Finally, Kant distinguishes rigorously between knowledge and history with the idea of preventing what Husserl later calls psychologism. Fichte, on the contrary, understands the subject within history.

Fichte, Practice, and History

The difference between Fichte and Kant is especially visible with respect to history. In this respect, it is useful to notice the difference between history and practice. History derives from the domain of practice, but practice is not yet history. Practice is an intermediary stage between theory, which preceeds experience, and history or the historical character of experience. Practice, as Kant understands it, is linked to morality, to what one should do, but what one should do is unrelated to the situation of a concrete being, a person rooted in the real world.

Fichte, who substitutes a more flexible ethical conception than Kant's moral dualism, does not follow Kant's analysis of practice. The latter proposes two incompatible analyses of the relation of theory to practice with regard to whether theory belongs to or, on the contrary, depends on practice. On the one hand, Kant absorbs (or reabsorbs) practice into theory in a semi-popular text on their relation,[19] especially in respect to moral theory. However, this line of analysis is very problematic. Kant suggests it is necessary that the principle motivating all moral action apply identically, without any distinction, to all rational beings, without taking into consideration the particular case or the consequences. The result is to overlook as significant, and even to "suppress" the specificity of practice. On the other hand, while maintaining the distinction between theory and practice, Kant tries several times, but as he concedes always unsuccessfully, to subordinate theory to practice.[20] There is hence reason to believe that, though he is aware of the problem, Kant is never able to provide a coherent analysis of the relation between theory and practice.

As concerns practice, Fichte innovates with respect to Kant. Fichte, who follows Kant's stress on the priority of practice over theory, is directly concerned with practice in critical moments of his career. These include his important analyses of the French Revolution: at the beginning of his career in a famous text defending the revolution, and later in an equally well-known text on the German nation where he again defends it.[21] But it is not the same thing to be interested in practice, even in concrete fashion, and to grasp it or to grasp it entirely; in a word, to grasp its historical dimension.

Like Kant, but to a lesser degree, Fichte experiences early difficulties in thinking theory and practice together. In the first version of the *Wissenschaftslehre,* he develops a circular analysis of the relation of theory and practice in concluding that the former is only appropriate to understand the latter. Practice, which cannot be understood without theory, hence requires it, and, on the contrary, for this reason and this reason only the existence of theory is justified. In other words, without practice, there can be no theory which depends on practice, according to Fichte, since theory is not autonomous. But missing on this level is a comprehension of what one could call the historicity of the practical. Indeed, the theme of history only later attracts Fichte's attention.

Fichte on Practice and the French Revolution

There is a difference between practice and history. Practice refers to history, in which it is situated, but which surpasses it. In Fichte's time, the most important historical event, and arguably the most important historical event in modern times, was the French Revolution. Since then everything which happened has been influenced by this event, which constitutes a political break, so to speak, in the modern world.

Just as in politics, in philosophy it is necessary to distinguish pre- and post-revolutionary theories. When the revolution broke out, Kant was already sixty-five years old. The main lines of his position were already in place. It is well said that Kant only has room in the critical philosophy for two revolutions: the religious revolution inaugurated by Luther and the Copernican revolution leading to his own epistemological revolution in philosophy. Though he approves in principle of the French Revolution, there is no place for it in his position.[22] At least in this respect, his theory is therefore detached from historical practice.

Other observers were concerned to link theory to historical practice. An example is Erhard, who though Kantian, immediately proclaims the right to revolution.[23] In the same way as Kant, Erhard insists on the need to realize reason in the social context. He understands revolution as the transformation of the basic principles [*Grundgesetze*] of a society,[24] which he recommends in order to amend the constitution in favor of the people.[25] Fichte enjoys the reputation of a Jacobin thinker. Erhard, who is even more radical, goes so far as to defend the right to revolution against Fichte. According to Erhard, Fichte's early text on the French Revolution introduces an ambiguity concerning the good to be obtained through revolution and the right to act in that way.[26]

Kant tries to anticipate practice on the theoretical level, whereas Fichte, in inverting this relation, places theory after practice. Since he subordinates theory to practice, a basic practical change should give rise to a theoretical change. This is what happens in philosophy after the French Revolution.

Like all post-revolutionary thinkers, Fichte is strongly influenced by the political revolution that has never ceased to influence the contemporary philosophical debate. His own historical turning follows from two influences: to begin with, the interest he has in the revolution itself before he formulates he position, and then the position that follows from it. Everyone knows the important text that Fichte devotes to the defense of the French Revolution as early as 1793. Like many others, Fichte understands this event as possessing universal significance. For this reason, he makes a distinction between what happens in France and France, between the event that takes places in one or another country and the country where the event takes place. He comes back to this in the *Addresses to the German Nation,* where he once more defends the revolution, this time against Napoleon, a man without a name who, according to Fichte, had betrayed it.

Fichte's interest in the French Revolution is very visibly reflected in his concept of the subject. Fichte is often compared to Descartes, but the contrast is more interesting. The Cartesian conception of the subject is more complex than is often acknowledged.[27] Suffice it to say here that Descartes at least "officially" describes a passive subject as a simple spectator in negating the very idea of history under the heading of a *fabula mundi.* In comparison, Fichte advances a basically active subject, which is anti-Cartesian. He underlines how the individual develops through its interactions with other individuals and the natural world. Human development is not theoretical but practical. It consists in extending the sphere of action of the individual in going beyond obstacles encountered, in surpassing all sorts of hindrances in acting freely.

Now individual acts always take place in a social context. In the *Wissenschaftslehre,* where he sketches the basis of an analysis of interaction, Fichte works out his analysis on the basis of the individual, the self (*das Ich*). Later he changes his mind.[28] In tacitly adopting the concept of a plural subject, like Kant, he insists on the development of the species (*Gattung*).[29] This process of development is never instantaneous but extends through time. The result is a tension in Fichte's position. For he sees very clearly that his own conception of an active human person, namely, the anti-Cartesian idea of a subject that he arrives at after his analysis of the French Revolution and which functions as a presupposition for the theory he proposes in the *Wissenschaftslehre* (1794), requires a historical turning that he never later makes, a theory of history.

Fichte and the Theory of History

Observers differ on their views of Fichte's view of history. According to Philonenko, Fichte never contradicts himself.[30] In fact, there seems to be a remarkable continuity in the progressive development of Fichte's thought from its origins until the end of his career. We have already noted that it takes shape in the post-revolutionary space, after the most influential event of the modern period, of which it never loses sight. In reaction, Fichte formulates a theory that, at least in its initial version, requires a historical dimension that he has not yet focused and that he arguably never later wholly grasps. But except implicitly, the concept of history is lacking in Fichte's early writings. And so far as I am aware, the term *history* does not even appear in the first version of the *Wissenschaftslehre,* the most influential version of his position, which was so often misunderstood that Fichte, after several efforts considered as insufficient, later gave up presenting in other than oral form.

If his position points to history, one can rightly ask: where is his theory of history? It is not easy to respond to this. According to Philonenko, who considers the Fichtean writings after 1807 as unworthy of their author, Fichte only wrote from 1793 until 1807.[31] From this perspective, his position begins and ends with his analyses of the French Revolution.

Fichte is not only a philosopher who thinks in the post-revolutionary space, but also and above all a thinker for whom politics is, so to speak, the central theme of his position. Among the German idealists, with the possible exception of Marx, Fichte is the one who most retains his revolutionary enthusiasm. One thinks here of Schelling or even of Hegel, two thinkers whose early revolutionary enthusiasm was quickly tempered. We recall the severe verdict that Hegel later rendered on the excesses of the Terror in a well-known chapter of the *Phenomenology of Spirit.*[32] But there is a nuance between an analysis of historical facts, an exercise that attracts Fichte more than once, and a theory of history.

Lauth situates the "true" Fichtean theory of history in the *Addresses to the German Nation.* According to Lauth, the historical turning in Fichte is the result of a series of events that put an end to the Holy Roman Empire, especially the victories of Napoleon at Auerstadt and Jena, which later require Fichte "to enlarge his transcendental perspective in completing it through a historical analysis."[33] On the contrary, there is wide agreement to consider *The Characteristics of the Present Age* (1806; *Grundzüge des gegenwärtigen Zeitalters*) as a major source of that theory.[34]

Fichte's View of History in the *Grundzüge*

Like all the Fichtean writings that appeared after the famous Atheism Controversy (*Atheismusstreit*), including the *Five Lectures on the Vocation of the Scholar* (1811; *Funf Vorlesungen über die Bestimmung des Gelehrten*) and the *Addresses to the German Nation,* the *Grundzüge* belongs to the popular writings. We do not possess a "scientific" presentation of the Fichtean view of history. However, and like the writings of William James, who also never gave a written form to his position, and who left no more than a series of popular writings, the *Grundzüge* is very important.

Fichte approaches the problem of history as a transcendental philosopher. In the "First Introduction to the Science of Knowledge," he says that the chemist[35] and the ordinary person see the same thing in two different ways, the former a priori in analyzing the whole, and the latter a posteriori and in detail.[36] This implies the possibility of setting out the general lines of experience a priori, that is, in independence of it. In *Some Lectures Concerning the Scholar's Vocation,* he anticipates the application of this approach to the problem of historical comprehension in suggesting that one can anticipate the precise stages through which human beings must pass in order to reach a precise phase of culture.[37] In the *Grundzüge,* Fichte elaborates this approach in a detailed argument.

This argument can be summarized very rapidly as follows. The present historical period, and in fact any period, can only be understood on the basis of a general principle. This principle is determined a priori by the philosopher. All historical periods point to time understood as a unity. In order to understand a single period, one must grasp the general thrust of history, or human history in general. Fichte specifies his view in claiming that "the aim of human life on earth is to organize all relations freely according to reason."[38] And this requires that we free ourselves from our instincts.

In the *Grundzüge,* Fichte distinguishes five historical periods corresponding to different degrees of rational action. These include the present phase, which functions as the hinge, so to speak, between instinct and reason. In place of a summary, in his last lecture, Fichte writes: "In the preceding lectures, we have interpreted the present moment as a necessary part of an overall plan concerning the terrestrial life of our species and revealed its hidden meaning. We have striven to understand present events on the basis of this concept, to deduce them as the necessary results of the past, and to foresee their immediate consequences for the future."[39]

What strikes any reader who knows German idealism even a little is the "Hegelian" tone of this work, the way it anticipates well-known aspects of so-called absolute idealism. Such an assertion is obviously controversial. According to Lauth, Fichte's view of history is distinguished from Hegel's in that it lacks a purely logical structure.[40] Yet in abstracting from experience, any a priori analysis, including Fichte's, is necessarily "logical." Yet Lauth is correct to call attention to Fichte's endeavor to combine rationality and freedom in his theory of history as the realization of the human species.[41]

Fichte, in effect, characterizes the present period as the historical moment in which freedom and necessity overlap. "Thus the contemporary moment unifies the ends of two worlds that are entirely different according to their principles, the world of obscurity and the other of clarity, the world of compulsion and the one of freedom, without belonging to either of them."[42] We see how Fichte, who is chronologically situated between Kant and Hegel, reproduces the Kantian antinomy between freedom and causality, in this case individual freedom and logical determinism, while anticipating the Hegelian idea, derived from Spinoza, of freedom as a manifestation of reason.

There are numerous parallels between Fichte and Hegel on this point. To think history, as Hegel will later do, Fichte stresses reason, freedom, and development as a conceptual and historical process, hence necessarily temporal, the way in which different nations momentarily incarnate the spirit of one or another period before being replaced by others, and the importance of the present period understood as the crucial moment of transition to a new world.

For both Fichte and Hegel, the present period is centrally important on political grounds. Though neither one nor the other speaks explicitly in this context about the French Revolution, it is difficult not to perceive that both think that, after a historical event that has transformed the modern world, new possibilities are at hand.

The difference between the two thinkers' perspectives concerns the difference between their respective analyses of the duality between reason and freedom. With respect to history Fichte, like Kant, comprehends freedom as a simple given. He understands history as the realization of the concept of reason. Fichte, who, like the Enlightenment thinkers, perhaps underestimates the difficulty of realizing freedom in the social world, describes what he calls "the plan" as an effort "to educate the species in this life to rational freedom."[43] For Hegel, on the contrary, history is rational in itself, since there is always a reason in history. But though often criticized on this point, Hegel never affirms that what happens is intrinsically rational in any final sense. From his perspective, freedom in a historical context is not a mere given, something we already possess, but rather the aim of history.[44]

Fichte and Historical Knowledge

Fichte intends to provide a transcendental deduction of history. "Deduction" means something like "make intelligible in proposing an a priori schema or general principle for the interpretation of all a posteriori facts." It is not intended to produce the objects relating to the facts, which is the objection that Kant brings against Fichte, but rather to understand experience, including historical facts. As concerns history, Fichte establishes a certain reciprocity between the a priori and the a posteriori levels. His schema permits an interpretation of facts it does not produce, which refer to it for their comprehension.

Is Fichte a positivist in this respect? There is an analogy, though only a superficial one, between Ficthe's approach and the positivist conviction that the intelligibility of history requires historical laws similar in all main respects to the laws of nature. According to Hempel, there are historical laws similar in all respects to laws of physics.[45]

In the positivist approach, nature and history are one and the same. Fichte, on the contrary, detects a basic difference between nature and history. Following Kant, he observes a distinction between nature, which is causal, and history that emerges from the free acts of human beings. His proposed law of history differs from the laws of nature in that it is an a priori description of the stages through which the human species must pass in order to become fully rational.

The transcendental deduction is intended to coordinate the theory as well as the knowledge of history. As concerns the latter, three aspects seem to be important. These include what one could call, in Hegelian terminology, the category of the whole (or totality), then the concept of reason with respect to the interpretation of history, and finally the status of the entire analysis. Fichte, as Hegel later does, insists on the need to understand facts with respect to a subjacent totality, which must necessarily be identified before turning to the facts of experience. Like Kant, Fichte denies there is an immediate or non-mediated given. Like Hegel, Fichte sees that all difference presupposes an underlying unity with respect to which difference appears. Finally, like the hermeneutical thinkers in our time, starting with Dilthey and including Heidegger, Gadamer, Ricoeur, and so on, he makes a distinction between the general idea of something prior to experience and the experience illustrating this idea.[46]

Let us suppose that we require such a principle, a general idea in order to grasp the multiplicity of experience. That is tantamount to saying that there is, as Hegel insists, reason (*Vernunft*) in history. According to Fichte, there is always a thread linking historical givens which can be determined not after but prior to experience as the condition of all interpretation. But how can we identity the idea in question in order to interpret historical givens?

According to Kant, human maturity consists in thinking freely.[47] Like Kant, Fichte postulates that all human life is directed toward the organization of human relations freely and according to reason. He has in mind a non-perspectival analysis of the present period independent of that period.[48] Since the historical analysis does not depend on one or another historical period, it has in principle a trans-historical status. In this way, and perhaps without being aware of it, Fichte comes back to the epistemological problem, more precisely the epistemological limits of hermeneutical analysis.[49]

Fichte's suggestion that his analysis "surpasses" the present period is controversial. Kant claims to deduce the only possible categorial structure. This claim remains controversial. Problems have been raised about the meaning of "deduction," alternative categorial frameworks, the problem of closure, and so on.[50] Since there are as many categorial systems as one can desire, it is always possible to create another one, always possible to provide another categorial analysis.

I see no way to prove that Fichte in fact identifies the characteristics of all history or even of the present historical period, which can be interpreted on the basis of other principles. Since there is no decision procedure in the strife of interpretations, any hermeneutical principle only offers a possible perspective, and no single perspective can reliably claim to exhaust the realm of possibilities. There is not a single but rather a multiplicity of possible principles which provide as many different perspectives. Fichte is right to think that any interpretation presupposes an interpretive principle. But he is wrong to think that there is only a single principle or that he has discovered it.

On the Limits of Fichte's Approach

The introduction of the concept of the epistemological subject at the dawn of the modern period, to begin with in abstract form, points to what will later be called an anthropological and historical interpretation, as well as a historical turning. Following Fichte, who insists on his relation to Kant, the *Wissenschaftslehre* is often understood as directly continuing the critical philosophy. Fichte, who parts company with Kant in many ways, doubtless goes further than Kant in considering the problem of history in greater depth and in greater detail. But like his illustrious predecessor, he is unable to grasp the historically relative character of knowledge, which is rooted, as all knowledge is rooted, in history.

With respect to the latter point, there is a tension in the Fichtean position. On the one hand, he understands the subject of knowledge as finite human being, caught up in time and presumably history. However, he also thinks that the philosopher is able to escape from time, and hence from historical limits, in maintaining the venerable fiction, which still persists after more than two millennia, of philosophy as leading to a-perspectival knowledge. For if Fichte makes the historical turning, he is unable, and after him no one has been able, to think the problem through to the end, to integrate knowledge and history, which remains to be accomplished.

Notes

1. For discussion of the relation between Fichte and the French Revolution, see the articles by Alain Renaut, Ives Radrizzani, and Alain Perrinjaquet in *La Révolution française dans la pensée européenne,* ed. Daniel Schulthess and Philippe Muller (Neuchâtel and Lausanne: Presses Académiques de Neuchâtel et L'Age d'Homme, 1989), 35–70.

2. See Jean Hyppolite, *Introduction à la philosophie de l'histoire de Hegel* (Paris, 1983), 79.

3. See, for discussion, Tom Rockmore, *In Kant's Wake. Philosophy in the Twentieth Century* (Oxford: Blackwell, 2005).

4. See Giambattista Vico, *The New Science,* trans. Thomas Goddard Bergin and Max Harold Fisch (Ithaca: Cornell University Press, 1970), section 331, pp. 52–53.

5. See Immanuel Kant, *Critique of Pure Reason,* trans. and ed. Paul Guyer and Allen Wood (Cambridge: Cambridge University Press, 1998), B xiii and B xviii.

6. See Martin Heidegger, "Die Zeit des Weltbildes," in *Holzwege* (Frankfurt: Vittorio Klostermann, 1963), 69–105.

7. A similar conception of the subject arises earlier in Christian thinkers concerned with the problem of moral responsibility. See, for example, Augustine, *On the Free Choice of the Will,* trans. Thomas Williams (Indianapolis: Hackett, 1993).

8. For a recent discussion, see Manfred Buhr, "Philosophische Geschichtsschreibung," in *Weltbürgerkrieg der Ideologien, Antworten an Ernst Nolte,* ed. Thomas Nipperdey, Anselm Doering-Manteuffel, and Hans-Ulrich Thamer (Berlin: Propyläen, 1993), 404–20.

9. H. Nohl, ed., *Hegels theologische Jugendschriften* (Tübingen: J. C. B. Mohr, 1907), 429.

10. Jean Hyppolite, *Introduction à la philosophie de l'histoire de Hegel* (Paris: Rivière, 1968), 14.

11. See Immanuel Kant, *Werke in zehn Bände* [= *Kants-Werke*], ed. W. Weischedel (Darmstadt: Wissenschaftliche Buchgesellschaft, 1975), 6:351.

12. See Immanuel Kant, *Opus posthumum,* in *Kants-Werke* (Berlin: Preussische Akademie der Wissenschaften, 1902–), 21:115.

13. See Johann Gottlieb Fichte, "Second Introduction to the Science of Knowledge," in *The Science of Knowledge,* trans. Peter Heath and John Lachs (Cambridge: Cambridge University Press, 1982), 50–51.

14. See Fichte, *Science of Knowledge,* 50–51.

15. See G. W. F. Hegel, *The Difference Between Fichte's and Schelling's System of Philosophy,* trans. H. S. Harris and Walter Cerf (Albany: State University of New York Press, 1977).

16. See Tom Rockmore, *Hegel et l'idéalisme allemand* (Brussels: Ousia, 1993).

17. See Kant, *Critique of Pure Reason,* B xxxviii.

18. See "Über den Begriff der Wissenschaftslehre," in *FW* 1:27–82.

19. See Immanuel Kant, "On the Common Saying: That May Be Correct in Theory, But That Is of No Use in Practice," in *Practical Philosophy,* trans. Mary J. Gregor (Cambridge: Cambridge University Press, 1996), 273–310.

20. See Immanuel Kant, *Critique of Judgement,* trans. James Creed Meredith (New York: Oxford University Press, 1973).

21. See "Beitrag zur Berichtigung der Urtheile des Publicums über die französische Revolution" (1793), in *FW* 6:37–288; and J. G. Fichte, *Addresses to the German Nation,* trans. George A. Kelly (New York: Harper and Row, 1968).

22. See André Tosel, *Kant révolutionnaire: Droit et politique* (Paris: Presses Universitaires de France, 1988), 14.

23. See Johann Benjamin Erhard, "Über das Recht des Volks zu einer Revolution," in *Über das Recht des Volks zu einer Revolution und andere Schriften* (Frankfurt, 1976).

24. See Erhard, "Über das Recht des Volks," 43.

25. See Erhard, "Über das Recht des Volks," 91.

26. See Johann Benjamin Erhard, "Rezension von Fichtes Revolutionsbuch" in *Über das Recht des Volks zu einer Revolution und andere Schriften,* 135–64.

27. See, for discussion, Tom Rockmore, *On Constructivist Epistemology* (Lanham: Rowman and Littlefield, 2005), 67–71.

28. See J. G. Fichte, *Die Grundzüge des gegenwärtigen Zeitalters* (Hamburg: Meiner, 1956), 26.

29. For a discussion of Kant, see Monique Castillo, *Kant et l'avenir de la culture* (Paris: Presses Universitaires de France, 1990).

30. See Alexis Philonenko, *L'Oeuvre de Fichte* (Paris: Vrin, 1984), 211.

31. See Philonenko, *L'Oeuvre de Fichte,* 212. On the contrary, according to M. Vetö, the most important phase of the evolution of Fichte's position is the third and last one from 1810 to 1813. See Miklos Vetö, "Les trois images de l'absolu: Contribution à l'étude de la dernière philosophie de Fichte," *Revue Philosophique,* no. 1 (1992): 34.

32. See G. W. F. Hegel, "Absolute Freedom and Terror," in *Phenomenology of Spirit,* trans. A. V. Miller (New York: Oxford University Press, 1977), 355–63.

33. See Reinhard Lauth, "Die Handlung in der Geschichte nach der Wissenschaftslehre," in *Transzendentale Entwicklungslinien von Descartes bis zu Marx und Dostojewski* (Hamburg: Meiner, 1989), 397–410.

34. See, for example, Ives Radrizzani, "Quelques réflexions sur le statut de l'histoire dans le système fichtéen," in *Revue de Théologie et de Philosophie* 123 (1991): 293–304.

35. This example is interesting since Kant, who regards physics as the basic natural science, understands chemistry as a simple art. See Immanuel Kant, *Metaphysical Foundations of Natural Science,* trans. Michael Friedman (New York: Cambridge University Press, 2004).

36. See Fichte, *Science of Knowledge,* 28.

37. See *EPW,* 44–84.

38. Fichte, *Grundzüge des gegenwärtigen Zeitalters,* 11.

39. Fichte, *Grundzüge des gegenwärtigen Zeitalters,* 248.

40. See Lauth, *Transzendentale Entwicklungslinien,* 399–400.

41. See Lauth, *Transzendentale Entwicklungslinien,* 409.

42. Fichte, *Grundzüge des gegenwärtigen Zeitalters,* 56.

43. Fichte, *Grundzüge des gegenwärtigen Zeitalters,* 20.

44. See G. W. F. Hegel, *Vorlesungen über die Philosophie der Geschichte,* in *Werke in zwanzig Bänden,* ed. Eva Moldenhauer and Karl Markus Michel (Frankfurt: Suhrkamp, 1980), 12:32.

45. See Carl Hempel, "The Function of General Laws in History," in *Readings in Philosophical Analysis,* ed. Herbert Feigl and Wilfred Sellars (New York: Appleton-Century-Crofts, 1949), 459–71.

46. See Fichte, *Grundzüge des gegenwärtigen Zeitalters,* 145.

47. See Immanuel Kant, "An Answer to the Question: What Is Enlightenment?" in *Practical Philosophy,* 11–22.

48. See Fichte, *Grundzüge des gegenwärtigen Zeitalters,* 253–54.

49. See Tom Rockmore, "Herméneutique et épistémologie: Gadamer entre Hegel et Heidegger," *Archives de Philosophie* 53, no. 4 (October-December 1990): 547–57.

50. See Stephan Körner, *Categorial Frameworks* (New York: Barnes and Noble, 1970).

Contributors

Johannes Brachtendorf is a professor of philosophy in the department of Catholic theology at the University of Tübingen. He holds the Augustinian Endowed Chair in the Thought of Augustine at Villanova University and is a codirector of the Tübingen Augustine Center.

Daniel Breazeale is a professor of philosophy at the University of Kentucky. A cofounder of the North American Fichte Society, he has translated numerous volumes of Fichte's writings into English. He is also the author of scholarly articles on Fichte and German idealism and the coeditor of eight volumes of essays on Fichte. His own collection of essays is titled *Fichte and the Project of Transcendental Philosophy*.

Yolanda Estes is an associate professor of philosophy at Mississippi State University. Although she teaches in all areas of philosophy, her scholarship focuses on Fichte's philosophy, particularly the relation between moral and philosophical consciousness. *Fichte and the Atheism Dispute (1798–1800)*, which she wrote with Curtis Bowman, is forthcoming.

Andrew Fiala is an associate professor of philosophy at California State University, Fresno, and the director of the Ethics Center at Fresno State. The author of *The Philosopher's Voice, Practical Pacifism, Tolerance and the Ethical Life,* and *What Would Jesus Really Do?,* Fiala is also coeditor of the journal *Philosophy in the Contemporary World.*

Steven Hoeltzel is an associate professor of philosophy at James Madison University in Harrisonburg, Virginia. A specialist in Kant and post-Kantian idealism, existentialism, and phenomenology, he has authored several articles on Fichte's and Schelling's early systems.

Angelica Nuzzo is a professor at City University of New York's Graduate Center and Brooklyn College. The recipient of an Alexander von Humboldt Fellowship, she has also been a Fellow at the Radcliffe Institute for Advanced Study at Harvard University. Among her publications are *Kant* *and the Unity of Reason, Rappresentazione e concetto nella 'logica' della "Filosofia del diritto," Logica e sistema,* and *System.*

Ernst-Otto Onnasch is a research fellow in the philosophy department at Vrije Universiteit Amsterdam. His research concentrates on the history of classical German philosophy, particularly on the notion of system in Kant, Fichte, Schelling, and Hegel. He conducts a larger research program on Kant's *Opus postumum.*

Tom Rockmore is a professor of philosophy at Duquesne University and a cofounder of the North American Fichte Society. He is the author of many books on various themes, problems, and figures in modern philosophy, including *Kant and Idealism.*

George J. Seidel is a professor of philosophy at Saint Martin's University, where he has taught since 1962. He is the author of several books on philosophy, the two most recent of which are *Knowledge as Sexual Metaphor* and *Toward a Hermeneutics of Spirit.*

Michael Vater is a retired philosophy professor at Marquette University. He occasionally teaches courses on Buddhist Meditation and Taoist Yoga at the University of Wisconsin–Milwaukee and Marquette University.

Violetta L. Waibel teaches transcendental philosophy and German idealism at the University of Vienna. Previously she worked with Dieter Henrich in Munich and Manfred Frank in Tübingen. The author of *Hölderlin und Fichte, 1794–1800* and *System der Systemlosigkeit,* she is also the coeditor of the series *Hölderlin-Texturenk* and a member of the governing board of the International Johann Gottlieb Fichte Society.

Holger Zaborowski teaches philosophy at the Catholic University of America. His main research interests include seventeenth-century English philosophy, modern German philosophy, and phenomenology. He has published widely in these areas and is coeditor of the *Heidegger-Jahrbuch* and of the new edition of Schelling's *Philosophie und Religion.*

Kevin Zanelotti is an assistant professor of philosophy at McKendree University. He is the author of articles on Spinoza and the pedagogy of teaching philosophy.

Günter Zöller is a professor of philosophy at the University of Munich. A general editor of the Bavarian Academy edition of Fichte's collected works and a member of the Fichte Commission of the Bavarian Academy of Sciences, he also serves on the board of the Kant Commission of the Berlin-Brandenburg Academy of Sciences. He has twenty-two books to his name, as either author, editor, or coeditor, and has written some 150 articles on classical German philosophy and the philosophy of art.